LAW AND SOCIETY IN VIETNAM

A unique analysis of the struggle to build a rule of law in one of the world's most dynamic and vibrant nations – a socialist state that is seeking to build a market economy while struggling to pursue an ethos of social equality and opportunity. It addresses constitutional change, the assertion of constitutional claims by citizens, the formation of a strong civil society and non-profit sector, the emergence of economic law and the battles over who is benefited by the new economic regulation, labor law and the protection of migrant and export labor, the rise of lawyers and public interest law, and other key topics. Alongside other countries, comparisons are made to parallel developments in another transforming socialist state, the People's Republic of China.

MARK SIDEL is Professor of Law, Faculty Fellow, and Lauridsen Family Fellow at the University of Iowa. He has also served as Visiting Professor of Law at Harvard Law School.

CAMBRIDGE STUDIES IN LAW AND SOCIETY

Cambridge Studies in Law and Society aims to publish the best scholarly work on legal discourse and practice in its social and institutional contexts, combining theoretical insights and empirical research.

The fields that it covers are: studies of law in action; the sociology of law; the anthropology of law; cultural studies of law, including the role of legal discourses in social formations; law and economics; law and politics; and studies of governance. The books consider all forms of legal discourse across societies, rather than being limited to lawyers' discourses alone.

The series editors come from a range of disciplines: academic law; socio-legal studies; sociology; and anthropology. All have been actively involved in teaching and writing about law in context.

Series editors

Chris Arup
Monash University, Victoria
Martin Chanock
La Trobe University, Melbourne
Pat O'Malley
University of Sydney
Sally Engle Merry
New York University
Susan Silbey
Massachusetts Institute of Technology

Books in the Series

The Politics of Truth and Reconciliation in South Africa
Legitimizing the Post-Apartheid State
Richard A. Wilson

Modernism and the Grounds of Law
Peter Fitzpatrick

Unemployment and Government
Genealogies of the Social
William Walters

Autonomy and Ethnicity
Negotiating Competing Claims in Multi-Ethnic States
Yash Ghai

Constituting Democracy
Law, Globalism and South Africa's Political Reconstruction
Heinz Klug

The Ritual of Rights in Japan
Law, Society, and Health Policy
Eric A. Feldman

The Invention of the Passport
Surveillance, Citizenship and the State
John Torpey

Governing Morals
A Social History of Moral Regulation
Alan Hunt

The Colonies of Law
Colonialism, Zionism and Law in Early Mandate Palestine
Ronen Shamir

Law and Nature
David Delaney

Social Citizenship and Workfare in the United States and Western Europe
The Paradox of Inclusion
Joel F. Handler

Law, Anthropology and the Constitution of the Social
Making Persons and Things
Edited by Alain Pottage and Martha Mundy

Judicial Review and Bureaucratic Impact
International and Interdisciplinary Perspectives
Edited by Marc Hertogh and Simon Halliday

Immigrants at the Margins
Law, Race, and Exclusion in Southern Europe
Kitty Calavita

Lawyers and Regulation
The Politics of the Administrative Process
Patrick Schmidt

Law and Globalization from Below
Toward a Cosmopolitan Legality
Edited by Boaventura de Sousa Santos and Cesar A. Rodriguez-Garavito

Public Accountability
Designs, Dilemmas and Experiences
Edited by Michael W. Dowdle

Law, Violence and Sovereignty among West Bank Palestinians
Tobias Kelly

Legal Reform and Administrative Detention Powers in China
Sarah Biddulph

The Practice of Human Rights
Tracking Law Between the Global and the Local
Edited by Mark Goodale and Sally Engle Merry

Paths to International Justice
Social and Legal Perspectives
Edited by Marie-Bénédicte Dembour and Tobias Kelly

Law and Society in Vietnam
The Transition from Socialism in Comparative Perspective
Mark Sidel

Constitutionalizing Economic Globalization
Investment Rules and Democracy's Promise
David Schneiderman

The New World Trade Organization Agreements: 2nd Edition
Globalizing Law Through Intellectual Property and Services (2nd Edition)
Christopher Arup

Judges Beyond Politics in Democracy and Dictatorship
Lessons from Chile
Lisa Hilbink

LAW AND SOCIETY IN VIETNAM

Mark Sidel

CAMBRIDGE
UNIVERSITY PRESS

CAMBRIDGE UNIVERSITY PRESS
Cambridge, New York, Melbourne, Madrid, Cape Town, Singapore, São Paulo, Delhi

Cambridge University Press
The Edinburgh Building, Cambridge CB2 8RU, UK

Published in the United States of America by Cambridge University Press, New York

www.cambridge.org
Information on this title: www.cambridge.org/9780521850520

First published 2008

Printed in the United Kingdom at the University Press, Cambridge

A catalogue record for this publication is available from the British Library

ISBN 978-0-521-85052-0 hardback

To Margaret, Rosie and Thea and to Kevin, Inge and Andy

CONTENTS

TABLES

ACKNOWLEDGEMENTS

Many people have contributed to this effort. In Vietnam and elsewhere around the world, I am grateful to Stéphanie Balme, John Bentley, Bob Burnham, Nittaya Poonpermpan Burnham, Nguyen Nguyet Cam, Nguyen Bich Diep, Dan Duffy, Luu Tien Dung, Trinh Tien Dung, Peter Geithner, John Gillespie, Tom Gottschang, Joe Hannah, Andrew Harding, Neil Jamieson, Sunanthana Kampanathsanyakorn, Fred Kauffman, Minh Kauffman, Ben Kerkvliet, Bill Klausner, Jim Kurtz, Viet-Huong Tran Kurtz, Bui Thi Bich Lien, Le Mai, David Marr, John McAuliff, Roy Morey, Pham Duy Nghia, Binh Ngo, Pip Nicholson, Hong Nhung Pham, Nguyen Xuan Phong, Sisamorn Plengsri, Nguyen Hung Quang, Matthieu Salomon, Ta Van Tai, David Thomas, Bui Van Toan, Phan Nguyen Toan, Karen Turner, Thaveeporn Vasavakul, Peter Zinoman, and Mary Zurbuchen.

At the University of Iowa, I have benefited from the superb scholarly environment at the College of Law and the Obermann Center for Advanced Studies, and from the support and counsel of Eric Andersen, John Bergstrom, Amanda Bibb, Sandy Boyd, Ken Cmiel, Marcella David, Carolyn Frisbie, Bill Hines, Carolyn Jones, Ke Chuanren, Linda Kerber, Richard Koontz, Lorna Olson, Jay Semel, Karla Tonella, Gordon Tribbey, Stephen Vlastos, my faculty colleagues in the College of Law, a number of excellent research assistants over the years, and the superb staff at the University of Iowa College of Law Library.

This volume was completed while I served as visiting professor at Harvard Law School and Vermont Law School; at those institutions I am grateful to Bill Alford, Juliet Bowler, Bruce Duthu, Laura Gillen, Emma Johnson, Tim Locher, Hong Nhung Pham, Jeff Shields, Melissa Smith, Hue-Tam Ho Tai, Ta Van Tai, and Stephanie Willbanks.

At Cambridge University Press, it is a pleasure working with Finola O'Sullivan, Brenda Burke, Helen Francis, Richard Woodham, and their colleagues.

I have taught or lectured on Vietnamese law at Harvard, the Institut d'Etudes Politiques de Paris (Sciences Po), Iowa, the University of Melbourne, the School of Oriental and African Studies in the University of London, the University of Victoria, and other institutions. I am particularly grateful to students and colleagues at each of those institutions for raising stimulating questions and encouraging new lines of thought.

INTRODUCTION

Vietnam's *doi moi* (renovation) era began twenty years ago, in 1986, and this volume is about Vietnam's struggles to strengthen law and pursue legal reform in that era of reform. Vietnam's efforts are part of a broader transformation of socialist societies, and this volume makes explicit comparisons to developments in China, a country closely watched in Vietnam and whose own reform efforts have sometimes paralleled (or presaged) some of Vietnam's struggles and policies (Cohen 1990).

Vietnam's current debates and activities in strengthening a role for law are, of course, closely related to its history, and understanding that history is crucial to comprehending the debates over legal reform in Vietnam. Nguyen Ngoc Huy, Ta Van Tai, John Gillespie and other scholars have illuminated the important roles that Chinese, French, Russian and (in the south), American law have played in the development of different historical stages of Vietnamese law (Huy and Tai 1987; Tai 1989; Gillespie 2006). In this introduction, we begin the exploration of the modern conflict over the role of law in Vietnam by exploring conflicting strands of legal thought in Vietnam in the 1950s, when the first in a series of debates and conflicts on law under Party rule took place.

Any attempt to unravel these strands cannot challenge the historical fact that law was severely repressed, undervalued and used as an instrument of Party policy during this era. The Vietnam Workers Party, later the Vietnamese Communist Party, directed the legal system, often down to the individual trial level, in much the same way that the Party not only led but directed, or at least sought to lead and direct, often at the micromanagement level, many other elements of Vietnamese economic, political, military and social life. But even as we acknowledge that the Party refused to recognize law as an autonomous force in society or, often, even the narrow roles that law could play within a Party-dominated system, it is important to note that different conceptions of law did exist (Gillespie 2004, 2006; Sidel 1997c). Vietnamese political and "legal" life from the 1950s well into the 1980s was certainly dominated by the Party (Ginsburgs 1962a, 1962b, 1963). But that clear Party instrumentalization of the government and its ministries, of the legal system, economic life, and social life masks other strands of thought and action that are important to understanding the development of law and the legal system in later decades. The work of David Marr, John Gillespie, Neil Jamieson, Ben Kerkvliet, Adam Fforde, Kim Ninh and others provides a more textured understanding of Vietnamese political, economic and social life in this era (Jamieson 1992; Marr 1995a; Fforde 1986; Luong 1993; Ninh 2002; Kerkvliet 2005; Gillespie 2006). Here we explore some of these complexities for law, strands that may help in understanding the debates and policy development of the period from 1986 to 2006 that form the core of this book's analysis. We do this with reference to similar developments in China and in the analysis of Chinese law, an important comparative base for understanding developments in Vietnam.

Law certainly lags behind history, economics and politics in this analytical understanding. The dominant paradigm in western understanding of Vietnamese law from the mid-1950s through the mid-1980s has been virtually complete Party domination, almost without opposition, and the virtual non-existence of countervailing forces and contending strands of thought (Sidel 1993, 1994, 1997b, 1997c). In the years of the cold war this paradigm was eagerly accepted by some scholars whose political support for American cold war efforts required an acceptance of the Vietnamese (and Chinese) tendency to deny internal conflict, to portray their own views as even more monolithic than they may have actually been.

In recent years, this paradigm for defining north Vietnamese legal development in the 1954–1975 period has been accepted by those working with the emerging Vietnamese legal system, many of whom are interested in the promotion of western models, structures and statutes. The introduction of western models largely without reference to Vietnamese legal traditions and practice is thus not only taken for granted but takes on a kind of nobility: by bringing in the new and modern, the aid-givers can dispense with the old (or, in its slightly more sophisticated version, help Vietnamese reformers discard the old), which is considered of little value by the donors of the new and the modern (Rose 1998).

Two strands of thought that provide contrasting approaches to the hardest of the Party's instrumentalist positions on the role and domination of law arose from intellectuals, journalists and other writers, many originally non-Communist, who joined with the Viet Minh and the Party in the 1940s and early 1950s. The individuals and their thought led in somewhat different directions. One clearly dissenting strand of thought on the role of law led toward a form of political opposition in the mid-1950s, and is already reasonably well-known to specialists. That conflict between the Party and its political/legal apparatus, and those who sought more legal protections for individual freedoms and a more autonomous legal system, is a relatively under-explored aspect of the *Nhan van Giai pham* movement of the late 1950s and its residues in critical and dissident thought beyond that era. The discussion here focuses not on the conflict over artistic and literary freedom that was, admittedly, at the root of the movement, but on the views that Nguyen Huu Dang, Nguyen Manh Tuong and a few others close to the *Nhan van Giai pham* core group published on a different, expanded, and more autonomous role for law and the legal system.

If this strand of dissenting thought on the role of law was buried under repression in the late 1950s, another strand of thought on the role of law was submerged for a long period in academic work and political powerlessness. In the early 1960s, a groups of intellectuals, including some from non-Party political backgrounds, came together in the newly-formed "law group" (*to luat hoc*) within the social sciences section of the State Sciences Committee in Hanoi. The writings of some members of that group evinced a respect for a comparative approach, for the role of strong legal systems in western societies, and for the role of law (in addition to Party policy) in promoting economic development. At one level the isolation of this strand in the academic world removed these views from day-to-day policy influence just as surely as repression would have done. But removal and isolation were not in fact repression, and the views and methods these scholars represented were left to hibernate and ripen until finding some vindication several decades later, once reform had begun.

A third set of contending approaches is the most difficult to analyze and perhaps the most controversial to discuss. That is the varying strands of thought on the role of law within the Party and its leadership. There are some who would deny that it is possible to identify anything but complete and monolithic convergence within the Party on the question of the role of law. But we know that monolithic convergence of view was not the case in economics, in artistic policy, even on the conduct of the war with the United States, and monolithic convergence of policy was not the case in law as well. In recent years other scholars (such as Gillespie 2004) have begun unraveling these strands on the role of law within the Party itself.

CONFLICT WITH "ENEMIES" OVER CONTENDING APPROACHES TO LAW: *NHAN VAN GIAI PHAM* AND BEYOND

The story of *Nhan van Giai pham*, the 1956–1959 conflict between the Party and a group of dissenting intellectuals that is often analogized to China's Hundred Flowers Movement and its repression, has been told since the late 1950s (Chi 1958; Mai 1958; Boudarel 1991; Tuong 1992; Ninh 2002). But I focus here on the group's visions for a different relationship between law and the Party.

Nguyen Huu Dang and Nguyen Manh Tuong were two of the intellectuals who had (in Dang's case) joined with Ho and the Viet Minh forces, and (in Tuong's case), initially adapted to Viet Minh and Party control. Nguyen Huu Dang joined Ho Chi Minh's first cabinet in 1945, and helped to plan the September 2, 1945 ceremony in Ba Dinh Square where Vietnam's independence was declared. Tuong was, in the 1950s, one of Vietnam's most prominent intellectuals, the famous "dual doctorate" from France, who had returned to teach in Hanoi. When the *Nhan van* and *Giai pham* periodicals began publication in 1956 they were important participants, especially Nguyen Huu Dang.

These figures expressed their approach to the role of law in the mid-1950s in two strands of thought. First, they emphasized the need for sharply strengthened, considerably more independent legal processes under considerably less day-to-day Party control, with more vigorous protection of individual liberties and system autonomy. As Nguyen Huu Dang noted,

> [W]e are used to looking down upon bourgeois legal principles, so that among a large number of people this state of affairs has turned into contempt for the law in general. It is also because, during our long and hard resistance, we were used to solving all questions within our groups, at our convenience. We were accustomed to resorting to a "rule of

thumb" to move things along every time our work ran into a regulation. We have been used to replacing law with "viewpoint".

(Dang 1956a)

The solution was not a firmer political "viewpoint," but the failure to embrace legal norms as a standard for conduct.

> To have a firm point of view is very valuable, but this is not sufficient in itself . . . A complete legal code would be a guarantee for the democratic nature of our regime. It will be the main track for the train smoothly speeding our people toward socialism. It is due to the lack of a legal code that our agrarian reform has bitterly failed. . . It is due to the lack of a legal code that a police agent can ask for a marriage certificate from a couple sitting on the bank of the "little lake" waiting for the moonrise, that a census cadre can watch at the door of a house, making its tenants so uneasy that they cannot eat or sleep . . . It is due to the lack of a complete legal code that shameless political slanders and threats can be made.
>
> (Dang 1956a)

And the measures proposed for reaching that solution were spirited and daring. They included a new Constitution that would replace the 1946 Constitution and further enshrine the rights embodied in that document; more authority for and more frequent meetings of the National Assembly, "because in peacetime there is no reason why the National Assembly should entrust all its work to its standing committee, which, so far, has been practically inactive"; and "reorganization of the judiciary, and giving it real power" (Dang 1956a).

Nguyen Huu Dang discussed the core problem of constitutionalism in the next, and as it turned out, last issue of *Nhan van*. Dang continues to argue that law and its enforcement are necessary for consolidation of socialism in the north, not an inconvenience or a luxury that can be deferred until reunification is completed. And consolidation of law requires promulgation of a new or amended Constitution adequate to current needs. At another level, however, Dang seems aware that he is fighting different forces: not only those who regard law as an incon-venience, but some who seek to roll back even the very limited protections provided in the 1946 Constitution and the laws and regu-lations promulgated under it. By late November 1956 that view is also of deep concern.

I only want to assert one thing, that no matter what the content of a future Constitution may be, the parts of the 1946 Constitution relating to guarantees of democratic freedoms cannot be changed, because this is the basis of a democratic regime.

Today ... some say about the 1946 Constitution, "the 1946 Constitution is a blanket, strategic concession to the gang of the Vietnamese Nationalist Party aided by the Chinese Nationalists, and to those who did not follow the revolution at the time ... It is all the more inadequate in the present situation, when the people's government has made great progress. Since the forces of the workers and the peasants are now greatly developed, of course one should be stricter, instead of falling back to the level of bourgeois democracy of 1946.

Actually, there is no opinion that is more anti-democratic than the one stated above.

(Dang 1956b)

Thus even in late 1956 the democratic dissidents were drawing distinctions between some in the Party leadership who favored the perhaps somewhat gentler instrumentalism of the early years of the Democratic Republic of Vietnam (DRV), and those who favored even less autonomy than already existed for an already highly controlled, instrumentalized legal system, and more repression.

Nguyen Manh Tuong made similar criticisms in his far-reaching and famous attack on the repressive land reform campaign, delivered before a meeting of the Fatherland Front:

Administrative measures, and particularly legal measures, when correctly used, can ensure the success of the Revolution. What did we want then? We wanted to discover the enemies of the peasants, of the revolution, in order to suppress them. But if we were prudent, if we wanted to safeguard the prestige and the success of the revolution, we should not forget that revolutionary justice must not miss its target: the enemy. A slogan has been put out: Better kill ten innocent people than let one enemy escape. This slogan is not only leftist to a ridiculous degree but it is also harmful to the Revolution ...

We have the means of discovering our enemies ... we must avoid mass repression and ... we must not kill innocent people.

(Tuong 1956)

Professor Tuong then outlined the safeguards that he believed would better serve the revolution. At the time these procedural steps were proposed (and proposed carefully, as is clear in Tuong's careful reticence from calling directly for judicial independence), they constituted perhaps the single most clear-cut call for legal reform in the Democratic Republic of Vietnam of the 1950s:

> The first principle is: Those who committed crimes many years ago should not be punished for those crimes now ...
> The second principle is: The responsibility falls on the guilty person only, not on wives, children or relatives ... None of the Western countries has proceeded in such a manner for four hundred years. Responsibility before the law is always individual ...
> The third principle is: We cannot condemn a man without valid evidence ...
> The fourth principle is: The interest of the defendant must be taken into consideration in the process of investigation and accusation. The prisoner at the bar has the right to be represented by counsel ...
> How can these principles be applied to our Land Reform? The reform could certainly continue, but the punishment of reactionaries should not be settled by the Special People's Court[s], obviously so full of shortcomings ... On the contrary, having mobilized the spirit of the people and listened to their denunciation, we should charge the ordinary People's Court to investigate, to examine, to interrogate, to judge, while the defendants should have the right to defend themselves and to be represented by counsel. We only hate the crime they might have committed; their human dignity we respect. We ought to have confidence in the court and to provide all necessary guarantees for the judge to enable him to perform his duty free from any administrative pressure and quite separate from the executive. I say separate but not independent.
>
> (Tuong 1958)

Tuong, however, went further. He sought to "analyze the causes of our errors," and among those causes one was stated in the strongest possible terms.

> We despise legality. A Polish professor, Mr. Mannell, when lecturing at the Ministry of Justice, reported that in Poland, immediately after the revolution, the politicians completely despised legality. They thought that they were talented enough to take upon themselves the direction of justice; to compel justice to serve political interests without paying any attention to fundamental principles of law ... All this does not surprise us. At the beginning the politicians were crazy with their successes, naturally, for those successes were imposing ... Our politicians are biased by their prejudice against legality, thinking that justice is only a spoke to be put into the wheel. They do not understand that, on the contrary, legality serves to prevent the car from being overturned ...

A great danger lies in the fact that the politicians think that they are above the law ...

Politics still considers justice a poor relative ... Although there exists in our country a Ministry of Justice as well as many tribunals, laws and regulations; a politics of legality seems to be totally non-existent ... Politics is leading justice – that is perfectly right – but politics is impinging on justice, replacing justice.

(Tuong 1958)

For these views Nguyen Huu Dang, Nguyen Manh Tuong and others were severely criticized, and their professional and personal lives crushed (Tuong 1992; Ninh 2002). The criticism of *Nhan van Giai pham* took into account the views of Dang, Tuong and others on problems in the role of law, and directly criticized those views (Huu 1958; Bon Nhan Van 1959).

There are few other episodes of direct expression of conflicting views on the development of the role of law and the legal system before 1975. The more closed political atmosphere after *Nhan van Giai pham*, and the unifying mobilization that came with the onset of the US war, are among the reasons for that. Among the very few other episodes in this period available to us that may be interpretable as involving contending approaches to the role of law is the 1967 trial of the philosopher Hoang Minh Chinh and a number of others charged with "revisionist" and "counter-revolutionary" activities. But that episode – the last major flare-up of political dissent in northern Vietnam before the late 1970s – still remains somewhat murky and insufficiently documented.

THE "ACADEMIC" STRAND IN VIETNAMESE LEGAL THOUGHT

While some intellectuals went into opposition in 1956 through *Nhan van Giai pham* and related developments, others chose more quietly to advocate contrasting approaches to the role of law. Some, such as Phan Anh, head of the Vietnamese Lawyers Association and a pre-1945 non-Communist intellectual, seem to have operated largely within the policy sphere. But a methodological alternative to the hardest of the Party instrumental visions of law came from a group of senior legal scholars, some of them non-Communist intellectuals before and after 1945, who gathered in the legal studies group (*to luat hoc*, later the Institute of State and Law, *Vien nghien cuu nha nuoc va phap luat*) in what was first known as the social sciences division of the State Sciences Committee (*Uy ban khoa hoc nha nuoc*) in the early 1960s.

In the Chinese case, the role of such senior scholars, trained abroad often in non-Soviet systems, has been the subject of foreign scholarly analysis for some time. And it is becoming clearer that these scholars were, in the Chinese case, a key nucleus for the hibernation and then development of new strand of legal thought, and new notions of the relative autonomy of law and the relationship between law and the Party (Sidel 1995b; 1996). The group of Vietnamese legal scholars that gathered in and around the "legal studies group" in the early and mid 1960s and its successor, the Institute of State and Law in the early 1970s was a fairly diverse collection of scholars and officials, some perhaps more closely tied to the Party and Party views than others. The original group included key Party intellectuals such as Professor Pham Van Bach, then a member of the State Sciences Committee responsible for the work of the legal studies group and later President of the Supreme People's Court and Vice Chairman of the Vietnam Lawyers Association, and others. That group also included such senior figures as Tran Cong Tuong, who has been identified by former Party official Bui Tin as a leading early voice for legal reform and served as Director of the Theory and History of State and Law Division of the Legal Studies Group from 1963 through 1966 and perhaps beyond. Bui Tin sets the scene:

> There were many scholars and intellectuals outside the Party who had a far better understanding of the country than the Communists ... Even within the Party, there were intellectuals who were sincere, upright and knowledgeable, but they were demeaned because they maintained high standards and refused to act as toadies ... Gradually the role of the intellectuals and technocrats within the Party and the government was eliminated by reducing them to impotence or to being symbolic and decorative ... [T]here were the ideas of Tran Cong Tuong in the 1950s and 1960s about building up a legal system and setting up a Ministry of Justice and a Law University. These too were ignored ... Since 1945, legal experts like Phan Anh, Tran Cong Tuong and later Nguyen Huu Tho have stressed that the development of a legal system is very urgent. But these ideas have been ignored.
>
> (Tin 1995)

These legal scholars also included originally non-Viet Minh, non-Communist scholars, lawyers and officials such as Vu Dinh Hoe, who had served as Minister of Justice in Ho Chi Minh's first, broad-based cabinet and then as a senior scholar specializing in economic and civil law at the Institute of State and Law for much of the 1960s. Vu Dinh Hoe had an extraordinary career, and as the Vietnamese political scene relaxed in the late 1980s and early 1990s he was able to complete and publish a volume of memoirs of his life as a journalist, editor, legal scholar and official since the 1930s (Hoe 1995). The group also included other accomplished legal researchers whose political affiliations were not necessarily clear.

Among this group the comparative orientation of Vu Dinh Hoe and several others stands out in contrast to the more militant approach of some in the Party and military apparatus toward the role of law. We have in Hoe and his colleagues a respect for a comparative approach, for the role of strong legal systems in western societies, and for the role of law in addition to policy in promoting economic development that goes beyond the Soviet models strongly promoted in Vietnam in the 1960s and which cannot be found in the work of a number of Party leaders and documents.

Vu Dinh Hoe's career is well-known to many Vietnamese intellectuals and officials. Born in Ha Dong, his father a teacher, Hoe studied in his home province and then in Hanoi, first in the French-run Yen Phu primary school, then in the famous French-run Buoi School beside the West Lake, and still later at the French Albert Sarraut School in Hanoi, in the buildings where the Party Central Committee now works. After graduation from Sarraut he entered the French-run Hanoi Law University, graduating after three years with a bachelor's degree in law. Hoe went to teach at the Thang Long and Gia Long private schools and was "active in the General Association of Students, participating in the … students' movement." Later he took leadership roles in several non-Communist newspapers and associations, and participated in the movement to spread romanized Vietnamese as Vice Chairman of the Association for the Propagation of Romanized Vietnamese (Hoi truyen ba hoc Quoc ngu), where he worked with Nguyen Huu Dang, who would much later come to grief in the Nhan van Giai pham movement and its repressive aftermath. Hoe became an editor of the non-Communist Thanh Nghi newspaper that was published between 1941 and 1945, and a leader in the SFIO, the branch of the Workers International Party, and later in the Democratic Party (Dang Dan chu).

After the 1945 revolution Hoe served for six months in Vietnam's provisional joint government, and "then Mr. Ho [Chi Minh] transferred me to [the position of] Minister of Justice in the joint government of resistance" (Hoe 1995). Hoe describes his approach to law and abuses of legal process, including extra-judicial killings in the years that followed:

> At the end of 1947, a few days after the French aggressors parachuted into Bac Can, President Ho sent me on his behalf to take the lead in a Special Group to inspect provinces and districts in the Viet Bac region, to bring his wishes and motivate the people for struggle and to increase production. I discovered some cases in which the administrative authorities at certain levels of power had unlawfully arrested and confined people. In my capacity as Chief of the Special Group and Minister of Justice I issued orders freeing at once those who had been wrongly charged, and I reported to the chairman of the government. Several years later, I took the initiative to inspect the delta regions, and did the same there, instructing regional directors of justice [bureaux] to follow suit, in order to protect the trust of the government and the people's physical freedoms, in accordance with President Ho's orders at the end of 1945 and the 1946 Constitution of the Democratic Republic of Vietnam. Of course this work produced contradictions with some Administrative Committees, and the activities of the justice sector met with difficulties. In the judicial reform of 1950, many worker-peasant cadres were sent into the courts in the capacity of People's Assessors; another aspect was the unification of the regular courts with the military courts, and these courts tried the political cases . . .
>
> In parallel with the legal situation, the activities of the Democratic Party also had some similar difficulties because of different viewpoints between some democrats [nguoi dan chu] and some Communist Party members (who were sent to "help" the Democratic Party), especially during the periods of land reform and industrial and commercial transformation (1953–1958) . . .
>
> The 1959 Constitution was promulgated . . . [and] in accordance with the model of the (former) Soviet state machinery the Ministry of Justice was abolished in 1960 . . . I left my position as Minister in 1960 . . . and transferred to work as a legal specialist . . . in the Institute of Law under the Social Sciences Committee, working on research, directly under the authority of Mr. Pham Van Bach . . . I wrote articles, books, compiled dictionaries, taught on several areas of law, especially economic law and civil law. The volume *Economic Contracts* that I edited was evaluated positively by the Institute of Law and the Social Sciences Committee, and for that I was elected and recognized as a "fighter worthy of emulation" in the legal field in 1963.
>
> (Hoe 1995)

It is not easy to square Vu Dinh Hoe's emphasis on comparisons to French and German civil law, and the utility of some of those models to a socialist economic system, with the harder commentaries, commentaries considerably less respectful of the role of law, of Nguyen Chi Thanh, Truong Chinh and some other Party and military officials. For Vu Dinh Hoe, law had a considerably more autonomous role in Party-led economic development, a considerably less instrumental role, in a system still dominated by the Party and that relied heavily on Soviet and Chinese models. For Nguyen Chi Thanh, Truong Chinh and others, law only had an instrumentalized role under the Party.

Even these more comparativist yet still cautious strands represented by Vu Dinh Hoe and a few others began to fade in the mid-1960s. By then even the careful academic explorations of the appropriate shape of law in a highly instrumentalized system were appearing less and less frequently. As part of the mobilization for the war against the United States, patriotic legal scholars turned willingly to assist the mobilization of legal arguments against US intervention, against American bombing, against the southern government, and for northern interpretations of the Geneva Agreements and events since 1954. During this period Vu Dinh Hoe and most of the other legal scholars in the "legal studies group" participated in war-related legal research, mobilization and evacuation work. The legal publications that re-emerged in 1971 and thereafter were considerably more distinctly political in nature, and it would be the mid-1970s before Hoe's published work returned to the comparativist focus of the early 1960s.

None of this will surprise observers of Vietnam or China or other socialist states. But the effects of the US war and other wars fought on Vietnamese soil on the legal sector, and particularly on legal scholarship, have not been the subject of frequent academic analysis within Vietnam. An early, short, and notable exception was an abbreviated essay by the legal historian Tran Thi Tuyet of the Institute of State and Law (the successor to the legal studies group) that appeared in a 1994 volume on issues of law and society (Tuyet 1994). At one level Tuyet agrees with other legal scholars who have blamed the political and mobilizational aspects of war for the lack of focus on a role for law, and a lack of obedience for legal norms. But Tuyet adds another view.

> When we speak of the effects of war, there is usually a tendency to emphasize its negative effects. But it would not be fair if we evaluate wars in Vietnamese history only as having negative consequences for the building of legal consciousness and a sense of living life under law. We do not hope or wish for war, but in the special historical conditions of

Vietnam the two forms of war – national and democratic – have not only had negative consequences but also, at least to a certain degree, have also had a effect on building legal consciousness and a sense of living life under law in the people of Vietnam.

In the cause of building the nation and defending the nation, as in the conquering of the harshness of nature, war … bonded small peasant village society with a strong stamp of rural communal life, bonded peasants into a community deeply attached to solidarity and unity, with a consciousness of responsibility for the interests of the collective, the national community and people. That is an important premise for the perception of building legal consciousness and the sense of living life under law in Vietnam's … conditions.

Resisting foreign aggression and resisting nature have been matters of common interest directly relating to the lives and the destiny of each [village] member, family, village and community. Thus each member and each community voluntarily participated, implemented and complied with the law of the state [*phap luat cua nha nuoc*] and village customary regulations [*quy uoc cua lang xa*] relating to resisting foreign aggression.

(Tuyet 1994)

This sense that national political mobilization was more conducive to local obedience to the norms of the state than was peacetime is not specific to Vietnam. Nor does it conflict with the narrowing of the different strands of thinking about law into a single, mobilizational strand between about the mid-1960s and the mid-1970s.

SHADINGS OF VIEWS WITHIN THE PARTY ON THE ROLE OF LAW

If we can at least identify strands of thought about the role of law that emerged through the *Nhan van Giai pham* group, and a comparativist approach that emerged in the academic world in the early 1960s, went into political hibernation until the mid-1970s and only truly reemerged in the mid-1980s, we come then to the most perplexing problem in unraveling strands of thought on the role of law. That problem is the need to begin to understand views within the Party itself, and particularly among senior Party officials, a task well begun by the scholar John Gillespie (Gillespie 2004, 2006).

There is some indication that contending approaches to the role of law must have reached Hanoi's Party officials as well as legal academics. We know, for example, that those with whom Vietnamese Party leaders

13

worked outside Vietnam, and those with whom Vietnamese legal academics worked, often had diverging perspectives on the role of law in Party-dominated societies, even if as a fundamental matter they accepted the Party's dominant role in society.

Through Chinese and western scholarship, for example, we know that divergent views existed within China on the appropriate role and power of law in Chinese socialist society; the Hundred Flowers and the Cultural Revolution brought some of those conflicts sharply into view.

We also know of the discussions in the Soviet Union, where hundreds of Vietnam's younger legal scholars and future officials studied from the early 1950s well into the 1990s. And these debates and discussions were perhaps even more heated in central and eastern Europe. Vietnamese Party students and scholars could not and did not emerge from their years of study at Prague, East Berlin, Cracow and Budapest – even Havana and Moscow – without some sense of the various roles that were possible for law.

In this complex area it is useful at least to begin with the perceptions of Vietnamese scholars and practitioners. Several of those choose to identify the military and political leader Nguyen Chi Thanh with expressing some of the strongest views for the harder instrumentalist notion of law, and the least accepting of various versions of legal autonomy in the 1950s and 1960s. Nguyen Chi Thanh headed the General Political Department of the Vietnamese People's Army, the main political and ideological headquarters within the military establishment, in the 1950s and the mid-1960s.

Thanh was certainly not alone, but Vietnamese scholars and practitioners identify Thanh's opposition to a more autonomous role for law with harder positions on strengthening the role of the Party and Party institutions and collective action, and minimizing the role of individual initiative and rights in other facets of national life. Some of Thanh's strongest statements in these areas were presented in the political context of Nhan van Giai pham and in the harder mobilizational years of the early 1960s. Years after Nhan van Giai pham, Thanh, in a speech in 1963, echoed the criticisms in a broader context, and in ways that cannot have pleased the more flexible academics.

> Rightist deviationist revisionism and opportunism are the main threats in the international communist movement at present . . . In the past and more recently it has been truly difficult for that to worm into the country, but some of our comrades have begun to show some small influences of it, especially in those sectors which have not yet firmed

up their politics [chua duoc cung ran ve chinh tri]. In politics these people are loose on class struggle and the dictatorship of the proletariat; in economics they do not clearly identify the essential differences between the laws of capitalist economies and the laws of socialist economies; in literature and the arts they deny or make light of Party spirit and the spirit of the people; in their views on humanity and on the individual, they hold views that deny class ... in class struggle with the enemy they stress the actions of individuals, and de-emphasize the role of the broad masses; in the great revolutionary movements they only pay attention to short-term interests and do not look more broadly, casting aside the final goals. ...

Is it not surprising that today there are still a few people who ask for re-evaluation of agricultural cooperatization within the country as they did before? Re-evaluation of whether Party spirit and people's spirit in arts and literature are correct or not ... re-evaluation of the priority on heavy industry, [whether] self-reliance is truly correct or not.

(Thanh 1977)

But other shadings appear as well, in the statements of other Party leaders. For example, several Vietnamese scholars and lawyers point to then-Prime Minister Pham Van Dong as representing, at least through the mid-1960s, a somewhat more sympathetic sense of the role of law and perhaps somewhat more autonomous institutions. Certainly Pham Van Dong's views were considered somewhat closer by some within legal academic circles in the mid-1960s, particularly on the importance of institutionalizing the role of the state and its machinery, and the role of law in the national development process, even if the Prime Minister could do little to implement these concepts.

Strengthening the State machinery means strengthening the organization and activities of the State in accordance with the provisions and spirit of the Constitution, the fundamental law of the nation. We must pay special attention to the activities of popularly-elected institutions ... It must be recognized that at present we have made many mistakes in our understanding and actions with respect to popularly elected institutions, especially at the local levels.

And special emphasis was placed on the importance and role of law, even if phrased in rhetorically correct ways:

Strengthening the people's democratic State means strengthening socialist legality. Under our system, law reflects the line and policies of the Party; law is the will of the people. The reflections of the line and policies of the Party are the will of the people, and thus law is a sharp weapon for suppressing the people's enemies, for improving socialism and building socialism, for building a new life. Some people confuse the Party and State and do not understand this aspect of the State. Making revolution means winning power and establishing a State system of our own, and using that State to promulgate laws, ordinances, resolutions, new regulations and new rules that have effect with respect to every person, and every person must obey them.

(Dong 1980)

LAW AND SOCIETY IN VIETNAM DURING *DOI MOI* (RENOVATION)

All these strands – differing views within the Party on the role of law; broadly open and comparativist views in some legal institutions and academic circles; and even a resurgent dissident community – have re-emerged with considerably more prominence in the two decades since the Vietnamese Party announced its *doi moi* (renovation) policy in 1986. Vietnam's current efforts to strengthen law implicate many of the conflicts that stand out so clearly in the 1950s and 1960s. The debates over the role of a constitution, about the degree of deference that should be given to legal institutions, the ways of enforcing constitutional principles and constitutional rights, strengthening economic law, punishing wrongdoing by government officials, the problems and possibilities of representing defendants, and the role of law in addressing issues of economic development and social inequality in Vietnamese society – all these have been core questions in the last twenty years of Vietnam's efforts to build its legal system. This volume addresses these questions and others. It explores the contradictory role of the Communist Party, debates over constitutional powers and rights, whether economic law protects weaker forces in society while stimulating economic development, and other important issues. It is based on a number of years of work in and research on Vietnamese law, and on teaching Vietnamese law at Iowa, Harvard, the Institut d'Etudes Politiques de Paris, the School of Oriental and Advanced Studies in London, and other institutions.

Throughout this book run several themes. One topic is the role of the Constitution and the many debates on its text, its enforcement, and the rights it provides. The Constitution is in many ways a key fulcrum for legal debate in Vietnam, particularly in recent years during a recent amendment process (discussed in Chapter 1), and a renewed debate on how constitutional rights should be protected and enforced (Chapter 2). Still more recently, citizens in Hanoi have publicly and loudly claimed constitutional rights, an important episode discussed in Chapter 3.

A second unifying theme is the role of economic law in Vietnam's development. This problem is explored through the theme of labor law (Chapter 4), the role of business, trade and professional associations (Chapter 6), the role of lawyers as economic and professional actors in Vietnamese legal reform (Chapter 7), and the focus of the international donor community on drafting and harmonizing Vietnamese economic law with international norms (Chapter 8).

A third theme is the role of law in enabling citizens to face the state and to serve as autonomous actors in Vietnamese society. I explore this role for law in state–society relations by looking at a famous case of wrongdoing by police (Chapter 5), the growing debate over the role of law in controlling Vietnam's burgeoning sector of associations and social organizations (Chapter 6), and the rapidly growing role of public interest law and public interest lawyers (Chapter 7).

Portions of some chapters have been substantially adapted and expanded from material originally published in the *Singapore Journal of International and Comparative Law*; *Voluntas*; and *The mass media in Vietnam* (Canberra: Australian National University, 1998) (David Marr, ed.).

CHAPTER 1

CONSTITUTIONALISM AND THE EMERGENCE OF CONSTITUTIONAL DIALOGUE IN VIETNAM

When a Communist Party dominates law and the legal system, what need is there for a Constitution – or, in Vietnam's case, four Party-drafted Constitutions since 1946? A theory of constitutional instrumentalism has dominated scholarly understanding of Vietnam's constitutions and other socialist constitutions since the 1950s. The instrumentalist approach is clear: constitutions in Communist Party-run states have been, and remain, a means of political control by a single party, a way of expressing Communist Party political, economic and social policy, a method for mobilizing action, and a malleable document subject to redrafting and adoption by a compliant legislature as times and policies changed. This analytical framework has dominated foreign as well as Vietnamese understanding of Vietnam's constitutions, as it has dominated our perception of Chinese and other socialist constitutions, and of the Soviet and east European constitutions before the end of Party rule (Vasiljev 1973; Sang 1974; Cohen 1978; Nguyen 1981; Barrett 1983; Saich 1983; Bach and Hoe 1984; Ainsworth 1992; Heng 1992; Thayer 1993; Cai 1995).

Traditional instrumentalist theory remains the lens through which most foreign understanding of Vietnamese, Chinese and other socialist constitutional processes have been understood. Even in earlier decades that doctrine was too simple, though it served some useful analytical purposes as a broad and basic understanding of the constitutional role. But the pure instrumentalist theory is now substantially unsuited to understanding the complexity of constitutional debate in Vietnam and other transitional socialist societies. As change has come to these societies, albeit slowly and under single party rule, our understanding of the role of their constitutions, constitutional dialogue and constitutional change remains largely mired in the past. This chapter disinters the instrumentalist lens through which we have traditionally viewed socialist constitutions and, through interpreting recent and active constitutional dialogue in Vietnam, advances beyond instrumentalist theory in our understanding of how Vietnam and other Party-controlled socialist and transitional socialist states move to update and redraft their constitutions. Instrumental theory can no longer effectively explain and analyze what is occurring in transitional states such as Vietnam, where constitutional dialogue and debate has assumed a transitional form as well. This process of transitional constitutional dialogue and debate is utilized with great effectiveness by multiple, overlapping, often conflicting forces within these states to achieve their purposes, all moderated and, to some degree, controlled by the ruling Party – though in different ways, and sometimes with considerably more difficulty, than under the instrumentalism of the past.

This chapter reviews the instrumentalist background to western understanding of Vietnamese and Chinese constitutionalism, and then discusses the goals and formulations that informed the constitutional dialogue that occurred in Vietnam in 2001 and early 2002, when a Party-led constitutional amendment process grew into a wide-ranging if managed debate on the substance of Vietnam's Constitution and the role of constitutional amendment and revision. The Vietnamese constitutional dialogue that emerged in 2001 and 2002 – and which has expanded in the years since – also helps us understand the spectrum of options open to a key political force like the Communist Party in managing this expanded transitional constitutionalism, and the ways in which such dialogue and debate can strengthen rather than weaken the legitimacy and the authority of the ruling Party.

THE TRADITIONAL ANALYSIS OF SOCIALIST CONSTITUTIONS

An instrumentalist analytical model has had substantial and lasting power in explaining the role of constitutions in Vietnam, China and other Party-dominated states. The parties themselves, as well as scholars within and outside Vietnam, China and other Party-dominated states, have always viewed constitutions as controlled, as rhetorically generous in rights and privileges granted but politically dominated and always subject to direction from the ruling party. Constitutions have been an important means of control, of expressing policy, of mobilizing unified action, and a changeable form subject to wholesale or piecemeal revision when Party policy has required. This analytical framework dominated western understanding of the Chinese Constitution for at least four decades after the founding of the People's Republic in 1949, as well as the understanding of Vietnam's constitutional processes for virtually all of the history of the Democratic Republic of Vietnam (1954–1976) and the Socialist Republic of Vietnam (1976–present) (Institute of Law 1977).

At the same time, there have been a few scholars and other observers dissatisfied with the simplicities of an analytical model in which a constitution is nothing but a tool of the Party, who sought an initial understanding of the role of constitutional dialogue in such states even at times when the socialist countries were ruled by authoritarian regimes far stricter than those now in place in such countries as Vietnam and China. Such observers did not deny instrumentalism, but they did seek to detail it and identify its complexities. For Vietnam, the distinguished journalist and author Bernard Fall sought to understand some of the complexity of Vietnamese constitutional discussions even at a time when little source material was available and the dominant western (and Vietnamese) view of these processes was fiercely instrumentalist (Fall 1954; Fall 1956; Fall 1959; Fall 1960a; Fall 1960b; Fall 1966; Fall 1967; Fall 1975).

Some western scholars have also sought to understand the debate on constitutionalism in China that has waxed and waned since the late 1970s (Waldron 1995; Nathan 1997). Yet the instrumentalist analysis of Vietnam's and China's constitutions has always remained dominant, not only because each ruling Communist Party remained dominant but also because of a lack of detailed source material, the almost complete absence of an understood context for and details of constitutional debate that might have informed a more nuanced analytical approach. And times change: Vietnam, like China, is a considerably more open state and society today than when Vietnam's 1959, 1980 or 1992 Constitutions were adopted. In the wake of the broad constitutional dialogue that took place in Vietnam in 2001 and early 2002 and has expanded since, scholars now have some of the data necessary to begin a reappraisal of the processes of constitutional dialogue in Vietnam and similarly situated states.

Vietnam's recent constitutional amendment and dialogue processes are not only instruments of Party policy, the puppetry of a dominant party. Recent constitutional amendment and dialogue processes in Vietnam – one might even call them struggles – also support a different analytical model. What emerges from an analysis of these debates is that, at least in Vietnam, and in recent years, the Constitution has become considerably more than a mechanism for control and mobilization. In the Vietnamese case, the Constitution has also become a platform for wide-ranging debate on political, economic, and social arrangements in a transitional state. The Vietnamese Constitution and its amendment and dialogue processes have become a forum for dialogue – moderated, bounded, and controlled dialogue – as well as a framework for management and mobilization. In each of these facets robust but controlled constitutional debate can serve to reinforce and enhance Party legitimacy and authority.

In this analytical framework, as this chapter shows, constitutional dialogue is coordinated and directed but not entirely controlled by direct fiat. A less restrained constitutional dialogue and constitutional amendment process can be effective in helping to preserve constitutional legitimacy, facilitating reasonably open discussions on constitutional forms and powers, enabling dialogue among elites and resolving their conflicts, and opening new paths for exploring constitutional implementation and powers, all while preserving political control over the boundaries and results of constitutional dialogue and constitutional amendment. In short, constitutional dialogue and constitutional amendment in a socialist transitional state like Vietnam serve both proto-constitutionalist as well as adapted authoritarian goals.

Vietnam has adopted four Constitutions since it declared independence from France in 1945 and established a socialist republic, first in the north and then extended to the south in 1975. Three of those Constitutions, promulgated in 1959, 1980, and 1992, were the product of a command economy and a single party state (of which the single party state today remains a central feature of contemporary Vietnamese political and social life) (Muoi 1992; Duiker 1992; Dung and Tuan 1999). The 1946 Constitution, adopted at a time in which the Democratic Republic of Vietnam was new, reflects a somewhat broader acceptance of diverse economic and social forces in Vietnamese society during a period of wider political alliance. Constitutional emendation played little role in Vietnam's first four decades: Each of the post-1945 Constitutions reflected the dominance of Party power, and minor tinkering with the machinery of state organization and the forms of command rhetoric were usually accomplished through "re-constitutionalization" – the enactment of a new and somewhat differently worded Constitution – rather than amending a more permanent document.

In the mid and late 1980s, Vietnam turned to market liberalization as a solution to pressing economic problems and international isolation. Like China but unlike later developments in Russia and eastern Europe, the Vietnamese Communist Party consciously and intentionally maintained Communist Party control over these economic and social processes. Vietnam's 1992 Constitution, the fourth adopted since 1945, began to reflect that growing space in Vietnam's economy and society. The 1992 Constitution also sought to recruit and harness entrepreneurial peasants, business people, southerners of Chinese descent, intellectuals and other formerly castigated groups to the Party's economic agenda, and began attempting to cautiously and gradually remake a state machinery to suit economic flexibility and continued political control (Heng 1992; Thanh 1993; Thayer 1993).

"CONSTITUTIONAL REVIVAL," CONSTITUTIONAL LEGITIMACY, CONSTITUTIONAL RELEVANCE: THE DIVERGENT ORIGINS OF CONSTITUTIONAL REVISION IN VIETNAM

In December 2001, ten years after adopting the 1992 Constitution, Vietnam adopted important amendments to that document for the first time. That process had a long gestation, and several overlapping goals. Party, government and academic discussions on amending the 1992 Constitution had begun some years earlier, and a Constitutional Amendment Commission was established in May 2001 to draft the amendments and explanatory documentation (Sidel 2002).

The constitutional amendment process originally had two goals, both primarily rooted in reaction to the substantial changes in Vietnamese society and state policies since the adoption of the 1992 Constitution. But one of those aims was arguably broader and deeper than the other. The more narrowly tailored aim was to "bring the constitutional and legal framework into line with the country's shift from a centrally planned economy to a socialist-oriented market system" (VNS 2001a). This was a reactive conception of constitutional revision that would infuse the Vietnamese process until its end in December 2001, a formulation that focused on strengthening the state machinery, reforming Vietnam's cumbersome and often corrupt national and local administrative system, reducing and shortening governmental procedures, decentralizing decision-making, reducing the size of government bureaucracy, making administration more responsive to citizens, and upgrading the civil service, all in response to substantial changes in the economy and society, but without explicitly addressing the broader and even more complex questions of political and structural relationships among Vietnam's executive, legislative, and judicial institutions as an element in reaching those goals. Yet even these more defined aims were substantial and difficult steps forward for Vietnam and the Party.

At the same time, a somewhat different and not altogether consistent formulation of the goals of the constitutional amendment process also emerged in the spring and early summer of 2001. These ideas went further, calling the goal of the constitutional process a "clarification of the responsibilities, functions and relations among legislative, executive and juridical bodies in conformity with the new situation" (VNS 2001b). This somewhat broader and deeper formulation might have implied a broader revision of the 1992 Constitution (or even, perhaps a new draft Constitution) rather than individual amendments. But that approach was quickly abandoned by the Party in the spring and summer of 2001 – though it would be raised repeatedly by legislators and other observers in the constitutional debate that followed in the fall and winter of 2001.

What seemed common to these overlapping approaches was the need to bring the Constitution into line with rapid economic and social change and current economic and social policy, to avoid a sort of creeping constitutional irrelevance. This would be a "constitutional revival" predicated on bringing the Constitution up to date with developments in Vietnamese society (VNS 2001a). But the amendment process was crucial not only for implementing the policies in question but also for the legitimacy of the Constitution itself after a decade-long period in which the realities of Vietnamese life had far outstripped older constitutional provisions (Sidel 2002).

In the summer, fall and winter of 2001, Party and legal personnel began publishing a series of articles and statements intended to prepare Party members, government officials and knowledgeable segments of the public for constitutional revision, highlight proposed constitutional amendments, explain decisions already taken by the Party and National Assembly, build support for the draft amendments and the amendment process, and deter amendments and debate that were outside the bounds the Party considered appropriate. Crucial among those articles was a series in the main Party political and theoretical journal *Tap chi Cong san* (*Communist Review*) in 2001 on constitutional amendment that reached many thousands of middle and senior Party members and officials (An 2001; Dung 2001a; Hien 2001; Le Hong Son 2001; Thao 2001a; Uc 2001).

In one of the first such articles, the prominent legal scholar Dao Tri Uc addressed a key debate in Party, government, legal and academic circles: the goals and extent of constitutional revision. Professor Uc gave a brief but respectful hearing to the view that a "fundamental revision" of the Constitution (i.e. a new document) might be needed, but strongly favored a more limited amendment approach. In so clearly supporting a limited approach to constitutional revision in the Party's primary journal, Uc also directly signaled the Party's decision against "fundamental revision." And in doing so he directly aligned himself, and by implication the Party itself, with the "reactive" or "catch-up" school of constitutional amendment: the purpose of this exercise was to "make the Constitution conform better to the realities of life" in a rapidly changing Vietnam, and thus assist Party, state and Constitution in retaining their legitimacy. This was not the time for more sweeping reappraisal through "fundamental revision." Professor Uc also signaled the Party and National Assembly leadership decision to endorse the insertion of the concept of a "state governed by law" (nha nuoc phap quyen) in Article 2 of the proposed revision, a matter that had originally been raised and endorsed at the recent Party Congress (Uc 2001).

At the same time, the Party journal's discussion of constitutional amendment provided an opportunity for raising considerably more controversial and long-term issues of constitutionalism, albeit in carefully worded terms. Legal scholar Nguyen Van Thao, who would later pen one of the more trenchant commentaries on the draft amendments, sought to raise awareness of the need for "constitutional protection" in an October 2001 Tap chi Cong san article. In Vietnam "constitutional protection" means constitutional enforcement. This was a sensitive issue, for Vietnam had not yet developed a system for passing judgment on the constitutionality of laws and other legal documents, as well as Party and state action that might violate constitutional norms. Thao raised, publicly and in print in the key Party journal, the possibility of a constitutional court (toa an hien phap) or constitutional commission (uy ban hien phap) to "adjudicate unconstitutional documents." He also raised the controversial issue of allowing the new administrative courts, first established only in 1995, the broader authority to judge whether "the activities of administrative institutions are based upon the Constitution and the laws" (Thao 2001a). Thus even within the

Party, there was some continuing pressure for at least the discussion of constitutional revision, and perhaps its themes and goals as well. This conflict would continue until the National Assembly adopted constitutional amendments at the end of 2001.

KEY ISSUES IN THE CONSTITUTIONAL AMENDMENT PROCESS

From the beginning, Party and government leaders also sought to channel constitutional revision into limited areas, by rejecting the prospect of "fundamental revision," by turning away from broader formulations of the amendment process, and by limiting debate to certain key areas in which the 1992 Constitution had clearly fallen behind the times. Five key areas dominated debate throughout 2001. These were narrower issue areas than "fundamental revision," "constitutional protection," the leading role of the Party under Article 4 of the Constitution and the broader problems of fundamental authority in Vietnam, but they were still substantial and important topics of constitutional debate and governance.

THE ROLE, FUNCTIONS AND AUTHORITY OF THE NATIONAL ASSEMBLY

A key continuing problem throughout the 1990s had been the capacity of the National Assembly to carry out real oversight and examination of the work of the government, prompting drafters to articulate a specific goal for the amendment process: "The National Assembly has the role of supervision but it does not possess directly subordinate auditors so that such supervision can be carried out effectively." Calls, echoed in part by Assembly Chairman Nguyen Van An, a senior Party organizational figure who also headed the Constitutional Amendment Commission, focused on expanding the number of "professional" (*chuyen trach*) delegates in order to strengthen Assembly oversight committees and debate, authorizing and supporting an Assembly legal drafting agency in order to wrest away law drafting from ministries pursuing their own parochial agendas in the drafting process, expanding Assembly supervisory and approval and auditing power over national budgets and devolving authority over local budgets to local legislatures, and expanding the professional staff of the Assembly devoted to audit and examination functions (Vietnam News Service 2001c). Throughout

25

the constitutional amendment process the extent, scope and pace of this process of strengthening the National Assembly engaged the Commission and the delegates; the fundamental point that such a strengthening was necessary seemed to be agreed upon by all forces. But the pace and force of that strengthening caused extensive debate and conflict. And that conflict centered on proposals to allow Assembly delegates to hold senior government leaders (including ministers and the heads of Vietnam's key legal institutions) accountable through "votes of confidence." Whether or not to allow "votes of confidence" – and then later how to implement and control such a process – would emerge as a lightning rod in the Vietnamese debate on constitutional change.

DEVOLUTION AND CONTROL: PROBLEMS IN LOCAL DEMOCRACY AND GOVERNANCE

Issues of control within and devolution to local representative and legislative bodies elected by citizens were increasingly a strong concern, particularly the role of people's committees performing executive functions at the district level in cities and in the countryside. These concerns mirrored discussion throughout the 1990s in Vietnam on the appropriate role of local executive and legislative committees in a state long dominated by Party and state appointees. Some Assembly delegates called for the devolution of some budgetary authority to institutions in order to enable officials and representatives to respond to local issues (and to enable the National Assembly to increase its supervision at the national level). Some delegates argued for abolition of the district-level committees as a "superfluous level," supporting a strengthening of the committees both above (provincial, municipal) and below (village) the district committees. Others called for more central control of the appointment of leadership of province-level people's committees, and more province-level control of the leadership of lower-level councils. These issues aggregated to a wide-ranging debate on the role of local democracy and central control in a transitional state.

THE TRANSITION OF A SOCIALIST LEGAL INSTITUTION: THE PROBLEMS OF THE PROCURACY (STATE PROSECUTORS)

Throughout the 1990s, and particularly in the five or six years before the convening of the Constitutional Amendment Commission in 2001, substantial public and official dissatisfaction had grown with the effect-iveness of the Office of the Public Prosecutor (Procuracy), a powerful Vietnamese institution with origins in Soviet legal theory and practice. For nearly fifty years the Procuracy, headquartered in Hanoi with offices down to the provincial and district levels, had been responsible for criminal investigation and public prosecution, as well as for func-tions that had no direct analogue outside the traditional socialist context: monitoring the legality of activities by organizations through-out the legal sector (a sort of legal sector inspectorate over the judiciary and other agencies), and for monitoring compliance with the law on the part of state institutions, mass organizations and commercial firms as a kind of national inspectorate general (Ginsburgs 1979).

A consensus had emerged that the public prosecutors' offices had failed in many of its assigned tasks. Some criminal investigations and public prosecutions were handled shoddily, and a gradually resurgent judiciary and defense bar occasionally pointed that out in arguments and even judgments. Several significant corruption scandals hit the public prosecutors' offices at national and local levels. The prosecutors' ill-defined and even more haphazardly implemented inspection roles in the legal sector and the broader society were regarded with derision and suspicion, wholly ineffective but also a throwback to Stalinist times, and a new array of state institutions (including a national inspectorate and auditing agency) represented more "modern" approaches to these accountability problems. Over many years a debate had raged – as in China – on eliminating criminal investigation and broader political, social and economic monitoring duties from the public prosecutors' portfolio, leaving only public prosecution and an inspection role in the legal sector as the prosecutors' primary tasks. The 2001 constitu-tional amendment process was intended clearly to resolve this debate, with the Party and the National Assembly leadership forcefully sup-porting a sharp reduction in the role of the public prosecutors to undertaking and improving public prosecution and inspection in the legal sector.

But the prosecutors and their allies were not giving up so easily, struggling to maintain the scope and extent of their authority in a new and vastly different era from the Stalinist period in which procuracies had emerged dominant in socialist legal systems. There were multiple and conflicting views as the debate raged at the National Assembly, a debate that would infuse the entire constitutional amendment process and produce legal and political ripples after its completion.

ECONOMIC REFORM

Although economic reform did not dominate the 2001 Vietnamese debates to the degree other issues received attention, it remained an important theme and one that emerged in several different contexts. One conflict centered on the extent to which constitutional language should be amended to reflect Vietnam's economic changes, with some emphasis on labor concern about the breadth of constitutional wording endorsing market-based competition and the freedom of business activity. A second emphasized the role of key institutional actors and interests in the economic reform process, and the use of the Constitution to give such groups prominence and authority. The national trade unions and the Peasants Union were among those pressing on this issue. A national umbrella group representing intellectuals, business people and other non-Party forces, already featured in the Constitution, lobbied for even stronger treatment. Although somewhat muted in the debate, an interesting debate about class would appear, as different forces supported or opposed constitutional terminology referencing class and stratum.

SOCIAL JUSTICE AND THE ROLE OF THE CONSTITUTION: THE DEBATE ON SCHOOL FEES

Many of the themes already identified are fundamentally related to issues of social justice in the Vietnamese transition. Certainly debates on government accountability, the role of local elected representatives and councils, the power of prosecutors, and the role of class are themes of social justice. But social justice also arose explicitly in the Vietnamese constitutional debates of 2001 in the form of many months of intense debate over a short clause, Article 59, in Vietnam's 1992 Constitution that banned collection of tuition fees for attendance at public elementary schools. Proponents of amending that clause – "primary education is compulsory and dispensed free of charge" – focused on Vietnam's changing realities: fees in fact were being charged for primary education throughout the country, and the Constitution appeared increasingly irrelevant to practices on the ground. Opponents viewed the Constitution as the bulwark against unjust policies, demanding that the Constitution continue to stand for social justice even where practice deviated from that goal.

THE AMENDMENT PROCESS, CONSTITUTIONAL
LEGITIMACY, AND CONSTITUTIONAL DIALOGUE

From the very first stages of the 2001 constitutional amendment process, delegates, scholars, retired officials and citizens called for broader
constitutional reforms and raised issues of constitutional legitimacy,
while Party and National Assembly leadership sought to channel and
rechannel the constitutional amendment process back into more limited
paths. And even the range of officially-sponsored amendment proposals
threatened to throw the process into disorder. At the May–June 2001
Assembly session at which constitutional revision was initially on the
agenda and the Constitutional Amendment Commission was established, a senior Assembly official "urged" the delegates to "focus on
three main issues: the goals, requirements and guiding concepts for
revision of the Constitution; the scope of constitutional revision; and
the scope of study of the revision and supplement to the organization of
the state machinery." He did not succeed. "Of course," as Lao Dong
newspaper dryly noted, "the delegates spoke out far more broadly" than
that (Bao Lao Dong 2001a). Discussion ranged from the role and
professionalization of the National Assembly to structures of local
democracy, the role of the people's councils and committees, decisional
power on public finance, the appointment or election of provincial
people's committee heads, and other questions. Delegates called for
constitutional amendment to accelerate strengthening the quality of
judges, allowing local levels of government to nominate judges to the
lower courts, and empowering single judges at the lowest level of courts
to try relatively simple criminal, economic and civil cases, rather than
the three-judge panel currently in use. Opponents of the plan to limit
the jurisdiction of the public prosecutors signaled that they would not
depart the arena, rising to make their case for maintaining the multiple
roles of the Public Prosecutor, while others harshly criticized the public
prosecutors for ineffectiveness, overly broad authority, and corruption
(Bao Lao Dong 2001b).

Even this discussion went further than Party and Assembly leaders
might have preferred. But Assembly delegates went still further, rising
to question the effect of constitutional amendment on the legitimacy of
the constitution in an implicit challenge to the Party and Assembly's
attempt to re-legitimize the Constitution by bringing it up to date with
some of the transformations of Vietnamese society and economy.
Delegates complained that discussions of less important, technical or

even trivial constitutional amendments might damage rather than enhance constitutional legitimacy. One delegate put the problem of constitutional legitimacy clearly:

> On hearing the view that the Constitution should be amended ... I did not understand why we are amending successively like this. In the spirit of a democratic system, the Constitution is enormously important and sacred. In 1946 we adopted a Constitution, and subsequently we have continued to revise it, and so now we have the 1992 Constitution. On this revision, I think there are not many urgent issues that require such urgent revision ... [W]e should study [and work out] a strategy [for] the issues that require amendment. And then we should revise once until it is completed.
>
> (Bao Lao Dong 2001c)

Other delegates concurred, calling for the National Assembly to reaffirm the "correct spirit" of the 1992 Constitution. The Party and government shared this concern for limiting the scope of the revision process, though perhaps their motivation was avoiding the expansion of constitutional debate in addition to the maintenance of constitutional legitimacy. The Vice Chairman and senior legal official of the National Assembly sought to return the debate back into defined and approved territory:

> The recent Ninth Party Congress came to a conclusion [on these matters] and we ... have a duty to systematize the viewpoints and line decided by the Ninth Party Congress. So we must revise the chapters on state organization, some economic, scientific and technology issues ... and on the state machinery. We cannot just separately legislate on separation of powers and the powers of the state machinery like this; first and foremost because we must ensure the reality of the effectiveness of the State.
>
> (Bao Lao Dong 2001c)

After the May–June 2001 Assembly session ended, the Assembly leadership quickly sought to rechannel and limit the amendment process. An Assembly leader spoke directly to delegates through the National Assembly's newspaper, seeking to provide clear guidance: "[T]his amendment ... of certain articles in the 1992 Constitution must ... continue to affirm the ... form of the state machinery currently in effect and concentrate only on amending some articles that are really necessary and urgent and related to the organization, functions, duties and authority of the organizations of the state machinery" (Nguoi Dai bieu Nhan Dan 2001).

Between early June and mid-July 2001 the Constitutional Amendment Commission finished drafting most of the constitutional amendments and their rationales. On August 15, 2001, the Commission released a draft of the proposed amendments with a request for comments from citizens and organizations throughout Vietnam, as well as overseas Vietnamese abroad, in a comment period to end on September 30. The proposed amendments were reprinted in a number of newspapers.

The comment process on this constitutional revision has resulted in the availability of a public debate on constitutional amendments of a sort hitherto unknown to scholars of socialist constitutions, and in which interests and forces in Vietnamese society sought to mould the constitutional amendment process. Comments and commentary on the proposed constitutional amendments and on the amendment process appeared in newspapers and were sent to the National Assembly, which later posted a selection on its website. A range of other, generally much more negative comments were also written and posted for reading by Vietnamese dissidents resident abroad, as well as a few by dissidents resident in Vietnam. These focused primarily on the retention of Article 4 stipulating the leading role of the Communist Party and related issues (Quang 1992; Chinh 1992; for other overseas views see Nhan Dan 2001d). Many of the organizational comments published in Vietnamese newspapers or sent to the National Assembly endorsed the amendment process and the specific proposed amendments, in some cases seeking heightened constitutional attention (including formal identification in the Constitution) for the commenting group.

Organizational opinions split sharply, both within and between organizations on some of the more controversial institutional reform amendments under discussion – shifts to the functions, powers and appointments of people's committees, particularly at the district level, and the role of the public prosecutors. At a Fatherland Front meeting in Ninh Binh reported at length in the Party newspaper *Nhan Dan*, for example, "many views" supported the public prosecutors' position that "the general procuratorial [inspectorate] functions . . . should not be removed, but instead the level of procuracy cadres should be improved and upgraded." Others directly disagreed, "suggesting that this function of the procuracy be eliminated, because the current situation of abuse of position and authority, the procuracy generates difficulties for production and business units. And in circumstances in which the procuracy acts mistakenly, who will monitor the procuracy?" (Nhan Dan 2001a). An unsurprising and strong organizational dissent came from the Office of the Public Prosecutors (Supreme People's Procuracy).

At times organizational comments sharply criticized the efforts of the Constitutional Amendment Commission. For example, the 1992 Constitution had stipulated clearly that school fees may not be charged in elementary schools. In the ten years since 1992, many Vietnamese public schools had begun charging a wide range of tuition and fees. This was a controversial development, but to the Constitutional Amendment Commission the Constitution appeared out of date and out of touch with developments in society, and so the Commission proposed, in reactive mode, eliminating the constitutional ban on school fees. This proposal came in for fierce debate, both at the comment stage and when the National Assembly met to consider the constitutional amendments. This approach – the notion of bringing the Constitution in line with an unjust policy, no matter how widespread – came under stinging attack from a number of organizations.

Among the institutional discussants, the trade union exchanges went perhaps the furthest in criticizing the draft amendments and the amendment process. Although trade union officials recited their agreement to bringing the Constitution up to date through amendment, their 'seething' discussion attacked many of the specific proposals in addition to their fierce opposition to the proposal to allow school fees: the draft's class-biased term "intellectual stratum" should be changed to "the ranks of intellectuals." The endorsement of "healthy [economic] competition" in the draft ignored worker protection concerns, and should be changed to "competition within a legal framework," reflecting worker protection concerns. The trade union officials "unanimously" called for retention of the language prohibiting school fees, an issue that increasingly captured the attention of organizations and delegates concerned with the proactive power of the Constitution to direct and affect policy. The trade unions also opposed reducing the number of judges needed for less complex trials at the grassroots level to one on the ground that such a change would lead to injustice and mistakes (Bao Lao Dong 2001d).

Organizational comments also directly sought to bolster the commenting organizations' status in the Constitution. The Supreme People's Procuracy, of course, fought to retain its wide jurisdiction and expansive powers. The Fatherland Front requested that the Front's constitutional definition be clarified and upgraded with a longer description and a specific notation that the "VFF is the political foundation of the people's administration." The Vietnam Peasants Union also called for constitutional recognition of its role as representative of Vietnamese peasants, a call echoed by the Fatherland Front as well in a kind of informal alliance-building in the muted but serious constitutional amendment status-enhancement campaign (Nhan Dan 2001b). In turn the Peasants Union, also engaging in alliance building, called for constitutional recognition and definition of its role as well as that of a key organization representing intellectuals, the Federation of Science and Technology Organizations. And at several meetings, trade unions called for a considerably more detailed and broadened constitutional recognition and discussion of the key role of the trade unions and the lawful rights of working people (Bao Lao Dong 2001d). Overseas Vietnamese called for more favorable treatment in the Constitution and government policy, including representation in the National Assembly (My 2001). In virtually each of these instances, organizational calls for constitutional recognition of their role were carefully paired with endorsements of the constitutional draft, not surprising in a process in which collective and national interests are supposed to come before organizational interests.

Individual comments focused on particularly important or controversial proposed amendments. Individuals, many highly placed, supported and opposed the plans to narrow public prosecutorial discretion, decentralize local budgetary authority to local people's councils, called for a clause ensuring compensation to domestic and foreign investors in the event that changing policy or law harms their interests, and asked for a stronger provision on the right to conduct private business than the 1992 stipulation, which was considered "too dependent on the will of public authorities." Other individual comments proposed language on social policy to emphasize the duty of the state to protect the poor, unemployed, elderly and others who have suffered in Vietnam's reform era, while a National Assembly delegate from a mountainous province called the 1992 constitutional provision prohibiting school fees "very progressive, creating conditions for children to go to school." For him, there was a clear social justice aspect to the problem, as well as a firm sense that the constitutional provisions should help promote progressive policy rather than merely disappearing when the policies became too expensive. "[I]f this section is eliminated, then when will education in the mountainous areas catch up with the lowland areas?" A Foreign Ministry cadre chimed in on this issue, noting that the commentary draft released by the Constitutional Amendment Commission provided "no interpretation or reasons" for this amendment and that international experience was moving toward, rather than away from, tuition exemption in both primary and secondary education. They were joined by overseas Vietnamese and other commenters as well, in statements posted on the National Assembly constitutional commentary website.

Others went still further, seeking to use the opinion process to broaden the range of potential constitutional amendments, establish an agenda for broader reform, or to put deeper constitutional and political issues on a longer-term agenda. In a stinging commentary published in early September, for example, a senior government official noted the confusion and inefficiency in legal and judicial organization throughout Vietnam and urged that the constitutional amendment process consider fundamental change in these structural relationships.

> Who stands at the head of the legal system? . . . Legal institutions should not belong to the executive system . . . What is the position of the public prosecutor? . . . The organization of the court system is inappropriate . . . So in these amendments to the Constitution . . . we must study issues such as establishing a legal commission with an attorney-general as chair (standing at the head of the legal system . . .); establishing a public prosecutors' office belonging to the Government in place of the procuracy; and organizing the courts in accordance with jurisdiction over trials, and not based on administrative levels, and strengthening the functions of the administrative courts.
>
> (Diep Van Son 2001)

The expression of these kinds of opinions clearly implicated a different role of a constitutional amendment process. Rather than reactively conforming the Constitution to changes that had occurred in Vietnam over ten years, these commentators and others sought to utilize the amendment process as a proactive opportunity to rework inadequate and inappropriate state functions and relationships and to substantially alter the functions of Vietnam's legal and judicial agencies. This was constitutional amendation as the beginning of a reform process, not merely its compromise-laden summarization.

Other commentaries raised broader issues of constitutionalism. The prominent constitutional scholar Nguyen Dang Dung wrote that the Constitution is not an ordinary law, and called for a clear recognition of the differences between constitutional and statutory drafting so as to "permit the Constitution a long life, and so it can serve as the basis for other laws, because Constitutional stability is one of the fundamental measures of the stability of a political system" (Dung 2001b). A senior staff member at the National Assembly supported this view and its implications for the 2001 amendment drafting process, harking back to 1946 rather than 1992. In an implicit slap at all of Vietnam's post-1946 constitutions, he called upon the Commission to "inherit the essence of the progressive and scientific terminology and arrangement of the 1946 Constitution, to the level of substance. For example, some of the substantive terms that ensure democracy, on holding referenda, testimony before the National Assembly . . ." None of these were matters that the Party or the National Assembly wished to include in the constitutional amendments. Firmly echoing the comments of other liberal constitutional critics, he noted:

> The Constitution must have long vitality, embody a high level of generality in accordance with the proper meaning of a Constitution, avoiding being trivialized and petty matters. All these details should be made vivid in individual laws. I think that in this Draft of the Constitution, we are using a bit too much of the language of mobilization.
>
> (Tri 2001)

Among the most far-reaching and important individual comments were those provided late in the opinion process by the noted legal scholar Nguyen Van Thao, writing in a domestic development policy journal. Thao raised publicly the knotty question of determining the "constitutionality" and "legality" of legal texts.

> In nearly ten years of Constitutional implementation, we have never once seen the National Assembly or its Standing Committee abrogate, cancel, or suspend the implementation of a single document issued by the President, the Government or the Prime Minister. The system of monitoring is almost never exercised by the Government or the Prime Minister with respect to the ministries or local authorities, despite the fact that some legal documents issued by ministries and local authorities evidently violate the Constitution or laws.
>
> (Thao 2001b)

For Thao, the fundamental reason was clear: "The 1992 Constitution did not delegate to any institution judgment on the constitutionality of laws," and the 1992 Constitution remained unclear on the extent of the National Assembly's abrogation and cancellation powers. For Thao, the question of adjudicating constitutionality should now be on the agenda for debate – but the Constitutional Amendment Commission and the Party did not agree. Thao shifted from constitutional adjudication to rights, raising objections to the Commission's rather brief and (in his view) weak proposal that the Constitution include wording that "a defendant's right to counsel is guaranteed." "This is insufficient," Thao wrote, quoting directly from and relying on the International Convention on Civil and Political Rights. "Instead we must clearly declare that defendants have the right to counsel, and institutions undertaking legal process must guarantee that defendants are able to exercise this right." Then Thao went a step further, coming close to demanding that the provisions of this international human rights convention be noted as a form of constitutional legislative history in domestic law so that the origins and basis for this provision would be clear (Thao 2001b).

Professor Thao was also one of many to endorse the restriction of the procuracy's (public prosecutors') powers, ending its decades-long jurisdiction of monitoring compliance with law of economic, social and political institutions and organizations outside the legal sector. But Thao went further, warning that even leaving the public prosecutors authorized to "monitor activities in the legal sphere" required "clear definition of scope." He warned, fairly directly, of the potential for fierce conflict between the public prosecutors and the Ministry of Justice and local bureaus of justice if the scope of the prosecutors' remaining legal monitoring role was not clearly defined. Thao strongly endorsed the now widespread view that 'public prosecution' should be the 'primary function' of a reformed procuracy. But, again, he went further than many others, coming to the as-yet largely unaddressed and highly controversial problem of allowing an independent, traditionally powerful, now somewhat restricted procuracy to remain as an independent branch of the state in a new era. "In almost all countries of the world," he noted pointedly, "these are called 'prosecution offices' [*vien cong to*], with the responsibility of bringing law-breakers before the courts for trial. Prosecutorial institutions are ordinarily sited within the government, and prosecution activities come within the executive sphere" (Thao 2001b).

Faced with numerous useful comments on the amendments the Party and Assembly leadership sought to consider, and with a number of opinions urging broader reforms and strengthening of the Constitution, the leadership sought to rechannel discussion back toward formal amendments under consideration. In important review meetings in mid-September in Ho Chi Minh City and Hanoi, National Assembly and Constitutional Amendment Commission chair Nguyen Van An reaffirmed the Party and government's intent that the amendments "concentrate on issues that are truly urgent, that are ripe for adoption and practical testing, and must ensure a high spirit of unity." Focus remained on the amendments that would clarify and improve the functioning of the state machinery (Nhan Dan 2001c). Yet almost immediately critics rebounded, urging the Constitutional Amendment Commission to broaden the scope of the amendment process, including deeper recognition of economic reforms (Quang 2001).

Even as critics sought to broaden the amendment process, the leadership continued their efforts to narrow consideration to approved amendments, this time directed toward critics both abroad and at home. In an interview in the key legal newspaper *Phap Luat (Law)* in late September, the Assembly Chairman (and Chair of the Constitutional Amendment Commission) reiterated the Party's view that the 1992 Constitution should (and would) not undergo wholesale revision nor replacement, a direct counter to the fundamental revision view. But the real message of An's September 19 interview was to address what became known as the Article 4 issue.

Article 4 of the 1992 Constitution had, like other Vietnamese constitutions before it, stipulated the Party's leadership role over Vietnamese state and society. During 2001 dissident overseas Vietnamese and a few domestic dissidents had called for the deletion or substantial revision of Article 4, writing numerous commentaries on the constitutional amendment process that were republished on overseas Vietnamese and dissident websites and thus available (through firewalls) to some within Vietnam. Even some domestic commentators (though none published on the official National Assembly comment site) had argued that the Party's role as defined in Article 4 should be supplemented (*bo sung*) by discussion of the "process" (*phuong thuc*) by which the Party leads state and society. An firmly rejected any consideration of deleting, substantially revising, or supplementing Article 4 on the primacy of the Communist Party, a position consistently maintained by Party and Assembly leadership throughout the constitutional amendment process (Bao Phap Luat 2001).

The Constitutional Amendment Commission worked quickly in October 2001 to digest and determine which of the comments should affect the amendment proposal scheduled to go before the National Assembly in late November. Before revised amendments could go before the National Assembly, there was another crucial step that provided the impetus for the Constitutional Amendment Commission's hard work throughout October of 2001. The amendments revised by the Commission had first to be discussed and approved at the highest reaches of the Communist Party at a Party Central Committee meeting held in early November, and at related meetings of the Party's Political Bureau. At the November Party meeting, Party General Secretary reaffirmed the narrowing of discussion on constitutional amendment to certain key areas. "Revising the Constitution [is] a must," Manh told Party officials and others around the nation in widely publicized remarks, "but for the time being efforts should focus only on urgent issues which had already been clearly determined and approved by the majority of the people." The General Secretary's closing statement also once again closed the door on broader constitutional revision. "The question is not posed as to the comprehensive revision of the Constitution," but only specific amendments, likely reflecting a reassertion, and then deflection, of the "fundamental revision" viewpoint within the Party (VNS 2001d; Nhan Dan 2001e). The Party also made clear that it would continue to review and approve the amendment process when it reached the National Assembly,[1] and the Constitutional Amendment Commission and National Assembly Standing Committee proceeded to finalize the amendment proposal on the basis of the Party's views and instructions, for presentation at the National Assembly nine days later (Nhan Dan 2001e).

With the Party's instructions now in place, the debate on Vietnam's Constitution moved into the National Assembly. The Assembly Chairman opened the proceedings on November 21, 2001 with clear instructions echoing the Party's discussions: "Only amend and supplement certain articles that are truly urgent and necessary, and that have sufficient foundation and have high unanimity; do not undertake the issue of fundamental revision, or of the entire Constitution" (Nhan Dan 2001f).

In reality this meant that a host of controversial issues were now off the amendment agenda. They included the structure for people's committees and councils at various levels, and the transfer and appointment of the chairs of people's committees; "the Amendment Commission asked that they be withdrawn." That left several key controversial issues, on which the Party and Assembly leadership had specific recommendations arising out of the Party plenum. Seeking to end the bitter struggle over the jurisdiction of the public prosecutors, the leadership recommended that the Procuracy's jurisdiction be severely curtailed in accordance with the earlier proposals; and the inclusion of a "vote of confidence" for government ministers in the Constitution as "an aid to the National Assembly in exercising its powers better" (VnExpress 2001a).

Thus the stage was set for constitutional debate at the National Assembly. The issue of public prosecutorial jurisdiction was virtually settled when, in addition to the clear Party and Commission recommendation that its jurisdiction be limited, the Public Prosecutor-General's report to the National Assembly was "ploughed to bits" under severe criticism. In a fierce report, the Assembly's Law Committee "exposed a multitude of limitations in this report, reinforcing the nation's determination to adjust the jurisdiction of the Public Prosecutor." Brutal and fierce criticism of the public prosecutors' office would continue later in the session, when the public prosecutor's report came up for delegate debate (VnExpress 2001b, 2001c, 2001d).

One key topic of Assembly debate was the Preface to the Constitution. Delegates concerned for permanence in the interest of constitutional legitimacy opposed changing the Preface to emphasize "patriotic traditions" and "national solidarity" and to reflect foreign policy and economic diversification; another group viewed the 1992 Preface as "disconnected and inappropriately structured" and pushed for updating Article 16, in which the Amendment Commission recommended specifying diverse sectors of the national economy came under debate. Opposition mounted to prime ministerial appointment of the chairs of province-level people's committees, while delegates supported some devolution of local budgeting authority to local people's committees. A majority of delegates seemed to support restricting the broader jurisdiction of the public prosecutors to oversee fidelity to law in non-legal government and business organizations, though a stubborn minority still opposed this amendment: "With many violations of law occurring, and the prosecutorial sector having accomplished much in this area, if this work is not delegated to the Public Prosecutor then to which institution can it be delegated?" The proposal to allow school fees came in for wide-ranging criticism.

But discussion was not limited to the areas set out by the Party and the National Assembly leadership. Reaching considerably beyond the channeling and narrowing efforts of the Party leadership, delegates raised issues of constitutionalism far beyond the boundaries of constitutional amendment acceptable to the Party. In perhaps the most prominent example, an Assembly delegate and senior legal official in Ho Chi Minh City called for establishment of a constitutional court (*toa an hien phap*) to "defend the Constitution ... against the many forms of constitutional violation that at present cannot be investigated or adjudicated" (Bao Lao Dong 2001e). Speaking to a southern newspaper, a former Deputy Prime Minister pointedly praised the efforts of the judiciary to increase its role and capacities and emerge from "stagnation," while forcefully calling on the judiciary to overcome its "timidity" in the use of administrative courts to protect citizens from official abuses (VnExpress 2001e; see also Nicholson 1999; 2001; 2002a; Nicholson and Quang 2005).

By the first week of December 2001, after the Amendment Commission and Assembly leadership met to finalize amendment language and as the Assembly leadership labored to contain discussion, the leadership once again sought to refocus discussion on the limited amendments favored by the Party and the Amendment Commission, forced once again under delegate pressure to reiterate that "the issue of a fundamental revision of the entire Constitution is ... not posed" (Nhan Dan 2001g).

After months of Party, National Assembly, media and overseas debate, the National Assembly met on December 11 for a final review and debate on the Assembly leadership's adjustment of the constitutional amendments, and to vote on the final version of amendments. Despite months of sharp controversy, in the end the Party leadership won the day on virtually all issues. The amendments to the Constitution's preface emphasizing patriotic traditions and national solidarity passed with a wide majority. After the Assembly leadership accepted delegate proposals to change the term "intellectual stratum" – regarded as class-biased by trade unions and others – to "the ranks of intellectuals," and another proposal eliminating the usage of "class" as applied to workers and peasants, the Assembly adopted the Constitutional amendment identifying Vietnam as a "law-governed state" with another wide majority. The Assembly voted to adopt the amendments on education after the leadership agreed to retain the ban on tuition – a decision popular with the delegates. The devolution of local budgetary authority to provinces and votes of confidence on government officials also passed, after the Amendment Commission brokered a compromise agreement to specify the procedures and time limits for Assembly votes of confidence in government officials in the Law on the Organization of the National Assembly also up for revision at this Assembly session (Nhan Dan 2001h; Bao Lao Dong 2001f).

The Assembly took up the remainder of the proposed amendments the next day, December 12. The Amendment Commission and the Assembly leadership acceded to delegate and public requests for a more liberal provision on firms engaging in business, accepting a formula that firms are "permitted to engage in any business not prohibited by law" and re-emphasizing equal treatment of firms under the Constitution by adding the word "equal" (Vietnam News 2001). When the question of public prosecutorial jurisdiction came up, procurators and their allies once again criticized the proposed amendments. The National Assembly Chairman was forced to step in for a final time on this highly contentious issue, forcefully "stating that this issue had been discussed thoroughly and a majority of the views have supported the draft [amendment]" (VnExpress 2001f). Other amendments also passed, including a provision granting emergency war declaration authority to the Assembly Standing Committee after the Commission revised the wording to emphasize the seriousness of the circumstances in which the Standing Committee might exercise the war power. The Assembly completed its voting by adopting the package of amendments in a resolution.

TOWARD SOCIALIST CONSTITUTIONS AS A PLATFORM FOR DIALOGUE AND DEBATE

After all the fierce debate, the amendments adopted by the National Assembly in mid-December, 2002 reasonably closely matched those proposed by the Constitutional Amendment Commission and the Party in the summer of 2001. They had been the subject of months of spirited dialogue, but in only one significant case – the elimination of the 1992 constitutional ban on school tuition – was the proposal of the Amendment Commission and the Party overturned by public opinion and the National Assembly. Focusing on this mere single refusal, however, miscomprehends the process that emerged in 2001 – a debate on constitutional legitimacy and values unprecedented in Vietnam since 1946 and perhaps unprecedented in the recent Party-dominated socialist community.

How did the Party and Assembly leadership come to manage the constitutionalist debate so clearly evident before and during the National Assembly's debates on the constitutional amendments? Some issues – such as the Article 4 affirmation of the Party's leading role – had been taken off the political agenda by fiat. Others had been taken off the agenda for the time being – such as "constitutional protection," the calls for founding constitutional courts, or strengthening the role of the National Assembly in interpreting the Constitution – but they had sufficient support that Party and Assembly leaders could not mark them as taboo for future discussion. And some constitutionalist issues with potential for sharply enhanced democratic participation and supervision had been incorporated into constitutional amendments. The amendment providing for Assembly votes of confidence on senior government officials came into this category. It now fell to Party and Assembly leaders to implement the provisions for votes of confidence in ways that conformed to the letter and spirit of the amendments while remaining within approved and controlled bounds, illustrating some of the ways in which post-adoption implementation can limit and channel constitutionalist impulses.

POST-ADOPTION CONTROL THROUGH IMPLEMENTATION

The leadership's implementation role would not be easy, for both liberal and more conservative Assembly delegates were watching carefully. Assembly and Party leaders had agreed that detailed provisions on the votes of confidence would be included in the revised Law on the Organization of the National Assembly, to be discussed and adopted in the days after the constitutional amendments were passed, a move they had made to reduce delays and opposition to the votes of confidence amendment but also to retain more control over the scope and shape of the specific procedures to be used in undertaking votes of confidence.

More liberal Assembly delegates demanded institution of a procedure bringing votes of confidence directly to the floor of the Assembly on the proposal of a certain percentage of delegates for debate and vote by all Assembly delegates. They also tactically demanded substantial specificity from the Assembly on provisions for votes of confidence in the revised law on the National Assembly. Assembly and Party leaders opposed votes of confidence on direct motion from the Assembly floor, urgently seeking to devise a process they could manage more easily, and preferring indirect proposal of votes of confidence by the more easily controlled Assembly Standing Committee. Strong debate erupted in the Assembly on these alternatives – direct proposal of votes of confidence based, or indirect power resting in the Standing Committee. The leadership prevailed in delegating that "heavy responsibility" to the Standing Committee, substantially softening and limiting the votes of confidence power stipulated in the constitutional amendment (Bao Lao Dong 2001g). The resulting language in the revised Law on the Organization of the National Assembly rested primary responsibility to undertake votes of confidence in the Standing Committee, blocking direct proposal of votes of confidence in senior government officials in the National Assembly. Acceding to demands by more activist delegates, the leadership did compromise to the extent of agreeing that the Standing Committee would "investigate and present" a vote of confidence motion to the full Assembly "upon the proposal of at least twenty percent of the ... delegates to the National Assembly" or an Assembly committee (Organization Law 2002). By separating the constitutional amendment process from the process of drafting implementing language on those amendments, Party and Assembly leaders had an opportunity to limit the significant constitutionalist spirit on display during the debate on the constitutional amendments in the Assembly – a process made easier by the concern of Assembly delegates, most of them government officials and Party members, for social and political stability.

The ripples of Vietnam's 2001 constitutional debate continued into 2002. Without context, they were difficult to spot. But it is perhaps not coincidental that on the day after the constitutional amendments were promulgated by Vietnam's President in mid-January 2002 and published in major newspapers, National Assembly Chairman Nguyen Van An paid a visit to the Office of the Public Prosecutor-General. An spoke at the wounded national prosecutors' office, its work battered by the National Assembly and its jurisdiction publicly and sharply curtailed. He congratulated prosecutors nationwide on their "achievements" and pointedly "analyz[ed] the amendments to the 1992 Constitution, among them the readjustment to the functions and tasks of the Office of the Public Prosecutor-General." He praised prosecutors' plans to concentrate on the reduced jurisdictional tasks and called upon it to serve actively and faithfully (Nhan Dan 2002a). But even so, National Assembly leaders were still answering pointed questions in mid-March on how the general legal inspection role of the public prosecutors could possibly be undertaken by other agencies, and proposing a redefined role for the public prosecutors as 'attorneys general' in civil and economic cases (VnExpress 2002a). The adoption of a new organizational law for the public prosecutors reaffirmed the amendments in a statute, quieting the debate for the time being (Nhan Dan 2002b).

In January 2002 the Political Bureau of the Party also issued a new resolution on legal reform, likely taking advantage of the readjustments in executive, legislative and judicial institutions to launch a new move for efficiency in legal and law enforcement activities (Nhan Dan 2002c). And in late January the Standing Committee of the National Assembly released a resolution implementing some technical elements of the Constitutional amendments, among them decreeing that the general jurisdiction of the public prosecutors would end as of April 15, 2002 and would thereafter be delegated to government offices, the National Assembly, and local legislatures. For the judiciary, on the other hand, the constitutional amendments appeared to provide some benefit. In the wake of the amendment process, the National Assembly adopted a revised organizational law for the courts broadening the authority of the Supreme People's Court over lower courts and reducing the role of the Ministry of Justice in the management of lower courts.

TRANSITIONAL AND INSTRUMENTAL CONSTITUTIONALISM

In the wake of the 2001 Vietnamese constitutional debate, it is difficult to view the constitutions of such transitional states as Vietnam in a traditional light. Traditional analysis has focused on political control of constitution making and substance, the highly changeable nature of such documents as political policy shifts, the mobilizing role of constitutional documents, and their aspirational role in granting rights and privileges that often seem currently unattainable. Only in rare moments has a constitution itself been the topic of such broad discussion and debate in Vietnam and perhaps in China: perhaps in mid-1940s Vietnam, perhaps in the Beijing of 1988 and 1989, as legal scholars and political activists fiercely debated constitutional protection and the normative role of a constitutional document (Sidel 1995a).

In the wake of the 2001 Vietnamese constitutional debate, an instrumentalist analytical framework for understanding constitutional processes in Vietnam and other similarly situated Party-controlled transitional states must give way to an analytical framework that fully embodies the transitional nature of constitutional debates, society, and the state in these countries. In the new analytical framework of constitutional dialogue that emerges from the recent Vietnamese experience, the Party coordinates and ultimately controls, but through a spectrum of direction and coordination that ranges from high levels of control, to substantial direction, to strong pressure, to relatively open debate – and always maintaining a role in post-debate, post-adoption implementation processes. In this framework a substantially broadened array of debate takes place, while the results of the process remain under coordinated direction and, if necessary, firm control.

That spectrum of control and coordination is clearly delineated in recent Vietnamese experience: In certain instances, the political leadership chooses to dominate and impose its will without any substantial discussion, a more traditional model of socialist constitution making. In Vietnam in 2001 chief among these was the question of Article 4 and the primary of the Party itself. On this issue the Party made its position clear and brooked no debate or drafting that differed from its views. Even under the somewhat more free-wheeling rules of transitional constitutionalism, certain issues are taboo because they threaten the dominant political force, and in this instance that was Article 4.

But there are other facets to the spectrum of transitional Vietnamese constitutionalism. Political leadership allows discussion of certain issues that go beyond its plans for constitutional drafting, such as "constitutional protection," the founding of a constitutional court, or an expanded role for the national legislature in constitutional adjudication, but makes clear that those ideas are not to find their way into the current process – though they are clearly on an agenda for future discussion with the tacit agreement of the Party leadership. In this way the political leadership manages discussion on sensitive and complex issues, rather than allowing liberal constitutionalist intellectuals, or dissidents at home or abroad, to take the lead in a debate that the Party recognizes must occur. And constitutionalist intellectuals are now part of the constitutional process – albeit in a controlled way, with one of the key issues both recognized and sidetracked – rather than marginalized with dissidents at home or outside.

At another point on the spectrum of transitional socialist constitutionalism, this process allows a political leadership the opportunity to lead and strongly urge a certain position, but also to allow vigorous debate and, if sufficient opposition exists, to allow a range of results to emerge. The range of discussion on the National Assembly and the courts illustrates this role for transitional constitutionalism: as long as true independence and autonomy are not on the political agenda, a range of constitutionalist options are acceptable to the Party, up to and including 'votes of confidence' in senior government officials. And, of course, the more controversial of such options can be moderated and managed later, through the implementation process, as we have noted above.

In yet other instances, this dialogue allows a leadership the flexibility to note sharply divided views and to decline to impose its will, allowing a legislature to undertake constitutional drafting through relatively open debate. The debate on school fees and social justice clearly illustrates this option for transitional constitutionalism and the dominant political force.

Thus while a socialist constitution in Vietnam has traditionally been an instrument for control, management and motivation, a transitional socialist constitution such as Vietnam's is now a more complex document, and its drafting and amendment a considerably more complex process involving pressure from different forces and interests. Such a constitution is now a platform for dialogue and debate over current policy issues and future constitutionalist directions, albeit a platform carefully moderated and still controlled. That platform allows legislators, legal scholars, activists and dissidents to press the boundaries of possible change by raising a host of issues for discussion as part of this constitutional dialogue. They do so, generally without fear of punishment or retribution, understanding that some issues may not be raised, others may be raised for future debate but not for current drafting, other issues are subject to substantial Party influence, and still others are relatively open for dialogue and decision. By becoming part of a substantially broadened but still controlled transitional constitutional dialogue, more liberal constitutionalists, legislators, legal scholars and even dissidents raise and legitimate certain issues for future discussion while also providing some enhanced legitimacy to a gradually more flexible system.

Does a ruling party such as the Vietnamese Communist Party that allows a constitution to become a platform for dialogue and modulated struggle weaken itself in this process? Allowing, even encouraging, certainly leading, effectively refereeing and clearly deciding the results of such a process may in fact confer greater legitimacy on the political party that sponsors such a platform and dialogue, perhaps even more effectively than the harder instrumentalist analysis provided control in decades past. By participating in constitutional dialogue, liberal constitutionalists and dissidents within Vietnam and their expatriate analogues outside the country also provide some legitimacy to the Party-led process of constitutional discussion and amendment. And in so providing some legitimacy to the processes of constitutional dialogue and negotiation in which they are participating, domestic and external liberal constitutionalists and dissidents also provide some legitimacy to the political force – a Communist Party remaining in power – that sponsors, allows, monitors and ultimately controls such discussion. Successful Party management of these complex processes can lead to a willingness to allow deeper – though still controlled – dialogue later, a dialogue that a ruling party is increasingly confident of controlling. For the Vietnamese Party, viewing a constitution and constitutional debate not merely as a tool for control but as a moderated platform for dialogue on important national issues can be a Party-legitimizing force rather than a weakening influence.

At the same time as Party and other political leaders have allowed a freer transitional constitutional dialogue to occur, leadership also seeks mechanisms to moderate discussion and control outcomes in the transitional dialogue process. The history of the Vietnamese 2001 constitutional debate illustrates some of those mechanisms. They include: allowing relatively open discussion but carefully controlling drafting processes both before and during legislative sessions; clearly closing off debate on controversial and major areas of constitutional reform (such as Article 4 Party primacy); deferring other constitutionalist options for later discussion but not rejecting them outright and thus provoking strong reaction (as in the discussion of constitutional courts and constitutional protection); and accepting certain constitutional reforms that might not otherwise have been acceptable to conservative forces, but softening and limiting their impact through control of constitutional drafting and control of the statutory processes of redrafting subsidiary laws and implementing documents (as in the issue of votes of confidence, and the general jurisdiction of the public prosecutors).

What propels authoritarian systems like those of Vietnam and China toward accepting a shift in the role of constitutional dialogue and constitutional text, from a blunt instrument of control and motivation to a somewhat more flexible (and perhaps dangerous) platform for constitutional debate and even struggle? At the root of the Vietnamese choice is constitutional and political legitimacy. It is the drive to update a constitution that opens the platform for debate and struggle, a deep concern that an out-of-date constitution may become a seriously delegitimized constitution that can help to delegitimize a ruling party. And so updating becomes a necessity. And it is, of course, safer to alter text – even under conditions of constitutional debate such as that occurring in Vietnam in 2001 – than to allow constitutional updating and relevance to changing realities through constitutional interpretation and constitutional review, whether in the national legislature, the Supreme Court, a separate constitutional court, or other body formally independent of the Party. In avoiding those alternatives, the Party is left with the updating of text, a process it must allow to preserve some legitimacy in the textual document. In turn, that process of textual updating propels the constitution and constitutional dialogue from text to platform, from Party's instructions to a framework and platform for dialogue and struggle. This is a transitional constitutional process for a transitional society, a process that, even while still strictly moderated and coordinated, holds the promise for an expansion of constitutional dialogue and constitutionalist options in the decades ahead.

In the years since the most recent revision of the Vietnamese Constitution, the role of constitutional amendment as a platform for the expansion of constitutionalist dialogue has persisted and deepened in Vietnam. Some key issues raised but sidestepped in the 2001 revision process have re-emerged as essential issues in the broader legal and judicial reform, such as the options for constitutional enforcement and review that are discussed in more detail in Chapter 2. And once again there are calls to re-revise the Constitution, either to incorporate greater rights, or to provide for a constitutional court (or some other constitutional review mechanism), or to rework the structure of the judiciary. Another significant revision of the Vietnamese Constitution is probably at least several years away, but the process of dialogue and debate on key issues is underway.

These events in Vietnam have important parallels in China, where constitutional amendment has also served as a platform for important dialogue, as a means to allow certain reforms while sidestepping more sensitive discussions, and as a means to bring newly powerful institutional and societal actors into constitutional discourse. As in Vietnam, Chinese constitutional revisions to incorporate more specifically the role of markets and private property, and to strengthen the textual protection of rights, serve to reflect the changes of a reform era, to solidify such reforms in practice into constitutional text, and, sometimes, to legitimize and strengthen the efforts of more reformist forces. But in both countries, socialist constitutions bend but do not break. The role of the Communist Party remains central to both constitutions, an element that may occasionally be discussed but has not undergone substantial change even during a period in which reforms have swept through virtually all other spheres of social and economic life. The goal seems clear: a paramount Party can allow such reforms, and their sometimes heated discussion, without giving up power, and while strengthening its legitimacy and its claims to authority through the process of dialogue and change.

NOTE

1. That role would be exercised through the Party's Political Bureau and through the Party group in the National Assembly. "The Central Committee delegated the Political Bureau to provide guidance to the Party group in the National Assembly (*Dang doan Quoc hoi*) and the [Amendment] Commission ... on finalizing the draft for presentation to the National Assembly" (Nhan Dan 2001d).

CHAPTER 2

THE EMERGING DEBATE OVER CONSTITUTIONAL REVIEW AND ENFORCEMENT IN VIETNAM

The Constitution is both a source of pride and an object of political battle in Vietnam. Its importance as a symbol of the Vietnamese nation, the victory over foreign powers, and the unification of the nation under Party rule, has also led to several substantial revisions – of which the most recent such process, in 2001 and 2002, led to significant debates on the role of the Constitution, state agencies, political accountability and other difficult subjects that were discussed in Chapter 1. But in Vietnam, as in China and other socialist states, the problem of constitutional enforcement and review has always been awkward: the Constitution is defined as the "fundamental law" of the nation, and yet it remains largely unused to rescind inconsistent legislation, to establish the hierarchy of legislation, or as a standard to judge acts that violate its terms or those who commit such acts.

In China, filling this important but symbolic constitutional vessel with substantive enforcement became a significant political issue during the 1980s and 1990s. In China as in Vietnam, the issues of constitutional enforcement – or "constitutional protection," as it is often called in Vietnam (*bao ve hien phap* or *bao hien*) – have primarily implicated three problems: what to do about statutes or actions by the national legislature that may violate the Constitution; how to handle national statutes, local laws, or other national or local regulatory documents that violate higher law; and how to treat acts by state or Party officials that may violate the Constitution. In Vietnam, these debates have been spurred by domestic calls for a constitutional enforcement mechanism, and by overlapping calls from Vietnamese dissidents abroad, who score rhetorical points by re-emphasizing the "fundamental" nature of the Vietnamese Constitution but its lack of enforcement processes beyond a rhetorical delegation to the National Assembly and its Standing Committee. The Chinese solution to the problem of constitutional review and enforcement holds some lessons for Vietnam as well. In China, Party concern for the potential independence of a constitutional court, the power that constitutional review could give the regular judiciary, and the tradition of leaving constitutional supervision to the national legislature (the National People's Congress), has led constitutional review and enforcement to be delegated to a unit of the Legal Affairs Commission of the National People's Congress rather than to a constitutional court, a constitutional commission, or the Supreme People's Court, at least for the time being. But the topic of constitutional review and enforcement has also sparked significant debate in China, a debate that is far from over (Xin 2003).

In Vietnam, calls for a mechanism for review of the constitutionality of government and Party acts and legal documents have arisen at various points in modern Vietnamese history. Fidelity to constitutional promises was one of the demands of those who pressed for democratic legal reforms in the 1950s during the *Nhan van Giai pham* movement, including an initial and brave call for constitutional review discussed in the Introduction. Demands for such a mechanism to review the constitutionality of government acts and documents have periodically been renewed since, including by overseas dissidents on a regular basis for several decades, sometimes through reference to other constitutionality review mechanisms (Lenduong.net 2004), and by domestic political critics since at least since the late 1980s (Human Rights Watch 1995).

In 1997, for example, three prominent domestic dissidents petitioned the National Assembly to establish a constitutional court "in order to have an institution with jurisdiction to review petitions and to adjudicate (*xet xu*) cases of Constitutional violations" (Petition to the National Assembly 1997). In 2002, another group of 21 domestic critics again petitioned the National Assembly to "establish a Constitutional Court to adjudicate violations of the Constitution," because, according to the petitioners, this is an institution "any state ruled by law must have" (Petition to the National Assembly 2002).

Beyond dissidents, the more official discussion of constitutional review and enforcement in Vietnam has recent roots in the revision of the Vietnamese Constitution in 2001. During that process, legal scholars, citizens, overseas Vietnamese and others called for the establishment of a viable mechanism for constitutional review and enforcement to replace the mechanism that has never been used effectively, which gives the Standing Committee of the National Assembly primary responsibility for constitutional interpretation, and provides general constitutional enforcement duties to a wide range of other bodies as well. That discussion was postponed in 2001, but it has re-emerged prominently in recent years, encouraged by Party and legal theorists. And the Vietnamese debate on constitutional enforcement and review has been spurred by increasing reports of provincial and local laws that violate national laws or constitutional norms, and of expanding complaints against the acts of government and Party officials.

CONSTITUTIONAL ENFORCEMENT AND REVIEW IN THE VIETNAMESE CONSTITUTIONAL SCHEME

In formal terms Article 146 of the 1992 Constitution stipulates that "The Constitution of the Socialist Republic of Vietnam is the fundamental law of the State and has the highest legal effect. All other legal documents must conform to the Constitution." The 1992 Constitution also stipulates that constitutional issues are the province of the National Assembly, through the provision in Article 83 that "[t]he National Assembly is the only organ with constitutional and legislative powers," and in Article 84, that the National Assembly has "obligations and powers" that include the "exercise [of] supreme control over conformity to the Constitution, [and] the law and the resolutions of the National Assembly." Article 84 also provides that the National Assembly shall "abrogate all formal written documents issued by the country's President, the Standing Committee of the National Assembly, the Government, the Prime Minister, the Supreme People's Court, and the [Procuracy] that run counter to the Constitution." (Constitution 1992).

More specifically directed toward constitutional enforcement, the 1992 Constitution also provides that the Standing Committee of the National Assembly holds the power to "interpret the Constitution, the law, and decree-laws" and "to exercise supervision and control over the implementation of the Constitution, the law, the resolutions of the National Assembly, decree-laws, the resolutions of the Standing Committee of the National Assembly; over the activities of the Government, the Supreme People's Court, the Supreme People's [Procuracy]; to suspend the execution of the formal written orders of the Government, the Prime Minister, the Supreme People's Court, the Supreme People's [Procuracy], that contravene the Constitution, the law, the resolutions of the National Assembly; [and] to report the matter to the National Assembly for it to decide the abrogation of such orders" (Constitution 1992).

But the Assembly and its Standing Committee had never undertaken, or been permitted to undertake, those constitutional tasks. And the frequent mentions of constitutional duties by the government, Prime Minister, state agencies and others result in a lack of responsibility and activity rather than in multiple, effective caretakers of the Constitution.[1] None of this was accidental, of course: Party officials took charge of the traditionally infrequent discussions of consistency between local and national laws and regulations and the Constitution, and the infrequent allegation (other than by harassed dissidents) that governmental and Party acts violated constitutional norms.

CONSTITUTIONAL REVIEW AND ENFORCEMENT IN THE CONSTITUTIONAL AMENDMENT DEBATES

In the 2001 and 2002 constitutional amendment process, calls for some sort of constitutional review and enforcement mechanism began to move into the mainstream. These appeals for a constitutional review and enforcement structure reflected a changed vision of the role of the Constitution, as well as a more activist perspective that saw the Party and government as at least partly subject to law, rather than law being subject to policy. The accelerating, but also highly sensitive Vietnamese discussion took as its reference points the development of constitutional courts in Thailand, Korea and other Asian states, and the eruption of major debates on constitutional review and enforcement in China.

In the 2001 process, the Constitutional Amendment Commission worked diligently to narrow the amendment debate and process to less sensitive issues than constitutional review and enforcement. But officials, academics and others continued to raise constitutional review and enforcement throughout the revision process. Speaking in September 2001 in Ho Chi Minh City, for example, Fatherland Front officials called for "the establishment of a Constitutional Defense Commission, or constitutional courts, or adding to the functions of the National Assembly's Law Committee" to handle issues of constitutional review and enforcement (Nhan Dan 2001b). And in October 2001, a wide-ranging call for strengthened constitutional protection was raised in the main theoretical journal of the Communist Party, *Tap chi Cong san (Communist Review)* – about as official a platform as could be imagined, and an early indication that stronger measures to enforce the Constitution had some resonance in at least some quarters of the Party and state.

In that October 2001 article, legal scholar Nguyen Van Thao mooted the two key options of a constitutional court (*toa an hien phap*) or constitutional commission (*uy ban hien phap*) to "adjudicate unconstitutional documents." He also raised the possibility of allowing the new administrative courts, established in the mid-1990s, broader authority to judge whether "the activities of administrative institutions are based upon the Constitution and the laws" (Thao 2001a). Writing in a domestic development policy journal, Thao again addressed the difficult problems of "constitutionality" and "legality" of government acts and texts in another fall 2001 article. "In nearly ten years of Constitutional implementation," he wrote,

> we have never once seen the National Assembly or its Standing Committee abrogate, cancel, or suspend the implementation of a single document issued by the President, the Government or the Prime Minister. The system of monitoring is almost never exercised by the Government or the Prime Minister with respect to the ministries or local authorities, despite the fact that some legal documents issued by minis- tries and local authorities evidently violate the Constitution or laws.
>
> (Thao 2001b)

For Thao, the fundamental reason for this failure was clear: "The 1992 Constitution did not delegate to any institution judgment on the constitutionality of laws," and it was vague on the National Assembly's abrogation and cancellation powers. For Thao and others, the question of adjudicating constitutionality should now be on the agenda for debate – but the Constitutional Amendment Commission and the Party did not agree. In a view echoed by Party General Secretary Ngo Duc Manh in a November 2001 Party meeting discussing the scope and wording of the constitutional amendments, National Assembly and Constitutional Amendment Commission chair Nguyen Van An reaf- firmed the Party and government's intent that the constitutional amendment process only "concentrate on issues that are truly urgent, that are ripe for adoption and practical testing, and must ensure a high spirit of unity" (Nhan Dan 2001c). Official focus remained on the amendments that would clarify and improve the functioning of the state machinery, rather than broader issues of constitutionalism.

When the constitutional amendments reached the National Assembly for debate in November 2001, delegates again raised issues of constitutionalism beyond the bounds of the Party's efforts to channel and narrow the discussions. For example, an Assembly delegate and senior legal official in Ho Chi Minh City again called for establishment of a constitutional court (*toa an hien phap*) to "defend the Constitution . . . against the many forms of constitutional violation that at present cannot be investigated or adjudicated."[2] And speaking to a southern newspaper, a former Deputy Prime Minister pointedly praised the efforts of the judiciary to increase its role and capacities and emerge from "stagnation," while forcefully calling on the judiciary to overcome its "timidity" in protecting citizens from official abuses (VnExpress 2005k).

THE DEBATE CONTINUES AND GROWS

These calls to strengthen constitutional review did not make their way into the 2001 revision of the Constitution. But the problems of "constitutional protection," the calls for founding a constitutional court, or a constitutional commission, or strengthening the role of the National Assembly in interpreting the Constitution or some other mechanism had sufficient support within the Party and state apparatus that they could not be shelved indefinitely. That debate persisted after the Constitutional amendments came into effect in early 2002. In mid-2002, domestic political dissidents protested "the arrest and harassment of fellow dissidents and call[ed] for democratic reforms, establishment of an anti-corruption body, creation of a constitutional court to examine violations in constitutional law, and publication of Vietnam's border treaties with China," among other demands (Human Rights Watch 2003). As noted earlier, the 2002 critics group petitioned the National Assembly to "establish a Constitutional Court to adjudicate violations of the Constitution," noting that "any state ruled by law must have" a constitutional court (Petition to the National Assembly 2002).

The 2002 petitioners brought more detailed arguments to bear than the 1997 group. They cited specific laws that, in their opinion, violated the Constitution and were appropriate for constitutional review. In their view, for example, Article 69 of the 1992 Constitution, which guarantees "freedom of speech and of the press, and the right to receive information," was violated by the later-enacted Law on Newspapers, which "does not recognize newspapers organized by the people or private newspapers." And in their view Article 79 of the 1992

Constitution, which prohibits imprisonment without a judicial verdict, was violated by the government's oft-criticized Decree 31 that has provided the state and security forces with a broad basis for administrative detention and punishments.

The 2002 petitioners' rationale for a constitutional court relied on the concept of the Constitution as the nation's "mother law." Citing the 1992 Constitution's concept of the Constitution as the "fundamental law of the state," the petitioners wrote: "[T]he Constitution is the mother law. Every other law must comply with the mother law, be consistent with the mother law, and may not violate the mother law . . . But who can the people appeal to? Who can resolve [such violations]? Who can try them? Because these 'offspring laws' do violate the Constitution!" (Petition to the National Assembly 2002).

In these early days of debate, official documents did not immediately confirm the need for a structure of constitutional review and enforcement. Thus the Party Political Bureau's Resolution 8 of 2002 on important legal reform tasks did not directly address these basic problems of constitutionalism (Communist Party 2002). And a major effort undertaken by the Ministry of Justice, the government and foreign donors to systematize priorities in development of the Vietnamese legal system discussed detailed legislative and other work but unfortunately did not address important issues of constitutionality and constitutional review, a failing of both timid donors and their domestic institutional partners (Legal System Needs Assessment 2002).

THE CURRENT DEBATE: DELINEATING OPTIONS AND MOVING TOWARD DECISIONS

In the years after the constitutional revision process of 2001 and 2002, discussion of the options for "constitutional protection" has accelerated, now firmly through Party and state initiative. Foreign contact has contributed to the discussion and to understanding of foreign constitutional review models, particularly those in neighboring or regional countries. And direct contact with foreign constitutional courts has also increased. A Ministry of Justice and lawyers' delegation visited the French Constitutional Court in early 2004, and in the summer of 2004, the Vice Chairman of the National Assembly, Nguyen Van Yeu (also a member of the Party Central Committee) received a delegation from the Thai Constitutional Court led by its President. Since 2001 numerous other references to the Thai Constitutional Court have appeared in the

Vietnamese press, including discussions of the Court's attention to charges against the Thai Prime Minister. Vietnamese newspapers have also discussed the German Constitutional Court, including its role in German political developments in 2005. And a senior delegation headed by the Minister of Justice explored constitutional review and related issues, including judicial reform, during a fall 2005 visit to the United States. That delegation included personnel from the Law Committee of the National Assembly, Office of the Government, Office of State President, Ministry of Public Security, and Ministry of Justice.

The dialogue on constitutional review continued to expand, particularly in 2004 and 2005, and now includes reformist figures arguing directly and in public fora for a constitutional court or constitutional commission as well as strong indications of official support in the Party and state. In April 2004, for example, one of the most popular newspapers in southern Vietnam carried a commentary about the roles of constitutional courts by Pham Duy Nghia, a law professor at Hanoi National University. Nghia reviewed the difficulties in establishing supervision by citizens over officials and official acts in societies that have "long been sunk in Confucian ideology," citing China, Japan, Korea and Vietnam, and noted the difficulties in adjudicating "acts by public institutions that violate the Constitution and the laws." He emphasized that the dominant model in Asia involves "constitutional courts, or as they may be called constitutional protection courts, constitutional protection commissions, or other similar names," explaining that in the United States constitutional review is carried out by the US Supreme Court without establishing a separate institution. Nghia also pointed out that a council for constitutional protection and oversight over administrative agencies was established in French Indochina in the 1920s (Nghia 2004).

Professor Nghia then turned to a particularly knotty problem in the Vietnamese discussions of constitutional review – the role of the National Assembly. He reaffirmed the constitutional provision that the National Assembly holds supreme constitutional power, and that "the oversight of acts that violate the Constitution or the laws by administrative institutions in Vietnam is fundamentally within the jurisdiction of the National Assembly." But Nghia continues, making his case step by step:

> Of course, undertaking that supreme supervisory power cannot be easy. With 498 delegates, of whom only one quarter are full-time deputies,

and meeting but two times each year, the Vietnamese National Assembly certainly has difficulties in supervising central authorities as well as dozens of ministries and agencies and 64 provincial authorities from the North to the South. For those reasons, studying the experience of neighboring countries in order to move step by step toward mechanisms for appropriate constitutional protection, may also be highly necessary.

(Nghia 2004)

Nghia points out that numerous "neighboring countries" have "imported the mechanisms of societies ruled by law" that also reflect their "Asian values." He notes pointedly that "the peoples of Japan, Korea, Thailand, Malaysia, Indonesia and the Philippines have all established constitutional courts, a mechanism for protecting the constitution, resisting illegal actions and unconstitutional actions by the government and legislature. The people of Campuchia have also established a constitutional protection commission along the French model" (Nghia 2004).

Later in 2004, after discussions over several years, then-President Tran Duc Luong, chair of the Party Judicial Reform Committee responsible for drafting a national Judicial Reform Strategy, announced that the Committee was prepared to recommend "study of the establishment of a Constitutional Court" (Bao Lao Dong 2004; Tuoi Tre 2004). This news sparked public discussion, at least on web dialogue sites, including detailed references to French, American, Russian and other models of judicial review, and differing views on the utility of establishing a constitutional court, commission or other form of constitutional review in Vietnam (TTVNOnline 2004).

But a number of issues and opposing views have also been raised in a difficult and sensitive discussion, particularly with respect to the role of the Communist Party and the potential problems with varying forms of constitutional review. Early in 2005, in a speech to the Party's Theoretical Council, President Luong noted that the Party's understanding of the rule of law in capitalist democracies included the division of power into legislative, judicial and executive power, and the Party's understanding that "for resolving conflicts between the three branches of power, there is the Constitutional Court." "But," President Luong continued, echoing some still powerful critics of a constitutional review system for Vietnam, "in our state system, we do not advocate such a division of power ... Isn't the task of harmonizing and coordinating among the areas of Party leadership?" (Luong 2005).

THE PROBLEM OF OVER-REACHING LOCAL LEGISLATION AND LEGAL DOCUMENTS

At the same time as legal and Party leaders were debating the need for a mechanism for constitutional review and enforcement, the contours of such a structure, and the dominant role of the Party, the Party and government began dealing with a key issue on which all sides could generally agree: the increasing tendency of provincial and local officials to legislate on all manner of matters, particularly administrative violations by citizens, often in conflict with higher law and, arguably, constitutional norms. Concern for this conflict between local and national law sprang into the open in 2001 and 2002, though the problem had long quietly existed. By 2003, it was serious enough that the government formed a General Department for Inspection of Legal Documents within the Ministry of Justice and gave it the primary task of ferreting out local laws that conflict with national law (and, conceivably, the Constitution itself), and seeking to force local authorities to annul them (VnExpress 2002b). That department worked under the authorization of a new set of regulations intended to help the government and the Ministry of Justice harmonize local and national law (Decision 135 2003).

The new department got to work quickly, surveying provincial and local laws and actively seeking to force local governments to withdraw conflicting legislation. In early 2004, for example, the Department sent documents to the Saigon city leadership "informing" Saigon that it should annul a local regulation on the treatment of property owned by overseas Vietnamese and confiscated by local authorities because of conflict with national law (Thanh Nien 2004). In early 2006, the department "suggested" to Ho Chi Minh City that it annul another eight legal documents that conflicted with national laws (Nguoi Lao Dong 2006). The problem was not limited to local authorities: in a report compiled for the National Assembly in the summer of 2005, the Department identified more than 400 legal documents promulgated by national ministries as well as by local authorities that conflicted with higher national law, a result the Minister of Justice called "startling." Based on the Ministry's report, the National Assembly increased the pressure by declaring that some of these documents violated the Constitution as well, including the Ministry of Public Security's 2003 circular limiting motorbike registration to one per person. It called the Ministry's motorbike regulation a restriction on citizens' right to own property guaranteed in Article 58 of the Constitution and Article 221 of the Civil Code (Vietnamnet 2005a).

The Department continued to press local authorities to comply with national law. In early 2006, it released another list of nearly ninety legal documents from 33 provinces and municipalities that violate the law specifically in the area of administrative punishments of citizens, a popular area for local regulation (Nhan Dan 2006). In January 2006, the department took on the powerful Hanoi People's Committee, announcing that three Hanoi legal documents – among them an unpopular rule allowing city authorities to seize motorcycles and other vehicles for legal violations and hold them for fifteen to sixty days – conflicted with national law (VnExpress 2006).

MOTORCYCLE RIGHTS: CONSTITUTIONALISM HITS THE STREETS IN HANOI

Until 2005, these discussions occurred largely within reasonably narrow circles of domestic Party, government, legislative and judicial officials, legal scholars, and some domestic and overseas dissidents. But a consciousness of constitutional rights appears to be increasing in the general population as well, and nothing illustrates that growing consciousness better than the great motorcycle registration debate of 2005. A brief discussion of this important debate is given here, but these events are also covered in significantly more detail in their own right in Chapter 3, with full citations provided in that chapter.

Chaotic and unsafe traffic conditions have long plagued Hanoi and other major Vietnamese cities, a deadly legacy of economic prosperity, the use of motorcycles as an outlet for social relaxation as well as work and family transport, insufficient road infrastructure, unsafe driver training, exceptionally lax driver licensing, and a host of related issues. In Hanoi, where the problem is particularly difficult because of highly concentrated prosperity and a road infrastructure largely unimproved since the colonial era, the city's police authorities have attempted many methods to exert some control over the increasingly chaotic traffic scene. In one of many such measures, the Hanoi police began limiting motorcycle registration to Hanoi residents with drivers' licenses in early 2003, while debating whether to limit motorcycle registrations to one vehicle per resident. Pressure increased during 2003, with the city police calling for a moratorium on all motorcycle registrations in Hanoi, and residents – including delegates in Hanoi's

People's Council – expressing firm opposition. In response, the police announced a pilot program to temporarily cease registration in the "saturated" four inner city oldest districts of Hanoi and began implementing that in September 2003. The Hanoi police sought to extend that moratorium to three more districts in 2004 and another two in 2005, but public criticism delayed that timetable; in April 2004 Hanoi announced that three more districts would be added to the registration moratorium in 2005, and another two in 2008. And Hanoi police began enforcing lower speed limits mandated by the national Ministry of Transportation.

But the real trouble began in 2005, when Hanoi and other local police departments began enforcing a legal provision in the national police force's regulations on the registration of vehicles that had originally been released in 2003. Under those regulations, implemented by local rules, "each person may register only one motorcycle or moped." The attempts to enforce this provision in Hanoi and Saigon met with substantial resistance – arguments with registration personnel, angry letters to officials and the newspapers, and complaints to government offices and local and national legislators. In August 2005 the Ministry of Justice entered the fray, arguing that the police regulations violate national regulations on administrative sanctions and on transport safety. Other critics – including members of the Law Committee of the National Assembly – took the fight further, arguing vociferously throughout the fall of 2005 that the local rulemaking and implementation of restrictions on motorcycle and moped registration to one per person violate the right to property enshrined in the 1992 Vietnamese Constitution, and the Vietnamese Civil Code.

This was arguably among the first mass claims to constitutional rights in recent Vietnamese history, and it had enormous public appeal. It centered on two areas of life close to the hearts of many Hanoians and other Vietnamese – encounters with the police, and the motorcycle culture that has enveloped Vietnam. The enforcement of the restriction was part of a broader attempt to limit the growth in motorcycle ridership that was already being resisted by many citizens. And it was a constitutional claim that may have infuriated the national police and the Ministry of Public Security, but posed no political threat to the Party – in short, it was a "safe" constitutional claim. For several weeks claims of constitutional rights and violations echoed in discussions in Hanoi, and in the Vietnamese press as well. In late November, one day before the Minister of Justice was scheduled to report formally to the National

Assembly on violations of law by national ministries, the Ministry of Public Security issued a directive annulling the provision in its earlier regulations that limited registration of motorcycles and motorbikes to one per person.

But the fight was not yet over, for Hanoi, Ho Chi Minh City, and other municipalities had promulgated similar one person/one motorcycle rules based on the national regulations, and those were not automatically ineffective merely because their original policy and legal basis in a public security ordinance had been removed. Hanoi and Saigon retained rights to regulate on such matters within their borders, and they were not committed to removing those restrictions, since these rapidly growing cities suffered from the worst glut of motorcycles, traffic accidents, traffic jams, and motorcycle pollution in Vietnam's history. But elite and public pressure began to grow again, particularly on the Hanoi authorities to annul their local rule. Again the claim of constitutional rights was in the forefront of the calls to annul the local regulations limiting motorcycle registration to one bike per resident.

Faced with the retreat by the powerful national Ministry of Public Security on its one motorcycle/one citizen rule, the Hanoi authorities had little choice on that matter, and announced in early December that its own one motorcycle rule was being abrogated. But once again citizens, the press and legislators upped the ante, setting their sights on the Hanoi regulation that had temporarily barred registration of motorcycles in four urban city districts in early 2004, and another three districts in 2005. Having emerged victorious using the argument that the one motorcycle rule violated the Constitutional protection of the right to property and provisions of the Criminal Code, opponents of the seven district registration ban now widened their target, arguing that the registration moratorium also violated the Constitution. City police and transport authorities now tried to stand firm, arguing that public safety and transport gridlock justified this temporary, lawful limitation on the exercise of "rights" to register motorcycles that passed constitutional muster. But they were swept away by public sentiment that was both reflected and fanned by Hanoi local legislators and by the local press. At the end of December 2005, the "constitutionalist" forces were victorious again: the Hanoi People's Council and the local government decided to annul the temporary moratorium on motorcycle registration in seven Hanoi districts, sending police and transport authorities back to search for other methods of controlling traffic growth and accidents in Hanoi.

This episode was striking in the use of the Constitution as a means of argument and a political bludgeon against opponents. The conflict was fueled by multiple forces: the Ministry of Justice, in assertively and publicly comparing local regulations to national law; an increasingly active press; local legislators eager to satisfy constituents and become part of a broadened political process; and citizens for whom a heady sense of "constitutional" rights and a down-to-earth sense of the differing value of their motorcycle investments with or without Hanoi registration. They combined in a mix lethal to rational regulation and confused – but highly active – in their sense of constitutional wrongs. Nor was this a politically dangerous form of constitutional argumentation to be suppressed: motorcycles are not multi-party democracy, or opposition to police torture, or other topics on which constitutionalist arguments can be made in Vietnam that could well be far more risky to the speaker.

MOVING FORWARD

Beyond the issues of "motorbike constitutionalism," the Vietnamese discussion on constitutional review and enforcement focused on three key questions in 2005 and 2006: the role of the Party; the role of the National Assembly; and the role of potentially new institutions such as a court or commission. Theoreticians continued to raise the two key problems of the 1992 Constitution for constitutional review and enforcement: the Constitution gives the Standing Committee of the National Assembly the key role in constitutional interpretation and the Assembly a broad constitutional supervision role as well, while also requiring constitutional supervision by a number of other state agencies. Sorting out this basic text and the political and ideological problems it embodies has been a very difficult task.

As calls for some form of constitutional "protection" mounted, two meetings were convened in 2005 to study the issue. One was a conference on constitutional protection convened by a Hanoi law faculty. The other and almost certainly more important conference, on "the system of constitutional protection in Vietnam," was held in the coastal city of Vinh (far from southern or northern dissidents or politically aware students) in March 2005, under the auspices of the Office for Lawmaking Work under the Standing Committee of the National Assembly and the Party's Internal Affairs Commission. The meeting reviewed "the situation for supervision and protection of the

63

Constitution," comparisons from other countries, and suggestions for further research, with the goal of producing "an effective system of constitutional protection in the process of constructing a socialist state ruled by law in Vietnam" (Communist Party 2005b).

At the opening of the meeting, National Assembly Vice Chair and Central Committee member Nguyen Van Yeu reviewed the obligatory claim that Vietnam has a "relatively comprehensive" system for constitutional review. But for the first time he also provided in clear, public terms a definition of the three types of constitutional review under official discussion: "supervising the constitutionality and legality of legal documents; supervising the constitutionality of the execution, accession to and enforcement of international treaties; and supervising the resolution of petitions and accusations by citizens with respect to actions that violate the Constitution or the laws" (Communist Party 2005b).

The discussants quickly got to the nub of the problem: "Supervising the protection of the Constitution in Vietnam is different than many other countries around the world because Vietnam has not delegated to a specialized body the role of supervising the defense of the constitution (such as a Constitutional Court or Constitutional Protection Commission . . .) but has delegated this to a number of state bodies which have jurisdiction." The delegates' view, carefully stated in the Party statement, was that "the most important issue is the supervision and guarantee of the constitutionality and legality of legal documents," and that the problem of supervising the activities and statutes adopted by the National Assembly is particularly problematic – given that the National Assembly is also given primary responsibility for constitutional review under the 1992 Constitution (Communist Party 2005b).

Finding a workable system to suspend or cancel legal documents issued by state bodies that fail to pass constitutional muster was also a significant issue. After beginning with the obligatory refrain that Vietnam has a "relatively comprehensive" system for constitutional review, the statement concluded that "the researchers as well as many officials . . . felt that research on . . . effective solutions in continuing to perfect the system for supervision and defense of the Constitution in Vietnam was an urgent necessity." A "majority" of the delegates to the meeting believed that the "effectiveness was not high" in the current system of declining to assign constitutional review to a specialized body but relying on state bodies to carry out protection of the Constitution as part of their regular tasks, and that the current system "does not effectively heighten responsibility for constitutional protection in the state and society." The current structure of vesting supreme supervisory powers in the National Assembly "causes confusion between lawmaking powers and review powers (judicial powers)." And the practice of vesting these issues in subordinate offices of the National Assembly "makes it impossible to avoid dependency and passivity in the work of constitutional protection." The problem was clear: "The National Assembly is the important body for (structuring) State bodies and should itself abide by the Constitution and the laws, but has no body whatsoever to undertake supervision of constitutional fidelity (*tuan thu*) with respect to the Assembly [itself] and individuals acting in the jurisdiction of the Assembly; especially whether laws and ordinances that are being promulgated are constitutional or not" Based on these "shortcomings," the meeting agreed that it was "necessary to study the establishment of a mechanism for constitutional protection in Vietnam that will be more effective" under current Vietnamese conditions (Communist Party 2005b).

As the discussion continued in 2005, an important article in Vietnam's main law newspaper, *Phap luat Viet Nam (Vietnam Law)*, reviewed the terms of the debate. The article noted the continuing debate over the need for a constitutional review and enforcement structure: "there remain some views," the article noted diplomatically, that constitutional review should not be delegated to a specialized body because of the difficulties in defining that body's jurisdiction and the potential that resulting weaknesses in that body (a court or commission) would then weaken rather than strengthen constitutional review. But the remainder of the article seemed generally to assume that the primary question was not whether to form a structure of constitutional review, but which it would be. And the article usefully outlined the "three different viewpoints" on the appropriate mechanism for constitutional review. The first is to "establish a Constitutional Court under the Supreme People's Court." The second option "agrees with establishing a Constitutional Court but as an independent structure, not as a specialized court within the Supreme People's Court." The third viewpoint holds that "a Constitutional Court is a model that does not suit the current realities of Vietnam" (Phap luat Viet Nam 2005).

Four well-known senior legal officials or scholars provided their views on these options. Dr. Tran Ngoc Duong, Vice Chair of the Office of the National Assembly, echoed the views of the Vinh meeting, noting that the current system of dividing responsibility for constitutional review among state agencies is ineffective and that resting primary supervisory responsibilities with the National Assembly results in confusion between lawmaking and review powers. He cautiously agreed with the notion of "studying the formation of a specialized organization for Constitutional protection." Dr. Nguyen Van Thuan, Vice Chair of the Law Committee of the National Assembly, stated that "the task of determining whether [legal] documents violate the Constitution and the laws should be concentrated in one institution, [for instance] a Constitutional Court with the role of adjudicating and issuing orders rescinding legal documents that violate the Constitution or the laws."

Professor Nguyen Duy Quy, former President of the Vietnam Academy of Social Sciences "agreed with the viewpoint that we must establish a Constitutional Court to adjudicate legal documents that violate the Constitution," and left "for further study" the question of whether that new court should be part of the Supreme People's Court or separate. Professor Dao Tri Uc, Director of the Institute of State and Law in the Vietnam Academy of Social Sciences, seemed considerably more doubtful on the issue of "constitutional protection." In order to build an effective legal system, he told *Phap luat Viet Nam*, "we have traveled a road that is already fairly long but not yet completed. For that reason, we should not yet pose the question of the design of the form for inspecting and supervising [adherence to] the Constitution" (Phap luat Viet Nam 2005).

If the strength of the support for constitutional review (except for Professor Uc) seems surprising, it must be borne in mind that for most of its supporters that review is focused largely – often solely – on judicial review of statutes for constitutionality and compliance with higher law. Three of the four senior commentators cited by *Phap luat Viet Nam*, for example, cite judicial review of statutes as the sole reason legitimating a form of constitutional review in Vietnam. For senior officials, that is an easier form of constitutional review – of legislation, rather than governmental acts – to accept, and few senior supporters of constitutional review extend the notion to apply to constitutionality review of acts by state bodies, either at the national or provincial level. And there is no indication in these limited endorsements that any of the potential mechanisms for constitutional review and enforcement under discussion would apply to the Party's documents or actions.

As mentioned earlier, in 2004 the Party's Judicial Reform Committee chaired by then-President Tran Duc Luong had announced that the Committee was prepared to recommend "study of the establishment of a

Constitutional Court" (Bao Lao Dong 2004; Tuoi Tre 2004). In June 2005, the Party's Political Bureau adopted two important policy documents guiding development of the legal system up to 2020. One of those, Party Resolution 48 on Strategy for Development and Improvement of Vietnam's Legal System to the Year 2010 (Legal System Development Strategy 2005), was largely drafted by the Ministry of Justice and other government agencies and focused on specific legislative and other challenges. The other, the Resolution 49 on Judicial Reform Strategy to the Year 2020 (Judicial Reform Strategy 2005), was largely drafted by the Party Judicial Reform Committee and dealt in the main with courts and some other broader reform issues.

The Legal System Development Strategy did not deal in depth with constitutional review and enforcement, calling only generally for a mechanism "to protect the laws and the Constitution" and for a strengthening of the capacity of the National Assembly to undertake constitutionality review of legislation (Legal System Development Strategy 2005, secs. II: 1.3, III: 1.3). The Judicial Reform Strategy, drafted by the Party, also did not deal directly with constitutional review. And notably it did not contain any mention of a mechanism for constitutional review, such as a constitutional court or commission, though the Party Judicial Reform Committee had discussed those issues. The lack of specific discussion of a mechanism of constitutional review may reflect differences among powerful figures or institutions, or merely a lack of consensus on the issue. The Judicial Reform Strategy did propose the establishment of a "Judicial Committee" (Uy ban Tu phap) in the National Assembly charged with "assisting the National Assembly in exercising its oversight of judicial activities, with a focus on arrest, detention, prosecution, and adjudication." This is certainly not constitutional review or enforcement, but it may be a way of gradually establishing a group within the National Assembly that could begin focusing on constitutional issues, consistent with the model initially developed in China (Judicial Reform Strategy 2005, sec. II: 2.5).

Within months, however, discussion of constitutional review was prominent once again, and again an article in the official Party theoretical journal Tap chi Cong san (Communist Review) led the way. In an October 2005 Communist Review article treating legal reform issues that was reprinted in the main Party newspaper Nhan Dan, National Assembly Vice Chairman (and Party Central Committee member) Nguyen Van Yeu called for "building an effective structure for constitutional protection. We should study whether we can establish a

Constitutional Court (or Constitutional Protection Commission) with the responsibility for protecting the Constitution through jurisdiction to adjudicate and issue judgments on constitutional violations in legal documents, to adjudicate unconstitutional decisions and acts of agencies and individuals holding authority in state institutions and carry out the task of interpreting the Constitution and the laws (and ordinances where implementing ordinances have been issued)" (Yeu 2005).

Yeu's article was notable for once again broadening the definition of constitutional review to include not only the hierarchy and constitutionality of legislation, but also "unconstitutional decisions and acts of agencies and individuals holding authority in state institutions." It did not recommend a specific constitutional protection option, nor did it imply that the Party itself would be subject to the jurisdiction of any such mechanism, but it was important nonetheless for indicating clearly that the debate was still open and thriving.

Constitutional review and enforcement, at least of laws and other legal documents, and potentially also of official acts, fulfils several important roles that would help to buttress the developing Vietnamese state system – it would give some force to constitutional provisions, including force to the constitutional idea that the Constitution is the "fundamental law" of Vietnam superior to all others. A system of constitutional review and enforcement would begin to deal with the rapidly growing problem of contradictory legal documents, an issue exacerbated by the willy-nilly release of thousands of legal documents at national, provincial, metropolitan and local levels since the early 1990s. And, if extended to the review of official acts, it could begin to treat growing problems in state–society relations caused by the dictatorial practices of some officials, primarily at the local level.

So two interlocking sets of issues remain to be resolved. How far should the *scope* of constitutional review and enforcement extend in Vietnam? Only to the problem of legal texts? Or to actions as well? And, if to official acts, to acts by the Party as well as the state? Second, what *form* should constitutional review take and should that form be a constitutional court? And, if so, where should that court lie – as an independent court, or within the Supreme People's Court? Or should the National Assembly continue to perform this function, but at a higher level of intensity, attention and competence? (Cam 2003).

The second question – the form of constitutional review – may appear technical in nature and is often so considered by Vietnamese commentators. But like the issue of the scope of constitutional review it is, of course, fundamentally political in nature. As Ginsburg and others have shown, the construction of constitutional courts in Asia has frequently responded to popular demand as well as the growing sense that conflicts with a national constitution and laws require a powerful and specialized body to sort out those conflicts and relationships. But once the need and demand for such a structure is acknowledged by political elites, the construction of such bodies is a complex political process that is shaped by (depending on the state) political parties, popular organizations, lawyers and other professional interests, academics, and other forces (Ginsburg 2003).

In Vietnam there appears to be a growing acceptance both of the need for an institutional arrangement to sort out statutory conflicts with the Constitution and other laws, and of the demand for some sort of "constitutional protection" by business groups, academics, and others. And, somewhat more particular to the Vietnam case, acceding to that demand and need also enables the Party and state to wrest away a constitutional initiative from both domestic and overseas dissidents. But the key issues of scope and form remain; they are fundamentally political, and they are closely related to whether the Party will be subject to the constitutional review and enforcement that emerges.

In terms of scope, it seems broadly agreed that conflicts among and constitutionality of legislation need to be addressed; that form of constitutional review is clearly the least controversial of the issues of scope under debate, though even here the knotty problem remains of review of laws adopted by the National Assembly when the Assembly itself is stipulated in the Constitution as its interpreter. Debates continue on whether constitutional review and enforcement should include authority to review official acts – and, if so, whether that review power would include Party acts.

With respect to form, there remain several positions. The new structure could function as a specialized court of the Supreme People's Court based in Hanoi. That would be consistent with practice in some other Asian countries, but would make the new constitutional court part of a weak Supreme Court that lacks capacity as well as judicial independence. Yet that weakness might also be perceived as an advantage in Vietnam: the new constitutional court within the Supreme People's Court might be perceived as having little competition for authority within a weak Supreme Court, and might even be perceived as helping to strengthen the broader judicial structure of which it is a part. In starker political terms, there would be support within the Supreme Court and perhaps some other legal institutions for such an institutional arrangement; the National Assembly might well oppose this structure, and it is unclear how other elements of the Party and state would respond.

A related constitutional court option would be a separate constitutional court not located within and under the aegis of the Supreme People's Court. In organizational terms, a number of senior legal reformers support such an option because they want strong constitutional review and enforcement, and because they harbor strong concerns about the effectiveness of a constitutional court if it is part of either the existing judiciary or legislature. But a separate structure is a significant shock to the Vietnamese system – especially a structure such as a constitutional court that might embody, or come to embody, significant formal and expressive power, and thus a combination of institutional opposition and political anxiety may confront the independent option.

A third option, eschewing the constitutional court in any form, would be to strengthen the constitutional review and enforcement functions of the National Assembly. This is the option initially chosen by China through the formation of a constitutional review unit within the Legal Affairs Commission of the National People's Congress. And China is a jurisdiction Vietnam watches closely, in these and other matters. There are a number of ways to delegate these issues to the National Assembly while retaining political control of the outcomes. The Assembly could establish a constitutional review commission tied to the Assembly's Standing Committee, for example, or a constitutional review group tied to one the Assembly's committees, such as the law committee or the new "judicial committee" recommended in the Party's Judicial Reform Strategy, or a separate constitutional review committee. Strengthening the capacity and power of the National Assembly to handle some issues of constitutional review and enforcement would avoid the potential dangers of increasing the independence or authority of the Supreme People's Court or a new separate court. And such a structure within the National Assembly would be eminently controllable by the Party.

But there are also strong concerns in Vietnam about whether such a group could perform even the limited functions that the Vietnamese polity seems willing to delegate – the evaluation of statutes for conflict with the Constitution or other laws. It is that strong concern about National Assembly capacity to conduct constitutionality review – perhaps linked to political concerns as well, on giving the Assembly too much substantive capacity to go with its formal authority – that has helped to maintain discussions of a constitutional court either within the current judiciary or independent from it.

A fourth structural option – and the one currently chosen by default pending a different decision later – is to leave the system largely as it is with some additional administrative capacity to deal with pressing issues. This "status quo plus" option leaves the National Assembly formally responsible for "constitutional protection" and the government (delegating the Ministry of Justice) responsible for examining the immediate problem of over-reaching by provincial and municipal authorities beyond national law. While the administrative apparatus for harmonizing local and national law is active, the National Assembly Standing Committee, the relevant body currently responsible for these issues within the National Assembly, is highly limited. As Dr. Ngo Duc Manh, Director General of the Center for Information, Library and Research Services of the Office of the National Assembly argued in a 2005 paper:

> The constitutions of Vietnam, except for the 1946 Constitution, provide that the Standing Committee of the National Assembly reserves this right [of constitutional interpretation], but in fact, there has been no legal document ... officially interpreted by the Committee. In our understanding, this derives from the incompatibility between the function and legal status of the Committee. The Committee, as the permanent body of the National Assembly, primarily deals with the preparation for and organization of sessions of the National Assembly, while the body in charge of the interpretation of the Constitution, laws and ordinances should be granted ... an independent legal status.
>
> Other relevant legal matters also need to be clarified, such as the procedures of interpretation, including the proposal for interpretation, the study of the proposal by bodies of the National Assembly, the deliberation on the interpretation, the promulgation of interpretative documents. The implementing effect of and the relation between the interpretative terms made by the Standing Committee of the National Assembly and the provisions in the interpreted legal document should also be clearly defined, especially when the interpreted provisions are those of the Constitution.
>
> (Manh 2005)

Another legal scholar has raised even broader questions. Professor Bui Ngoc Son of Hanoi National University agrees with the common view that "Vietnam does not yet have a comprehensive system of constitutional protection ... and must have [such a] comprehensive system of constitutional protection." But, along with some others who have referenced Vietnam's 1946 Constitution, he holds that "because the power to make a constitution belongs to the people [the system of constitutional protection] cannot belong to the National Assembly." Implicit in his position is that a structure must be found that returns issues of constitutionality to "the people," or as close to the people as possible, but it is not at all clear how that would work in practice (Bui Ngoc Son 2003).

A crucial remaining question is whether constitutional review and enforcement would apply to the Communist Party at either local or national levels. The Party has played a leading role in discussions of "constitutional protection" and new potential mechanisms, primarily through the Judicial Reform Committee chaired by then-President Tran Duc Luong, and the Party's Commission for Internal Affairs. But for political reasons, the application of constitutional review and enforcement to the Party is rarely raised in the public discussions of these issues, and it remains unclear whether any constitutional protection structure would have any capacity to evaluate and adjudicate the constitutionality of Party documents, whether those documents conflict with current law, and the constitutionality or legality acts committed by the Party or Party officials. This limitation helps enable political support for a "constitutional protection" structure to begin to emerge – the Party may well be allowing, even encouraging discussions and planning of constitutional review and enforcement mechanisms to go forward on the understanding that the new structure will not include the Party within its jurisdiction. In other words, any new constitutional court or other structure would, like the remainder of the judiciary and the legal system, remain subordinate to the Party.

In 2006 and 2007, many of these questions remain unresolved in Hanoi. It will likely be several more years before Party, government, legislative and judicial officials make even some initial decisions about the structure and scope for a system of constitutional review and enforcement in Vietnam. Until then, the Ministry of Justice can be expected to strengthen its role in the harmonization of over-reaching local law with national law. And, as a temporary measure adopted with some reference to the current Chinese solution for these issues, it is possible that some additional capacity will be built into the Standing Committee of the National Assembly or other National Assembly committees to review constitutionality issues and citizens' complaints. But the contours of the debates on constitutional enforcement and review are now reasonably clear in Vietnam, and will require some resolution when politics allow.

The results may, at least initially, approximate the Chinese formation of a unit within the National People's Congress to investigate allegations of constitutional violations, both in order to resolve certain constitutional issues, to provide both the perception and reality of addressing these important issues, and perhaps to forestall broader calls for a constitutional court or another review mechanism. But in Vietnam the calls for a constitutional court or constitutional commission continue to grow, and the potential formation of a constitutional review unit in the National Assembly along the lines of the Chinese model is unlikely to stifle those calls for very long.

NOTES

1. The Constitution also mandates that "all Party organisations operate within the framework of the Constitution and the law" (Article 4), that the Government "shall ensure respect for and implementation of the Constitution and the law" (Article 109) and "ensure the implementation of the Constitution and the law in State organs, economic bodies, social organisations, units of the armed forces, and among the citizens, the Prime Minister, and state ministries and other agencies" (Article 112), that "all State organs, economic and social bodies, units of the people's armed forces, and all citizens must seriously observe the Constitution and the law" (Article 12), that the Prime Minister "suspend or annul" decisions, directives, circulars, resolutions and other legal documents issued by ministries, other national government agencies, and local government bodies "that contravene the Constitution, the law, and other formal written documents of superior State organs" (Article 114), that local People's Committees must "implement the Constitution," (Article 123), and that even the Vietnam Fatherland Front "ensures the strict observance of the Constitution and the law, strive to prevent and oppose all criminal behaviour and all violations of the Constitution and the law" (Article 9).
2. This clear call for formation of a Constitutional Court was accompanied by a strong tactical sense for potentially acceptable arguments in its favor. The rhetorical case for the court centered not on unconstitutional acts by Party and government officials (though those would be covered), but on "the many legal documents in effect that constantly violate the Constitution and the laws ... and cause harm to the people." The institutions responsible for investigating and acting on such documents are 'unable to do much', mentioning the public prosecutors along with the Assembly and the government. "A Constitutional Court could adjudicate unconstitutional acts. Any person against whom an unconstitutional document has been applied could appear before the Constitutional Court. In this way millions of people would have the power of supervision, and the system would be more democratic and more objective" (Lao Dong 2001).

CHAPTER 3

MOTORBIKE CONSTITUTIONALISM: THE EMERGENCE OF CONSTITUTIONAL CLAIMS IN VIETNAM

By the fall of 2005, Hanoi's motorcycle owners and riders were up in arms. Beginning two years earlier, in 2003, the Hanoi traffic police and the national police had promulgated a series of regulations that, they firmly believed, limited their autonomy and independence in owning, registering and riding motorbikes. First, in early 2003, the national police had announced a new national regulation stipulating that each Vietnamese citizen could legally register only one motorcycle, in an attempt to deal with rapidly increasing motorcycle congestion, accidents, deaths and pollution. Then Hanoi had enforced that national "one person, one motorbike" rule through a local regulation, angering Hanoi residents.

In early 2004, the Hanoi police sought other means to relieve motorcycle congestion, accidents and pollution in Hanoi. Concerned that the "one person, one motorbike" rule was difficult to enforce and that motorbikes were continuing to proliferate, the Hanoi authorities "temporarily suspended" new registrations of motorcycles in four of Hanoi's most congested urban districts. In early 2005, Hanoi extended that temporary suspension of registration from four to seven of Hanoi's districts. Hanoians were infuriated at both moves. The results were clear: "foreign" motorbikes – those registered in provinces outside Hanoi – were flooding into the city and dampening the resale value of motorbikes purchased but unable to be registered by Hanoi residents. And at US$3,000–8,000 per bike, Hanoians paid close attention to their motorcycle futures.

These new rules – "one person, one motorbike," and the suspension of regulation in seven urban districts sent Hanoi motorcycle owners and riders into open rebellion, and sparked Vietnam's first mass public assertion of constitutional rights in the reform era. Owners and riders began to complain, gradually more loudly, and they collected an unlikely but powerful alliance of supporters ranging from other citizens to legislators to national legal officials, united around the claim that these motorcycle regulations violated their right to own private property protected by Article 58 of the 1992 Vietnamese Constitution as well as the Vietnamese Civil Code.

The open assertion of constitutional rights by the public in Vietnam had previously been virtually unknown. A few isolated domestic political dissidents and some overseas Vietnamese dissidents regularly charged that the Party and government violated their own Constitution. But few heard them in Vietnam, because the regime took vigorous efforts to isolate, harass and sometimes jail domestic dissidents and few citizens appeared interested in direct political opposition to the Party. Constitutional claims had also been made in some rural land, tax and religious disputes, as in northern Thai Binh province in the late 1990s, but those claims had gained less attention at the time than was warranted or that urban citizens could muster. Motorcycles were different – for Hanoians and people throughout Vietnam, motorcycles have come to represent autonomy, freedom, convenience, a symbol of prosperity and a means to prosper, and a reflection of the more relaxed social atmosphere under *doi moi*. In short, Hanoians' love for their bikes and their riding freedom (and their motorbike values) resonated more immediately than direct political freedoms. And it did not hurt when citizens found they had allies in some of Vietnam's most powerful legal and political bodies and in the mass media.

REGULATING MOTORCYCLE CONGESTION: A CONSTITUTIONAL CONTROVERSY DEVELOPS

Hanoi's 2005 motorcycle constitutionalism debate has its roots in the Vietnamese love of motorbikes. Motorbikes became a prized symbol of autonomy, prosperity, and fun in new Vietnam – as well as the most convenient form of work and family transportation in the absence of a strong public transport system in many of Vietnam's rapidly growing cities. By 2003 the problem was getting out of hand in major urban areas like Hanoi and Saigon – the streets were literally filled with motorbikes, traffic accidents and deaths were on the increase, pollution was growing rapidly, other traffic was stifled, and, government officials charged, economic development was being slowed as well.[1]

The government responded with regulatory measures at both the national and local levels. In early 2003 the national police, the Ministry of Public Security, issued rules that limited motorbike registration to one motorbike for each citizen, and required that citizens carry a motorbike license, residence permit, and proof of insurance to register their cycles. The local police, the Hanoi Bureau of Public Security, promptly applied those rules in Hanoi via a local regulation (VnExpress 2003a).

These regulatory interventions reduced the number of Hanoians able to register new or repurchased motorbikes. In December 2002, according to the Hanoi traffic police, Hanoi residents registered about 700 motorbikes of various kinds each day. By the first week of January 2003, when the "one person, one motorbike" regulation went into effect, registrations dropped to about 300 per day. Hanoians also objected to the lack of notice and process as well – many motorbike registrants learned about the new restrictions and requirements only when they showed up at registration stations. And they objected to a twenty-day delay in obtaining motorcycle licenses that they believed might encourage corruption by police registration authorities. A Vietnamese press service reported that the new requirements had intensified a system in which private middlemen with ties to registration officials would facilitate the now more complex regulatory process for a fee of 500–600,000 dong (about US$33–40) per motorbike (VnExpress 2003a).

A month later, the Hanoi government announced nine new measures to reduce the growing rate of traffic accidents, deaths and congestion. The most controversial was the "temporary suspension" of motorbike registration in four of Hanoi's most congested and most prosperous urban districts, where about 40 percent of Hanoi's annual motorbike registrations took place (VnExpress 2003c, 2003d, 2003f). The registration suspension was intended to begin in June 2003, but it was pushed several months because of popular dissent. Hanoi police and city officials had wanted to go even further. Hanoi's police chief, Gen. Pham Chuyen, publicly proposed a complete suspension of motorbike registration throughout all fourteen districts of Hanoi beginning at the end of 2003, but opposition initially limited the ban to the four districts (VnExpress 2003d, 2003e, 2003f). The four district suspension went into effect over popular opposition on September 1, 2003, with senior Hanoi police officials still vowing to push for the fourteen district "suspension of registrations throughout the whole city during 2004" (VnExpress 2003d).

Hanoi police and transport officials continued to press for a citywide registration ban in 2004. Noting that 65 percent of traffic accidents involved motorbikes, the police chief warned that "if motorbike registrations are not halted this year, and we cannot develop infrastructure, then traffic jams and motorbike accidents will increase." But in the face of widespread public opposition, Hanoi police and transport officials could not muster enough political support to put the citywide registration ban into effect in 2004. They had to settle for a suspension of registrations in three more districts late in 2004, with the possibility of adding two more districts in 2005, later delayed to 2008 (VnExpress 2004a, 2004c). Hanoi police officials further angered the public by refusing to implement a national police document, issued in March 2004, that allowed the owners of lost or stolen motorcycles to register their replacement bikes without coming afoul of the "one person, one motorbike" regulation (VnExpress 2004b).

LOCAL AND CENTRAL: THE GROWING PROBLEM OF LEGAL CONFLICT

There matters largely stood until the summer of 2005 – widespread public dissatisfaction, adaptation involving "foreign" bikes, out-of-town registration, and the use of middlemen, but not a widespread rebellion. But other developments in 2005 sparked a much broader public discussion and, eventually, a debate on the constitutional rights of motorcycle owners. For years Party and government leaders had become increasingly concerned at the tendency of provincial and local officials and lawmakers to legislate on a wide variety of matters in conflict with higher law (and, arguably, constitutional norms). Conflicting legislation was particularly prevalent in areas of particular interest to local authorities, such as incentives for foreign and domestic investment, and provisions to fine or even jail citizens for local administrative violations. The courts had no explicit powers to decide these conflict issues.

By 2002, as discussed in Chapter 2, the problem was serious enough that the government formed a General Department for Inspection of Legal Documents within the Ministry of Justice with the primary task of ferreting out local laws that conflict with national law, and pressuring or forcing local authorities to annul them (VnExpress 2002c). The new department got to work quickly, surveying provincial and local laws and rapidly trying to force local governments to withdraw conflicting legislation. The problem was not limited to local authorities: In a report compiled for the National Assembly in the summer of 2005, the department identified more than 400 legal documents promulgated by national ministries as well as by local authorities that conflicted with higher national law, a result that the Minister of Justice called "startling." The National Assembly then stepped up the pressure, declaring that some of these local and ministerial legal documents violated the Constitution as well – and the Assembly followed the Ministry of Justice's analysis and included the Ministry of Public Security's 2003 "one person, one motorbike" regulation on its list of "unconstitutional" acts.

Representatives of the Law Committee of the National Assembly told the Standing Committee that the Ministry's motorbike regulation was a restriction on citizens' right to own property guaranteed in Article 58 of the Constitution and Article 221 of the Civil Code, citing the stipulation of Circular 2 (2003) that "each person may only register one motorcycle or motorbike" (VnExpress 2005b; Circular 2 2003).[2] The constitutional provision guaranteed the right to own private property; the Civil Code provision stipulated that ownership rights were not to be limited with respect to number or value. The Ministry of Justice upped the stakes by calling for "adjudicating the lack of [personal] responsibility by leading cadres in the lawmaking process" where legal documents under their control violate higher law or the Constitution (VnExpress 2005b).

The next day, the press paraphrased Minister of Justice Uong Chu Luu in "proposing" that the government "must revise or abrogate" the one person, one motorbike rule "because it violates the Constitution and law." In a more formal interview, the Minister was more careful than the media editors, declining to speak in constitutional terms: he said that the one person, one motorbike provision "does not yet conform to the Ordinance on Administrative Violations and ordinances issued by the Government on defending transport order and safety" and "suggest[ed] that the promulgating agency must revise or abrogate" the regulation. He explained that ministry regulation of this type fall primarily within the jurisdiction of the relevant minister, and "secondly" the Prime Minister and the National Assembly. At the local level, local legislatures and executive bodies have the power to promulgate, revise or abrogate legal documents. "Where the People's Committee [at the local level] does not abrogate [such a document], then the Prime Minister may do so" (VnExpress 2005c).

ECHOES OF PAST COMMAND POLICIES, AND THE ROAD TO RESISTANCE

In the days that followed, the press and public increased the pressure on the national and local police to annul both the "one person, one motorbike" rule and the registration suspension in the Hanoi urban districts. The constitutionality of the one motorbike rule was questioned frequently in the media. The temporary suspension of motorcycle regulations was an "imaginary achievement that confuses the truth!" according to Hanoi's leading newspaper, *Ha Noi Moi* (*New Hanoi*). Using the term "command administration" – a reference to past hard-line practices – to describe the police regulations, *Ha Noi Moi* pointed out that in 2005, after the suspension began in four Hanoi districts, registrations actually rose 17 percent across the city. "The goals have not been met," *Ha Noi Moi* said, and fees had risen for the purchase of the "rationed" registrations. Such echoes of the past – "command," "ration," and corrupt middlemen – would reverberate around Hanoi in the days ahead. And, returning to the increasing theme of constitutional violations, the constitutional attack was broadened from the issue of "one motorbike" rule to the question of registration. "The temporary suspension of motorcycle registrations violates citizens' lawful right to own and register property provided by the Constitution and the Civil Code," *Ha Noi Moi* said (Ha Noi Moi 2005a).

After consulting with the Prime Minister and, most likely, other Party and government leaders, the national police folded on the "one person, one motorbike" rule. On November 21, 2005, the Ministry of Public Security formally withdrew its rule that "each person may only register one motorcycle," as well as an unpopular requirement that citizens provide a copy of their insurance certificate covering civil liability for the owner of the motorized vehicle (Circular 17 2005). Under recently promulgated transparency rules, these retreats from earlier policy came into effect fifteen days after publication in the official Gazette, or on December 14, 2005.

The national police decision was greeted with glee by newspapers and the Hanoi public. Newspapers pointed out that the Ministry's decision had come but one day before the Minister of Justice had been scheduled to present another report to the National Assembly on conflicts between local and national law and potential issues of constitutionality (VnExpress 2005d; Ha Noi Moi 2005b).

FROM VICTORY TO VICTORY: UPPING THE
PRESSURE ON HANOI

In the days that followed the Public Security Ministry's abrogation of the "one person, one motorbike" rule, the city of Hanoi came under increasing pressure to annul its own local regulations suspending motorcycle registration (VnExpress 2005e; Ha Noi Moi 2005c). Quoting legal specialists, one newspaper noted that "the Hanoi People's Committee's decision to suspend motorcycle registration also violates the Constitution and the Civil Code." The regulations are "inappropriate," one legal specialist said, merging issues of constitutionality, conflict with national law, and reasonable regulation for health and safety purposes. "Buying and registering motorcycles for circulation [in commerce] is a right of citizens for which [favorable] conditions must be created." The Hanoi restrictions not only violated property rights secured by the Constitution and the Civil Code, but also "caused inequality in society." "Citizens have the right to purchase any property at all and the state may not prohibit that in any way." And, a news service slyly intervened, the Hanoi restrictions were not only illegal and unconstitutional but also ineffective, citing a "decline in record keeping by management authorities" and an increase in motorcycles on the road (VnExpress 2005e).

The national police had given up on the "one person, one motorbike" rule, but the Hanoi police chief stuck bravely to the Hanoi suspension of motorcycle registrations. He argued that in the two years since registrations had been suspended in the four urban districts, "the number of registered motorcycles has gone down each year compared with the previous year. Before [the suspension] ... the city was registering 1,500 motorcycles per day at its height but now there are only about 300 on average each day." And he declined to reverse the suspension of motorbike registrations on the ground that the national police had lifted the "one motorbike" rule, on the grounds that the Public Security Ministry's retreat on that provision did not apply to local restrictions on registration. He bowed only to the strict terms of national police decision on the "one motorbike" rule, noting that Hanoi "will strictly implement the Ministry of Public Security's new circular, meaning that we will abrogate the provision that 'each person may only register one motorcycle'." Hanoi would not, however, go further and lift its four district ban on registrations (Ha Noi Moi 2005c).

But popular pressure continued to build, calling on Hanoi officials to abrogate the additional local restrictions on registration. In response, local political officials called for a report within a week on the effectiveness of the suspension of registrations in seven city districts. "If the prohibition on motorcycle registrations is ineffective," a prominent news service reported, "the Hanoi People's Committee will issue a decision abrogating it the next day. If it has been effective, the city will suggest to the Prime Minister that Hanoi be permitted to apply measures ending the registration of motorcycles in the city proper" (VnExpress 2005f; Ha Noi Moi 2005d).

Debate raged among the city's senior leaders. Some argued that the registration suspension was ineffective, leading to the "purchase of registration certificates to violate the law, with motorcycles from other provinces continuing to steam into the city." Local legislators echoed the argument that the Hanoi district registration suspensions were unconstitutional. Others, including the police chief, called the restrictions effective in reducing the number of vehicles (VnExpress 2005f). As the Hanoi debate continued, a Hanoi newspaper printed a dispatch from Saigon noting that the Saigon authorities would abrogate local enforcement of the "one motorcycle, one person" regulation, and simplify registration procedures so that only a residence certificate and license were required.

Into this distressed arena once again strode the Ministry of Justice, once again forcefully raising the issue of constitutionality. The Director of the Ministry's General Department for Inspection of Legal Documents told the press in late November that "Hanoi's temporary suspension of motorcycle registrations is a violation of law" and that the Department, along with other agencies, would "investigate the constitutionality (tinh hop hien) of that document." "The policy is good," the Ministry official said. But "implementing that policy through local administrative measures that restrict individuals' means of transport in a way that arbitrarily prohibits and restricts the property rights of individuals is incorrect." He said that any such restriction must be made by the national legislature, if at all. And he called for strengthening provisions for direct citizen complaint or petition against such regulations, and for "institutional liability" for damages caused by such legal provisions (VnExpress 2005g).

As the pressure mounted, Hanoi officials promised again that they would abrogate the local version of the "one person, one motorbike" rule as soon as the Public Security Ministry's abrogation of the national rule went into effect on December 14, and they promised to decide quickly on whether to continue the suspension of motorcycle registrations in seven districts. Showing responsiveness was important, and the tide was beginning to shift: "The people of Hanoi will not need to wait long; within ten days, the delegates of the Hanoi People's Council will be working actively to unify and issue a decision on this difficult problem." Another senior city official sought to signal a result: "The measure of suspending registrations ... over the past two years was a situational measure in reality it did not reach its goals. ... We must not only summarize when we have achieved victories but we must also straightforwardly draw out experience when ... we have made mistakes" (Ha Noi Moi 2005e).

Meanwhile, the Hanoi motorcycle market remained in a "gloomy" state because the city had not yet indicated that it would lift the suspension of registrations. The Public Security Ministry might have helped to "open" the motorcycle market when it annulled the national "one motorbike" rule, but Hanoi's motorcycle commerce remained "closed," with "as yet no intention to annul the prohibition on registration of motorcycles in seven city districts." Sales remained very slow, for the question of registration – rather than the "one motorcycle, one person" rule that was about to disappear – was more significantly dampening the markets (Ha Noi Moi 2005f).

The debate continued to rage over the effectiveness of the registration suspension in the seven city districts. "The card game is not worth the candle" used to light it, bannered one prominent news service at the end of November. Had registrations, motorbike congestion, accidents and deaths declined because of the city registration suspension, as the police claimed, or had city residents just found other ways to buy and ride their bikes – such as using external registrations, for such registrations were easily buyable for two or three million dong (US$125–190)? (VnExpress 2005i). The motorcycle market was "holding its breath," "frozen," waiting for the Hanoi People's Council to meet. One resident of Dong Da District was waiting to buy a Vespa. "I hear that the city is preparing to permit citizens to begin registering again. If that happens it will keep me from losing 2–3 million dong in buying a rationed registration from other people." A motorcycle dealer said he expected motorbike prices to rise if the city allowed registrations to resume, perhaps one or two million dong (US$63–125) per bike. Currently Hanoi residents had to buy the registration and pay a middleman to help in the registration (VnExpress 2005j).

Positions continued to harden in early December, as the Hanoi People's Council prepared to meet to decide on the "unconstitutional" suspension of motorcycle registrations. The Hanoi Public Security Bureau "continued to maintain its view that the registration suspensions had resulted in fewer registrations" and fewer cycles clogging the roads (Ha Noi Moi 2005g). As the national Public Security Ministry's revised regulations annulling the "one person, one motorbike" rule came into effect in mid-December, Hanoi's main newspaper pointed out that the Hanoi authorities had still not taken any decisions on the suspension of registration and had not even received a full report from police and transport agencies on the effects of the suspensions (Ha Noi Moi 2005h). But city officials continued to defend both the legal basis for and the effectiveness of their restrictions (VnExpress 2005h).

In the first public comments from a national leader, a spokesman for the Prime Minister weighed in, calling for calm and analytical deliberations. "If they are going to continue to prohibit [registration], Hanoi must explain clearly whether those provisions violate the law or not and their effectiveness. If they abrogate the prohibition order then they must also have a strategy for reducing traffic congestion and limiting traffic accidents ... We may not unanimously support the regulation suspending motorcycle registration in Hanoi. An individual may buy ten motorbikes, but none of us can go onto the streets on ten bikes at once." (VnExpress 2005h). And in response to a highly loaded question from journalists – "the Ministry of Public Security has issued a circular abrogating its regulation that each person may only register one motorbike but Hanoi continues to shilly-shally" – the Prime Minister's spokesman left his Hanoi colleagues twisting in the wind: "The Prime Minister knows about this matter and has called Hanoi's attention to it!" (Ha Noi Moi 2005i; Vietnamnet 2005b).

THE HANOI LEGISLATURE MEETS, WAVERS, AND INCITES MORE ANGER

Hanoi's municipal legislature, the Hanoi People's Council, opened a three day session on December 7, 2005 with one burning issue on the agenda. "There are still some views suggesting that we should limit [registrations]" under the Hanoi rules, a legislative official said as the session opened. And Hanoi's Public Security Bureau "maintained its view" that the registration suspension had been effective. But public opposition remained strong, and higher authorities were deliberating on the issue. In the run-up to the legislative session, the question had been brought to Hanoi's key political body, the Hanoi Party Committee, for decision (Tien Phong 2005).

As the session opened, a poll of Hanoi residents conducted by the news service VnExpress found 4,941 of the 6,113 respondents (80.8 percent) favoring lifting the suspension on registrations, and 1,061 of the respondents (17.4 percent) favoring the restrictions. The Hanoi government's view diverged sharply from the popular voice: the Vice Chairman of the Hanoi People's Committee reaffirmed that the People's Committee would still "favor . . . continuing to suspend registration of motorcycles in seven city districts." And the city was preparing to propose extending the registration ban to rural districts of Hanoi as well. Under sharp questioning at the legislative session, the Vice Chairman firmly rejected the view that the city was "disobeying higher law," saying that the city had considerable autonomy in taking measures to regulate its own affairs and control traffic. And he rejected the view that the city's actions violated the Constitution and the Civil Code: "The duties of city leaders are to ensure traffic safety and to promote beauty and modernization for the city," including various measures to control traffic (VnExpress 2005h).

Meanwhile, a Hanoi lawyer argued that "localists" should not be permitted to violate "principles of socialist legality" in adopting a "situational measure." He lauded the powerful Ministry of Public Security for abrogating the "one person, one motorbike" rule, an act "very much worthy of praise because it may be the first time that a state agency has been bold enough . . . to correct the mistakes it committed itself." He criticized Hanoi officials for their unwillingness to take the same step (Vietnamnet 2005c).

In the legislative session, Hanoi officials argued that "Hanoi's temporary suspension of motorcycle registration does not conflict with provisions issued by the Center," and is a "correct policy" (Ha Noi Moi 2005j; Tuoi Tre 2005). Other legislators argued instead for "financial measures" to control motorcycles, including increased license fees and tolls on certain roads. But on December 9, in a "burning" session, the Hanoi People's Council refused to abrogate the Hanoi regulations suspending motorcycle registrations in seven urban districts. Seven of the twelve deputies who spoke on the issue favored lifting the registration regulations, according to a domestic news service, but the Chairman of the People's Council "bolted the door again" and declined to accede to the view in favor of lifting the suspension, siding with the

Hanoi police and political leadership. Other deputies called for a vote, but it appears that no formal vote was held (VnExpress 2005o; Ha Noi Moi 2005k).

The decision seemed to be made – Hanoi's restrictions on motorcycle registration would stay in place, even though the national rule of "one person, one motorbike" had been annulled. Instead, Hanoi would continue studying the issue, with the Chairman of the People's Council promising to lead the abrogation effort in January 2006 if the suspensions proved to be ineffective in controlling motorcycle traffic and safety (VnExpress 2005p; Ha Noi Moi 2005l). Popular opinion still seemed to side strongly moving quickly to reopen motorcycle registration in the affected districts.

UPPING THE STAKES ONCE AGAIN IN THE NATIONAL ASSEMBLY

At the national level, other political figures had plans different from the Hanoi leadership. The chairman of a committee of the National Assembly spoke angrily to the press the day after the Hanoi legislature adjourned. "Hanoi's suspension of motorcycle registrations violates the Constitution and the law," he said, and threatened to "send a report to the Standing Committee," the highest body of the National Assembly. "Hanoi must implement the provision of the Ministry of Public Security [annulling the "one person, one motorbike" rule] and immediately abrogate the provision for temporary suspension of registrations" (VnExpress 2005o).

Meanwhile, on December 12, Saigon formally abrogated its local application of the "one motorcycle one person" rule and the insurance certification requirement (Tien Phong 2005; Ha Noi Moi 2005l). On December 13, Hanoi abrogated local application of the "one person, one motorbike" rule for city residents beyond the seven districts in which motorcycle registration was suspended, in line with the national police action, while maintaining the registration suspension within the seven city districts (VnExpress 2005q).

On December 13, the question of the constitutionality of Hanoi's motorcycle regulations reached the Standing Committee of the National Assembly, Vietnam's highest legislative body. The atmosphere was tense: "Today, ... if the committee members approve, the National Assembly will issue a document requesting that the executive of the Hanoi People's Council issue a report ... evaluating the effectiveness of the regulations suspending motorcycle registration, and clarifying its views on whether to maintain or annul" those regulations (Ha Noi Moi 2005l; Vietnamnet 2005d). The Chairman of the National Assembly assigned the task of "inspecting" the work of the Hanoi People's Council on this matter to the chair of the committee who had brought the matter to the Standing Committee, effectively supporting those who sought to annul the Hanoi rules (Vietnamnet 2005d).

A VICTORY FOR HANOI MOTORCYCLISTS – BUT A VICTORY FOR CONSTITUTIONALISM?

In the face of this political pressure from above, the Hanoi government's resistance collapsed the next day. The Hanoi People's Committee issued a decision annulling its suspension of motorcycle registration in seven city districts, with immediate effect. The result of both victories – both on the "one person, one motorbike" rule, and on registration, was that "residents throughout the city of Hanoi may once again register their motorcycles without restriction as to number" (VnExpress 2005r). The news service continued, perhaps putting the best face on Hanoi's capitulation – and carefully providing a non-constitutional, more limited legal justification for Hanoi's decision without mentioning the issue of constitutionality:

> After two years of implementing the decision on an experimental basis to suspend motorcycle registration in seven districts, the Hanoi People's Committee has annulled the decision because temporary suspension was not effective as was hoped. In addition, this provision violated the Civil Code with respect to property and assets owned by citizens."
>
> (VnExpress 2005r)

As VnExpress pointed out, "only five days after" the Chairman of the People's Council refused to overturn the unpopular regulation, the Hanoi executive branch (the People's Committee) overturned it on its own motion (VnExpress 2005r). Ha Noi Moi put it even more gleefully in its headline: "Ha Noi: Motorbikes can get registered again!" (Ha Noi Moi 2005m).

The motorcycle markets of Hanoi had been "relatively quiet" in recent days, as buyers "waited for the city of Hanoi to annul the regulation suspending registrations." Motorcycle dealers expected prices to rise between 500,000 and one million dong (about US$32–63) in the short term (VnExpress 2005r; Ha Noi Moi 2005m).

Initially, the lines at registration stations were short, and markets remained quiet as resident absorbed the news that the registration suspension had been lifted (Ha Noi Moi 2005m). But in a few days the situation "changed suddenly," as Hanoians began to flock into registration stations (VnExpress 2005s). And the Hanoi police claimed that obedience to traffic rules declined as motorcycle traffic picked up (VnExpress 2005t). Within a week, Hanoi's registration stations were "overloaded" with hundreds of eager motorbike owners. 500 new motorbikes were registered on December 15, 646 on December 16, 679 on December 19, and 750 on December 20. And the "middlemen" were back, charging fees of about 70,000–240,000 dong (US$10–31) to assist with and speed up registration (VnExpress 2005n). By December 22 the registration stations were falling behind, and the middlemen were targeting the impatient, or those without time or correct information (Ha Noi Moi 2005n).

The motorcycle market began to rise each day, as the number of motorbikes registered quickly doubled the daily totals during the restriction period (Ha Noi Moi 2005o). And by early January 2006, the registration process had gone from prohibited on December 13 to "miserably hard." The prices for assistance by the middlemen were rising as well, to about 700,000 dong for assistance with registration. The main Hanoi newspaper called on the Hanoi traffic police to "strengthen their administrative measures, assign more officials to handle registrations, in order to resolve the . . . overloaded situation and the plague of the 'middlemen' who perform at the registration stations" (Ha Noi Moi 2006a).

By the end of January 2006 motorcycle registrations had increased to 12,666 in the month after the restrictions were eased, up over 200 percent (8,474 registrations) above the 3,792 registrations issued in the month before the suspension ended. Almost all of this increase – 7,488 of the 8,474 new registrations – occurred in the seven suspended districts. On a citywide aggregate basis, registrations were up from 200–250 vehicles per day to 700–800 vehicles each day (Ha Noi Moi 2006b).

IMPLICATIONS OF THE MOTORBIKE CONSTITUTIONALISM DEBATE

What can we draw from this story of urban regulation, popular resistance, and an unlikely arena for struggle over constitutional principles?

In 2005, Vietnam was ready for discussion of constitutional principles, at least in an initial form. And the regulatory activities of national police and local traffic police were the perfect foil for a rebellion of a certain kind, a demand for individual rights that was unrelated to broader political demands or other constitutional principles such as the right to free speech or a free press. This was safe constitutionalism, the fight for the right to be free to own, register and ride one's own motorcycle (or ten of them). And it was closely related to economic interests. The Hanoi motorcycle market wilted when the authorities imposed a widening ban on registrations, bringing to bear a powerful combination of economic and emotional interests – a sense of freedom being limited in both economic and personal life – that galvanized both the public and the press.

If the motorbike battle was powerful economic and political theater, it was not necessarily powerful constitutionalism. But the earliest ink-lings of constitutional rights may well be personal and economic in nature, not more broadly political. This was a constitutionalism of individual rights that the Party could live with in a way that it could never tolerate dissidents' assertions of political rights, or separation of powers. And the rebellion resonated with a highly personal, rights-based, individualistic sense among younger Hanoians that outspokenly claimed the right to be left alone by the state, rather than the right to carry out forbidden political activity. That right to be left alone, to ride one's motorbike, to buy and sell them, without interference from the authorities, was easier to observe and satisfy than any broader political complaints.

Yet there are problems here. In the 2005 debate over motorcycle constitutionalism in Hanoi, constitutional rights were claimed with a breadth that would astonish many foreign scholars. And they were claimed not only by ordinary citizens untrained in constitutional law, but also by knowledgeable officials in the Ministry of Justice, the National Assembly, and other legal institutions. The core public asser-tion was that any restriction on the rights contained in the Constitution – here, the right to own private property – was uncon-stitutional. In the public discourse, that was mixed murkily with another debate on the "effectiveness" of Hanoi's regulatory interven-tion. And the brew was further confused by multiple references to conflicts of law – between the local regulations and the range of regulatory action Hanoi is permitted to use, between the local regula-tions and national traffic regulations issued by the Ministry of Public Security, between the local regulations and national laws such as the Civil Code, and between local regulations and the Constitution.

Of these various overlapping debates, the "unconstitutionality" provision had the most public resonance but made the least sense either in Vietnamese or in broader constitutional terms. The notion that *any* restriction on a constitutionally protected right is *per se* unconstitutional is neither part of Vietnamese constitutional jurisprudence nor broader constitutional theory. Rather, the targeted regulation must generally be measured, at least in some form, for its appropriateness in furthering a legitimate governmental goal and in the extent of its effects on a constitutionally protected right. So the public (and sometimes legislative and governmental) proponents of a baldly stated "unconstitutionality" position in the motorbike debate had little solid footing.

The debate on "effectiveness" was more valuable, for it implicitly acknowledged the need to balance a constitutional right against the government's power to regulate for the public good. And, not surprisingly, that was a more sophisticated and fact-based debate, relying on dueling statistics on motorbike registrations in Hanoi and dueling interpretations for registration shifts. In the end, a sophisticated debate on the effectiveness of governmental regulation and its incidental or substantial intrusions on constitutional rights did not carry the day. Instead, when the pressure became too heavy, the Hanoi authorities had to fold to overwhelming public opinion backed up by political and legislative officials who, often for institutional interests, issued broad constitutional statements that helped inflame the public.

Thus many factors were at work in Hanoi's debate on motorbike constitutionalism. The public was safe in depending autonomy from the state and freedom both to enjoy and profit from their beloved motorbikes – the individualist and market bases for constitutional assertion. The Ministry of Justice and the National Assembly supported the public's appeals, at least partly in order to strengthen their own legally defined roles as arbiters of conflict between local, ministry and national legal documents (in the case of the Ministry of Justice), and constitutional supervision (in the National Assembly). And a beleaguered, plainly unpopular Hanoi city government was left to defend an even more unpopular cadre of traffic police and transport officials who, seemingly in good faith, had imposed strict restrictions on motorcycle registration in Hanoi's great colonial and modern capital, a city rapidly being overrun by motorcycles and motorcycle culture. Put in those terms, perhaps the outcome of Vietnam's first major debate on constitutionalism and constitutional principles should have been entirely foreseeable from the beginning.

In Vietnam the first major, popular debate over constitutional rights developed as an urban and largely middle class phenomenon – the province not just of city-based motorcycle owners, but in some cases of urban dwellers who wish to own more than one motorbike, and to maximize their resale potential. At least in this case, constitutional appeals were led by those who arguably have gained the most from the *doi moi* process, and who have the most to gain from a limitation of government regulation in this area. For those winners in the economic reform process, the assertion of constitutional rights provides a shield from government regulation, even while it promotes possibilities for strengthened corruption. But here too the costs have been clearly weighed: in effect, the cost of corruption (in the purchase of motorbike registrations) may pale beside the gains to be made from a freer system of registration, ownership and motorcycle transfer.

In China, constitutionalist appeals have already begun to move from the middle class interests of Hanoi's motorcycle owners (with emotional as well as economic appeals to poorer urban residents as well), and toward a constitutionalism of rights for those who have so far not so fulsomely gained from reform. Chinese poor urban dwellers whose homes are being demolished for private developments or public works projects, or peasants subject to overwhelming taxation, corruption or the demolition of residences, have raised constitutionalist appeals. We may see a progression in Vietnam from a constitutionalism for the economic rights of the middle class to a constitutionalism for the rights of the disenfranchised. In Vietnam, as in China, the Party and government may well accede to the constitutionalist claims of wealthier urban residents who have found their voice. But in China, the response to the constitutionalist assertions of poorer citizens has been less forgiving.

Only institutions – not senior Party and government intervention – can help to ensure that the response to constitutionalist assertions by the poor is as accommodating as the claims of the wealthier. But in Vietnam such institutions are virtually non-existent, which is why the decisions in the motorbike episode were made by a politicized legislature and by senior officials. And the process of building such institutions has not, as we have noted in Chapter 2, developed much further. Without autonomous institutions to weigh constitutional claims, the winners in Vietnam's coming constitutionalist battles may, like the winners in the motorbike story of 2005, be those who are already winning the struggle for prosperity and the voice of the Party and government in a rapidly marketizing nation.

NOTES

1. Because of the unusually broad coverage and discussion of these issues in the increasingly open Vietnamese press, newspaper reports cited as sources for this chapter are identified in the text by newspaper and date. All are available via the Internet; VnExpress is at vnexpress.net; Hanoi Moi (New Hanoi) is at www.hanoimoi.com.vn. Other documents, such as national and local regulations, are traditionally cited in the text with full references in the bibliography.
2. In early 2006, the department released another list of nearly ninety legal documents from 33 provinces and municipalities that violate the law specifically in the area of administrative punishments of citizens, a popular area for local regulation. And also in January 2006, the department took on the powerful Hanoi People's Committee, announcing that three Hanoi legal documents – among them an unpopular rule allowing city authorities to seize motorcycles and other vehicles for legal violations and hold them for 15 to 60 days – conflicted with national law (Nhan Dan 13 January 2006).

CHAPTER 4

ECONOMIC LAW IN THE SERVICE OF GLOBALIZATION: LABOR LAW AND LABOR EXPORT FROM VIETNAM

Economic law in Vietnam takes multiple forms, with multiple objectives. It can serve to strengthen Vietnam's integration into a global economy and to bring the benefits of that integration to Vietnam's citizens – either a narrow band, or a wide urban and rural community. The law governing the economy and various forms of commercial and business transactions can, however, also be used to restrict rights and opportunities in a rapidly marketizing economy, particularly rights and opportunities for the poorer and weaker in Vietnamese society, as it frees the creative forces of entrepreneurs and provides flexibility for the domestic business sector (Greenfield 1994).

Most recent academic work on Vietnamese economic law analyzes the role of law in corporate, commercial, contracting, foreign investment and related contexts. Here we look at an another important and recent example of Vietnamese economic law at work – the role of law in facilitating opportunities for Vietnamese workers in the globalizing economy, and in controlling and restricting workers' rights as well. The protection of export laborers under Vietnamese law and the cases that have arisen in this arena illuminate a key problem in Vietnamese legal reform: what and who does the law effectively protect? Is law intended to defend the rights of those with fewer protections in society, does it primarily serve as a tool for the extraction of economic profit by government and private interests from workers and other less powerful groups, or is it intended to balance these interests? And what are its actual effects?

For the law of labor export, those issues were illuminated most clearly in a case of over two hundred Vietnamese and Chinese workers who were held in involuntary servitude and mistreated at a Korean-owned garment factory on the American island territory of Samoa. That case, which became famous in Vietnam and around the world, illustrated failures in both American and Vietnamese law in protecting Vietnamese workers in the United States. If the expanding law governing export labor from Vietnam, *the law as text*, is drafted both to protect the rights of Vietnamese workers sojourning abroad to work, and the interests of the private and government authorities that dispatch them, it failed in the Daewoosa case. In the Daewoosa case, Vietnamese labor export workers and their supervisors were sent abroad under the Vietnamese legislative and regulatory system for export labor developed in Vietnam over the past fifteen years. That Vietnamese export labor legal regime is intended to earn export revenues for Vietnam, in which workers are now a kind of export commodity, help reduce rampant unemployment, provide worker training, and, at least rhetorically, protect the rights of workers sent abroad. In that case, practice trumped text, legal text remained unenforced, and law failed in its protective role.

The failures of law to protect the rights of the weaker and poorer in the Daewoosa case reflects broader problems both in Vietnamese law and in donor support for the revamping of Vietnam's economic law system. That modernization and renovation of Vietnam's economic law has resulted in a system that is more detailed, more legal, and arguably more regulated. But it has also been used and enforced largely by those within Vietnam with greater economic and political power and against those with less power. The conviction of the factory owner in American Samoa should not blind us to the failings of the labor law system in Vietnam that has served to provide legal protection to rapacious labor export companies, police and loan sharks. Such failings have helped to produce situations like that on Samoa, while giving workers themselves virtually no way to implement the general rights that legislation supposedly grants them.

There is something of a contradiction in these pictures. In the export labor case, the reform of a particular economic law regime – labor law and the system of sending export labor overseas – has clearly benefited the state, government ministries, the state export labor companies that make profits from sending laborers abroad, and the loan sharks, police and local officials who earn profits from the amounts charged or gouged from workers as fees, loans or blackmail for being allowed to go overseas. That economic law regime regulating export labor was also intended to facilitate economic opportunities and, at least rhetorically, to protect Vietnamese workers from exploitation by forces at home and abroad – at home, from loan sharks, local officials, and labor export companies; abroad, from rapacious foreign factory owners and managers. That part of the system is clearly failing, because the legislation embodying it requires implementation by state authorities that have, as their primary duty, the serving of government ministries and labor export companies rather than the protection of workers' rights, and because that legal regime provides not even the hint of permission for any sort of even semi-autonomous advocacy on behalf of export workers.

In recent years, however, the Vietnamese authorities have taken significant steps to reform and detail the text of laws dealing with labor export – most notably by adopting a new Labor Code in 2002, adding to that Code in 2003 with detailed implementing procedures through a new national decree and circular (Labor Code 2004), and adopting a national law on export labor in 2006. Thus the text of law is considerably stronger and more detailed than when the Daewoosa events occurred. The new Labor Code, the implementing regulations under it, and the new labor export law speak directly to the issues raised in the Daewoosa litigation and, at least in textual form, re-emphasize worker protection. The question that remains is whether stronger text will in fact be implemented. Enforcement has been a significant problem, and the implementation of detailed provisions on a regular and consistent basis is a key challenge for economic and labor law in Vietnam. Vietnam has begun that process, through charging and convicting illegal labor exporters and human traffickers, and undertaking programs with domestic and foreign organizations to improve enforcement and implementation. But the road to strong and consistent enforcement of law that protects rights in Vietnam is long and difficult (Sidel 2003, 2004; Gillespie 2006; Nicholson 2006).

VIETNAMESE SERVITUDE ON A PACIFIC ISLAND: THE DAEWOOSA CASE

We begin with the Daewoosa case – an American criminal prosecution – and the problems in recent Vietnamese legal reform that Daewoosa helps illuminate. On February 21, 2003, Kil Soo Lee, the owner and manager of Daewoosa Ltd., a garment factory located in US territory on the Pacific island of American Samoa, was convicted of multiple criminal charges involving involuntary servitude (a modern term for slavery) in connection with the trafficking, beatings, and other mistreatment of over 200 Vietnamese and Chinese workers, including the gouging out of an eye of one of the laborers. But the Daewoosa saga began years earlier, in the late 1990s, when Kil Soo Lee appears to have visited Vietnam (as well as China) and made contact with several export labor companies recognized and permitted by the Vietnamese Ministry of Labor, Invalids and Social Affairs to export workers abroad.

In late 1998 and early 1999, Lee opened a garment factory registered on the American Pacific territory of American Samoa. Lee was the majority owner of Daewoosa Samoa and the manager of the factory. Daewoosa held contracts with several important American retailers of clothes, including JC Penney and Sears, who could import from Samoa at lower tariffs and with products bearing "Made in American Samoa, USA" labels. Labor protection on American Samoa was weaker than on the American mainland. And Daewoosa's links to the American Samoan government appeared particularly strong. As the nongovernmental organization Vietnam Labor Watch later reported, "[o]ne of Daewoosa's directors [was] the wife of the Lieutenant Governor of American Samoa ... The company's [first] legal counsel ... [was] the brother of the governor of American Samoa." Senior Samoan officials or their relatives served as an incorporator of the company and as its lawyers (Vietnam Labor Watch 2001).

In early 1999 Daewoosa imported over 200 workers from Vietnam through the Vietnamese labor export companies International Manpower Supply (IMS), and Tourist Company 12 (TC 12). Those labor export companies were in turn owned and controlled by two Vietnamese government entities: the Vietnamese Ministry of Trade, in the case of IMS, and the General Administration of Tourism, in the case of TC 12.

Although many of the Vietnamese workers would later be mistreated on American territory, they originally came voluntarily, for economic reasons, and through a complex and circuitous route. Most of them came from villages in northern and central Vietnam, recruited by local officials or local agents for the labor export companies. Each had to pay large amounts in order to be selected for work abroad, usually US$4,000 or more. In order to collect these funds, virtually all the workers had to borrow from loan sharks who were often tied to local officials or police, or borrow money against their homes or land. Each signed a contract with one of the labor export companies that specified minimum wages, benefits and other protections guaranteed by Vietnamese law. The labor export companies, IMS and TC12, in turn signed agreements with Daewoosa in Samoa, and sent the workers off to work at the Daewoosa factory in 1999 and 2000. The workers held signed contracts, usually between them and the Vietnamese labor export companies. They were to be paid US$390–408 per month along with food and housing and overtime pay beyond forty hours work (Vietnam Labor Watch 2001).

The conditions the workers endured on Samoa were considerably different from what they had been promised. Vietnam Labor Watch picks up the story:

> The workers were paid according to the whim of the owner of the company, Mr. Kil-Soo Lee, in ... amount as well as frequency ... [T]hey were forced to work long hours under sweatshop conditions without any overtime pay for overtime work ... [They had] to live in crowded rooms in rat-infested barracks behind razor wire fences and under a curfew. They were not allowed visitors[;] even their attorneys were stopped by Daewoosa security guards when trying to enter the compound ... [T]heir food was often substandard or just inedible. According to a [U.S. Department of Labor report of December 2000], most workers suffered from conditions of malnutrition and overwork.

The female workers also suffered from sexual abuse. A US Department of Labor report noted that Daewoosa "exhibited a pattern of abuse to women, including assault and invasion of privacy" (Vietnam Labor Watch 2001).

WORKER RESISTANCE AND FEDERAL INTERVENTION

Worker protests began in the spring of 1999 and were immediately suppressed by the company with the assistance of Vietnamese supervisors sent by the Vietnamese labor export companies. Daewoosa "sought to physically isolate [the workers], barring them from leaving the factory compound and denying them outside contact, withheld food from them, physically assaulted them, and threatened and attempted to imprison and deport them to Vietnam" (Vietnam Labor Watch 2001). In late March 1999 one of the workers escaped from the compound and contacted a Christian missionary office on the island, which in turn contacted the Vietnamese Embassy in Washington. The Embassy appears to have contacted Hanoi and Samoa's delegate in the US Congress, requesting intervention.[1] The intervention by the Christian missionaries and the Embassy did not immediately help matters: "Upon arriving at Daewoosa [in late March 1999], we observed three or four girls sitting immediately inside the security gate. The Korean [sic] guards began kicking and hitting the girls. About five minutes later, approximately thirty Vietnamese girls came to the gate crying and begging for help. Many of the young women were scratched, bruised, and bloody. When I asked what was going on, the guards began hitting the girls again" (Vietnam Labor Watch 2001).

Beginning in the summer of 1999 the Daewoosa operation came under investigation by the US Department of Labor and the Occupational Safety and Health Administration. Large civil penalties were imposed for labor law violations and ignored by Daewoosa. The Samoan judiciary also became involved but, according to Vietnam Labor Watch, its efforts were "thwarted by the lack of support from the executive branch of the American Samoa government," which consistently support the company leadership and hindered the activities of the missionaries and lawyers who sought to help the Vietnamese workers (Vietnam Labor Watch 2001).

Disputes and skirmishes between the Vietnamese workers and Daewoosa continued into 2000, eventually culminating in a work stoppage in November 2000. Company security guards beat a number of workers, including female workers, and one female worker was blinded in an eye. Kil Soo Lee and several of his colleagues were arrested by the FBI on involuntary servitude, forced labor and other charges in March 2001 and brought to Honolulu to await trial (Honolulu Star-Bulletin 2001a, 2001b, 2001c, 2001d; VnExpress 2001g). The charges were later expanded to include extortion, money laundering, attempting to bribe a bank official, and making false statements on a bank loan application, all federal offenses (Honolulu Star-Bulletin 2001g). After a federal court in Honolulu ruled that the federal court in Hawaii (rather than the High Court of American Samoa) had jurisdiction to try Lee on federal criminal charges (Honolulu Star-Bulletin 2001e), and several other factory employees pled guilty, the trial of Kil Soo Lee and two of his colleagues began in October 2002. The federal jury found Kil Soo Lee guilty of involuntary servitude, extortion, money laundering and related offenses in February 2003 (Honolulu Star-Bulletin 2001e, 2001f, 2001g, 2001h, 2002a, 2002b, 2003; Guardian 2002, 2003; BBC 2003; Department of Justice 2003; CNN 2003; Vietnamnet 2003a).

In the midst of these disturbances, and with assistance from local lawyers on American Samoa, a number of the Vietnamese workers had brought a civil suit for back wages and damages against Daewoosa and the two Vietnamese labor export companies. In December 2001, a local court on Samoa ruled that Daewoosa and the two Vietnamese labor export companies were jointly liable for damages to the Vietnamese workers, ordering payments totaling over US$3 million, or about $7–15,000 per worker. Until now those damages have not yet been collected – Daewoosa's accounts were emptied in 2000 or 2001, and attempts to secure the damages from the Vietnamese labor export companies have not yet taken place. The verdict was affirmed in April 2002 (New York Times 2002).

Beginning in 2000 and 2001 some of the Vietnamese workers petitioned to return home, while Hanoi sought to arrange their return. Vietnamese press reports turned from criticizing the workers for laxity in discipline to criticizing the labor export companies for their practices. Some of the workers eventually returned home, while others were resettled in the United States by the US Justice Department under the 2000 Trafficking Victims Protection Act to enable them to testify in the criminal trial of Kil Soo Lee and his colleagues (Washington Post 2003; Dallas Morning News 2003).

TEXT AND REALITY IN VIETNAMESE LAW: THE CASE OF LABOR EXPORT REGULATION

The Vietnamese workers at the Daewoosa plant on American Samoa were victimized by Kil Soo Lee, the owner of the factory, by the American Samoan government, and by an American system of labor regulation that accords lower protections to labor in territorial factories. But they were also victimized by a rapidly changing Vietnamese regulatory system for labor export. That is a system that ostensibly, rhetorically protects workers while also protecting the interests of the state and labor export companies, but is implemented largely to protect the joint economic interests of the state and private companies in expanding labor export. The exposure of the labor export scandal on American Samoa, and its relationship to the regulation of legal export in Vietnam, provides a window into the gap between legal text and the reality of legal implementation, between a rhetoric of equal rights and a reality of exploitation, exploitation that is facilitated rather than hindered by an economic law system in reform.

EXPORT LABOR AND ITS REGULATION IN VIETNAM

To understand the Vietnamese legal aspects of the Daewoosa case, and the problem of text and implementation in the branch of Vietnamese economic law that governs labor export, we must review some history. Vietnamese labor export in the modern era dates from about 1980, though Vietnamese workers did work in the Soviet Union and other countries friendly to the then Democratic Republic of Vietnam (DRV) in the 1950s, 1960s and 1970s. In the 1980s, skilled and unskilled workers were usually sent abroad under official bilateral agreements by the Vietnamese government rather than by labor export companies. From 1980 to 1990, almost 300,000 "workers and specialists" were sent abroad, of whom the vast majority – over 244,000 – went to the former Soviet Union, East Germany, Czechoslovakia and Bulgaria. During the decade 7,200 workers and specialists also went to Africa, and 18,000 to the Middle East, mostly construction workers to Iraq. The table below shows the flow in labor export to the four key socialist allies in the 1980s.

TABLE 4.1   Vietnamese Workers and Specialists Sent to the Former Soviet Union, East Germany, Czechoslovakia and Bulgaria, 1980–1990

Year	Number sent abroad
1980	1,070
1981	20,230
1982	25,970
1983	12,402
1984	6,846
1985	5,008
1986	9,012
1987	48,820
1988	71,830
1989	39,929
1990	3,069
Total	**244,186**

Table 4.1 data: official Vietnamese data from www.dafel.gov.vn, the official website of the Department for Administration of Foreign Employed Labor (DAFEL) of the Ministry of Labor, War Invalids and Social Affairs (MOLISA) of the Socialist Republic of Vietnam.

The early 1990s were a turning point in Vietnamese labor export. The downturn in relations with the former Soviet Union, declining economic prospects and demand for labor in Eastern Europe, and unsettled conditions in the Gulf and Africa (including the Gulf War) all contributed to a transformation in the flow of Vietnamese laborers abroad. The rapid Vietnamese response to these changing conditions smoothed the way toward the emergence of the state-related labor export companies that dominate the Vietnamese labor export market today. The official Department for Administration of Foreign Export Labor (as it was then named) described the changes in the early 1990s: "Vietnam decided to reform its manpower export mechanism in 1991, which was marked by the separation of manpower export management from the administration of the State. The State will exercise its administration over manpower export through legal instruments like policies and regulations. Vietnamese companies granted specialized license for manpower export are allowed to enter into manpower-export contracts with foreign agencies" (www.dafel.gov.vn).

Since 1991, Vietnam has increased labor export and diversified export markets, which now include Northeast Asia, Southeast Asia, the Gulf and the Middle East, North Africa, and the Pacific Islands.

In the mid-1990s, the Vietnamese Communist Party and government determined that a rapid increase in the export of workers from Vietnam could help resolve several pressing problems. One was the persistence of high levels of unemployment; another was the need for worker retraining; and a third, though less well publicized, was the need for national and local government authorities to begin earning additional revenues through labor export enterprises built upon governmental authority (Vietnam Investment Review 1999; 2002a; 2003a; 2003c).

As Table 4.2 shows, the number of workers sent abroad rose dramatically in the late 1990s, initially to South Korea, Japan, the Middle East, and Laos. Today the greatest numbers are sent to Malaysia, Taiwan, South Korea and Japan, though in total they are exported to more than forty countries and territories. In 2003 Vietnam planned to export 55,000 workers, including 15,000 from Ho Chi Minh City alone, and in the end exported about 75,000 because of sharply increased demand from Malaysia (Econet 2003; Vietnam Investment Review 2003b; 2004c). The 2006 target was also about 75,000.

Increased competition in the labor export market, and a downturn in the demand for export labor in Asia, the Middle East and the Gulf

TABLE 4.2   Official Vietnamese Labor Export,
1991–2006

Year	Number sent abroad
1991	1,022
1992	810
1993	3,960
1994	9,230
1995	10,050
1996	12,660
1997	18,470
1998	12,240
1999	21,810
2000	31,500
2001	37,000
2002	46,100
2003	75,000
2004	67,400
2005	70,590
2006	31,000 (through June 2006)
	2006 target = 75,000

Table 4.2 data: official Vietnamese data from
www.dafel.gov.vn. 1991–2001 from DAFEL historical
tables; 2002–2004 data from DAFEL releases and
Vietnamese news reports, including Vietnam Investment
Review, various issues 2003 and 2004; VIBForum, January
15, 2005 (for 2004); Vietnamnet (Vietnam News Agency),
July 1, 2004; 2005; Thanh Nien.com, January 20, 2006;
2006, Vietnam Investment Review, June 2006. These are
official data, but I believe that they may underestimate the
total number of Vietnamese workers sent abroad through
various channels since the early 1990s because
of inconsistencies in reporting of data to DAFEL and the
availability of new, less-controlled channels of labor export
in the last decade.

(some due to the Iraq war) in 2003 and 2004 dampened projections for
2004. In the first seven months of 2004, labor export dropped 26
percent from the record-setting pace of 2003, largely because of reduc-
tions in demand from Malaysia and problems encountered by
Vietnamese and other Asian workers there (Vietnam Investment
Review 2004b). The export statistics rebounded in 2004 and 2005,
though they have not yet reached the high goals set by Vietnamese

government agencies, and problems have continued to develop: In a number of countries Vietnamese workers left their jobs for new jobs, provoking sanctions from local authorities. Demand also fell in a number of countries, and the competition to provide export labor has heated up throughout Asia (Vietnamnet 2004a).

At a Party conference in 1999, Party leaders were frank about these reasons for Vietnam's upsurge in labor exports. In a key directive issued in conjunction with the conference that has continued to guide Vietnamese labor export policy, the Party Political Bureau spoke of the need to balance regulatory protections for the rights of those export workers with protections for the contractual and commercial interests of the companies sending them abroad.

> Apart from employment generation initiatives at home, the export of workers and specialists [is] an important and long-term strategy that helps develop the labor force for industrialization and modernization and promote international cooperation.
>
> The methods of and markets for exporting workers and specialists (hereinafter referred to as "manpower export") should be extended and diversified in consistent with the market-oriented mechanism and the requirements of the foreign partners in terms of quantity, quality, and professional skills. It is essential to improve the competitiveness of Vietnamese manpower for export by strengthening the quality of train-ing, increasing the proportion of highly-trained workers/specialists in manpower export, and improving the managerial skills of manpower-exporting companies. Equal attention is to be paid to the legitimate rights and benefits of workers consistent with Vietnamese laws and the laws of the receiving countries.
>
> (Directive 41 1999)

The earnings generated by labor export for government ministries and for state-owned and quasi-private labor export companies are impossible to measure but appear to be quite sizable. Local officials, state and private banks, loan sharks, police officers and others have also benefited from the economic accommodations these workers have had to make to go abroad (Daewoosa Judgment 2002; New York Times 2002). Some sense of the economic scale and stakes in labor export can be gleaned from the limited measure of worker remittances home: according to official Vietnamese statistics from the Department for Administration of Foreign Employed Labor (DAFEL), these totaled about $1.262 billion in 2001 and $2.4 billion in 2002, with remittances rising at 12 percent over 2002 in mid-2003 (Lam 2001; Vietnam Investment Review 2002a). Other figures (perhaps somewhat contradictory or based on other assumptions) pegged remittances at $1.5 billion in 2003 (Vietnam Investment Review 2003d), and the remittance figures have continued to rise quickly since then (Sidel 2007).

THE TRANSITION FROM "LABOR COOPERATION" TO AN EXPORT LABOR MARKET

The legal regulation of Vietnam's labor export industry has its roots in the 1980s, when Vietnam began exporting workers and some technical specialists to the Soviet Union, Eastern Europe, and to a lesser degree Africa and the Gulf. Most of that trade was conducted under bilateral labor agreements that specified, in fairly general terms, the obligations of state parties to the treatment of export laborers. On the Vietnamese side, regulation and management of export labor (then termed "international cooperation on labor affairs" in the less market-oriented days of the 1980s, *hop tac quoc te ve lao dong*) came within the authority of the Ministry of Labor, Invalids and Social Affairs (MOLISA) as early as 1987 (and likely before). In the 1980s labor export was almost entirely state-administered and was conducted in accordance with a series of annual plans.

The rapidly changing nature of labor export away from sending workers to the Soviet Union and other socialist countries resulted in substantial regulatory change in the early 1990s. A new set of *Regulations on Sending Vietnamese Labor Abroad on Fixed Terms* were adopted in 1991, beginning a process of defining both the "rights" (*quyen loi*) and the "duties" (*nghia vu*) of Vietnamese export workers that would continue throughout the 1990s and into the next decade (Decision 370 1991). MOLISA's primary role in administering labor export was reaffirmed in new organizational regulations adopted in 1993. Throughout the early 1990s Vietnamese government ministries and Party offices struggled with the process of bringing Vietnamese workers home from Eastern Europe in an increasingly chaotic market and employment environment in those countries, and the regulatory documents issued in that period reflected that priority and the difficulty of that work.

EXPORT LABOR UNDER THE 1994 LABOR CODE AND THE RISE OF THE LABOR EXPORT COMPANIES

The adoption of the 1994 *Labor Code of the Socialist Republic of Vietnam* provided an opportunity for Vietnamese policymakers to restructure the organization of Vietnamese labor export and to restate the rights and duties in the dispatch of Vietnamese workers abroad (Labor Code 1994). The 1994 Labor Code sought to maintain a balance between the rights of workers, their obligations, and the rights of state-related labor export institutions. But the Code and particularly its implementing legislation also confirmed the increasing role of labor export and recruiting firms, most tied to state organizations of various kinds, in the operation of an increasingly active labor export system. The Code provided that:

> Employment service organizations, which are set up in accordance with the provisions of the Law, have the tasks of providing consultancy, recommending, supplying and helping to recruit workers collecting and supplying information on the labour market. The dispatch of Vietnamese guest workers to foreign countries can only be carried out after due receipt of a permit issued by the relevant competent State agency ...
>
> The Ministry of Labor, Invalids and Social Affairs provides unified State management of employment service organisations throughout the country.
>
> Workers who are Vietnamese citizens have the right to work in foreign countries. If, according to the labour contracts, they work under the management of foreign organisations and individuals, they must abide by the labour laws of the foreign countries concerned ...
>
> The labourers of Vietnamese citizenship who go and work in foreign countries have the right to be informed of their interests and obligations and are protected by Vietnamese competent authorities abroad in the field of consular and civil affairs. They have the right to transfer their foreign currency earnings and private property to Vietnam, and to receive social insurance benefits and other benefits in accordance with laws in Vietnam and their countries of residence.
>
> The sending of Vietnamese citizens to work abroad must be permitted by the Ministry of Labour, Invalids and Social Affairs and other competent state agencies according to the provisions of the Law.
>
> It is strictly forbidden to send Vietnamese citizens to work abroad in contravention of the Law.
>
> (Labor Code 1994, Arts. 134(1), 135(1), 184)

New and important regulations promulgated in 1995 under the Labor Code spelled out these various rights and duties in considerably more specific terms. *Decision No. 07/CP of the Government on Detailed Provisions on Certain Articles of the Labor Code on the Sending of Vietnamese Labor to Work Overseas on Fixed Terms*, promulgated on January 20,

1995 (the "1995 Labor Export Provisions"), stipulated that export workers be granted rights to information on: their work conditions abroad, the term of the contracts, salaries and benefits, insurance and other information before signing contracts; the rights negotiated between Vietnam and their country of work; protection by Vietnamese embassies abroad of their lawful rights; social insurance and other protective policies adopted in Vietnam; and the rights to petition for redress of grievances to Vietnamese governmental authorities and the country of residence on contract violations by employers (Decision 7 1995).

The 1995 Labor Export Provisions also required that the workers pay required service fees to the entity sending them abroad for work as specified in Vietnamese regulations; to pay deposits or guarantee fees to sending entities "to guarantee the implementation of the contract," but not exceeding the cost of an air ticket back to Vietnam; to pay social insurance fees, income tax in Vietnam; to bear responsibility for contract violations and property damage to the sending entity; to "preserve state secrets and foster the excellent traditions of the Vietnamese people, seriously implement the regulations of the Vietnamese state on the administration of Vietnamese citizens abroad, and safeguard the management of the economic organization sending workers abroad for fixed terms" (Decision 7 1995).

Perhaps most important, labor export companies – economic organizations engaged in the labor export business – were formally recognized in the 1995 Labor Export Provisions. They were required to seek approval from the Ministry of Labor to begin operations, required to preserve the rights of workers as memorialized in contracts with overseas employers, "protect the lawful rights of workers during their terms working abroad," and report up to the Ministry of Labor in accordance with regulations promulgated for that purpose (Decision 7 1995, Arts. 6–10; Directive 20 1995).

But in the early years after the adoption of the 1995 Labor Export Provisions – and, some might argue, in later years as well – the labor export companies appear to have been only lightly administered by the Ministry of Labor, and many abuses occurred. As they sprang up throughout Vietnam, the labor export companies opened either as the wholly owned entities of ministries and other government agencies, or as semi-private companies with very close links to government bodies, police, and local authorities. For example, the two labor export companies at issue in the Daewoosa case, as described earlier in this chapter, were wholly-owned branches (or divisions) of the General Administration of Tourism and the Ministry of Trade, respectively (Sidel 2004).

Despite the provisions of the 1994 Labor Code and the 1995 Labor Export Provisions, and in part due to lax enforcement, legal violations began to multiply. In the late 1990s, a number of problems emerged. Some companies extorted high fees from unemployed workers eager to go abroad. Newly sprung up training schools – with enrolment mandatory to meet the requirements for going abroad to work – cheated hundreds or thousands of young workers and students eager to go abroad. Loan sharks, local police and others did a thriving business in loans to workers struggling to raise the funds to pay labor export brokers and the companies they dealt with. Some mandatory contracts were never offered to workers; others eliminated provisions required under the 1994 Labor Code and the 1995 Labor Export Regulations (Lam 2001; Inter Press 2003; Vietnam Investment Review 2004a).

THE 1999 RESPONSES TO LABOR EXPORT VIOLATIONS, THE 1999 PARTY CONFERENCE, AND THE AFTERMATH

Hanoi responded to the increasing spate of legal violations by labor export companies, loan sharks, local authorities and police and others with new regulations and directives issued in mid- and late 1999 and with a high-level Party meeting in September 1999 on problems in the administration of labor export. The terms of the *Provisional Regulations on Measures to Prevent and Handle Violations in the Field of Sending Laborers to Work Abroad* ("1999 Provisional Labor Export Regulations"), promulgated by the Ministry of Labor in June 1999 (Decision 725 1999), sought to protect the rights of both workers and labor export enterprises. Workers were prohibited from "participating in illegal activities, meetings or strikes," "going on strike in contravention of the law of the host countries [or] organizing, inducing or compelling other people to breach contracts or participate in illegal strikes."

The 1999 Provisional Labor Export Regulations also prohibited the labor export companies from carrying out a wide range of acts. They provide an indication of the abuses that some labor export companies had engaged in and that Hanoi sought to counter. The companies were forbidden from signing partial contracts or refusing to enter into contracts with workers, "recruiting laborers through an intermediary," over-recruiting and cheating recruits out of funds, sending untrained workers, "collecting money in contravention of regulations, or collecting money through an intermediary," and "letting disputes occur without settling them properly, thus causing bad consequences" (Decision 725, Art. 8).

These new provisions were laudable. But violations seem to have continued, to the point that a Deputy Prime Minister had to issue an official document in the name of the Prime Minister in August 1999 requiring that "ministries, agencies, and localities with [institutional] units active in labor export must strictly observe the management duties that have been stipulated." The Deputy Prime Minister also ordered the Ministry of Labor to strengthen its weak administration of labor export (Document 3828 1999).

It was in the context of this rapidly changing and difficult environment that the Vietnamese Communist Party's Political Bureau discussed labor export in September 1999 and issued the Instructions that affirmed the commercial nature of labor export and its current administrative arrangements.

The Party discussions coincided with a new 1999 *Decree Stipulating the Sending of Vietnamese Specialists and Laborers Abroad to Work for a Definite Time* that reiterated most of these provisions and those of the 1995 Regulations. Workers retained the formal right "to make claims or complaints to competent authorities of Vietnam or the receiving country about any acts of breaching the labor contract by the Vietnamese manpower-exporting enterprise and the foreign employer." Labor export companies remained responsible "to make compensation in accordance with applicable laws and regulations to workers for any losses caused by contract violations of themselves or the foreign partner." Under the 1999 Decree labor export enterprises were allowed to charge service fees and to send supervisors abroad "to supervise and protect the workers." (Decree 152 1999; Directive 28 1999).

But problems continued. Later administrative guidance under the 1999 Decree sought to deal with a raft of violations of the financial arrangements for labor export – deposits and guarantee payments, service fees – and to impose some limits on the withholding and withdrawal of deposits, guarantees, service fees, and salaries that labor export companies were permitted to make. This *2000 Finance Directive on the Financial System for Vietnamese Workers and Specialists Going Abroad to Work for a Fixed Term* ("2000 Finance Directive") also permitted companies to withhold deposits and guarantee fees if export workers violated their contracts. Companies continued to withhold significant amounts of funds from workers, at times over the maximums permitted by the 2000 Finance Directive, and the government was forced to step in little more than a year later to reduce the maximum deposits that companies could withhold from export laborers (Joint Directive 16 2000; Directive 33 2001).

TEXT AND PRACTICE: THE RIGHTS OF VIETNAMESE WORKERS ABROAD

The difficulties in this system came to light perhaps most clearly in the Daewoosa case on American Samoa, where over 200 Vietnamese and Chinese workers were held in intolerable conditions, unpaid or under-paid, and at times beaten by sadistic managers of a garment factory. Back in Vietnam, Vietnamese loan sharks and police ignored the protections for workers built into labor export regulation and other laws. The labor export companies, responsible for protecting worker rights vis-à-vis foreign employers and seeking to uphold contracts the workers had signed, failed to do both. In fact, the labor export compa-nies that had sent workers to Samoa also dispatched company "repre-sentatives," a process authorized under the regulatory structure with the goal of helping to manage the workers and, ostensibly, helping to protect their rights.

The Vietnamese labor export company representatives on site in Samoa allied itself with the Daewoosa factory owner, ignoring their companies' obligations to defend the defined and contractual rights of workers. The company representatives in Samoa served as a link between the factory owner who sought to suppress the workers' uprising in 1999 and 2000 and the labor export company leaders in Hanoi.

In turn the labor export companies in Hanoi put intense pressure on the workers to give up their assertion of rights, sending messages to the workers through company representatives, and even pressuring work-ers' relatives to write to them begging them to work hard and quietly under the conditions presented to them. Workers on Samoa were threatened, directly and indirectly, with repercussions for family mem-bers in Vietnam, loss of property, taking of residences and other punish-ments if they did not acquiesce in their treatment on Samoa.

Perhaps most importantly, central government officials appeared to have leaned significantly toward the side of the labor export companies rather than the workers. This was most apparent in the earlier stages of the Samoa dispute, when Ministry of Labor officials were even quoted in the Vietnamese press as criticizing the workers and their complaints. Early in the Samoa case, through about the end of 1999, the Vietnamese press largely reprinted the Ministry of Labor's view that the Samoa workers were troublemakers, providing no alternative for different views to reach the regulators. Only later, when the extent of the Samoa problems became apparent to the Foreign Ministry and may have been brought into the government and Party at a senior level, did Ministry officials and the press begin to balance their presentation of the Samoa events (Daewoosa Judgment 2002; New York Times 2002; Seattle Post-Intelligencer 2003).

In short, the legal protections built into Vietnamese law for export laborers were largely ignored because the workers lacked a means to exercise their textual rights. The labor export companies, local authorities, police and others cited workers' obligations under labor export regulation to pressure the workers into accepting their treatment, and government officials, before the situation became a scandal, appear to have sided largely with the companies. The case raised public and political problems in Vietnam, and led to demands for strengthening of the system of managing labor export and protecting workers' rights.

STRENGTHENED ENFORCEMENT OF LABOR EXPORT LAW

As these matters escalated, the government sought to bring the situation under better control. The Ministry of Labor and the government bodies that owned labor export companies supplying workers abroad were ordered to strengthen their management of the situation through a host of regulatory measures that flowed from the Ministry of Labor in 2001 and 2002 seeking to exercise some firmer control over export labor.

The government tried to step in during 2001 to stop labor export companies from sending unauthorized workers abroad (Directive 1366 2001). And in a move partly prompted by the role of a tourist company affiliated with the General Administration of Tourism in the Samoan debacle, the government sought to tighten control over tourism companies in mid-2001 and on several occasions thereafter (Decree 27 2001). In October of 2001, the Ministry of Labor convened a National Meeting on Strengthening the Export of Workers and Specialists. A Deputy Prime Minister emphasized a new theme – that "the strategy for labor export ... is an important and long-term responsibility, aimed not merely at economic goals, but also at serving the development of foreign relations." And he called upon the Ministry of Labor to decertify labor export companies that violated the law (Notice 147 2001).

Other steps to ameliorate abuses were underway in Hanoi as well, beginning back in 2001 and continuing to the present. These included a range of useful policy initiatives that may assist in protecting export laborers' rights when they are fully funded and implemented:

- Plans for a loan fund to enable export laborers to pay the fees required to go abroad,
- A national support fund to help bring back laborers laid off overseas,
- Loans from the National Fund for Hunger Eradication and Poverty Reduction to help workers go abroad,
- Strengthened professional training schools for export workers,
- Rehiring by labor export companies when workers are laid off by overseas employers, and
- Informal loan funds generated by labor export companies.

PROSECUTIONS OF LABOR EXPORTERS AND CONTINUING CONTROVERSIES

Beginning in 2001 and 2002, and continuing to the present, a number of prosecutions have been brought against labor exporters and labor export companies that have violated Vietnamese law, often by defrauding workers out of money through spurious training classes and promises to place them in work overseas. It appears that thousands of Vietnamese workers have been defrauded in this manner, and press reports indicate that the government has sought to fight against this phenomenon with criminal sanctions up to and including the death penalty.

In 2001, for example, the Hanoi People's Court sentenced two former officials of the labor export firm IMS for their actions in the Samoa matter. Le Cong Tam, former director of IMS, was sentenced to six months imprisonment for irresponsible criminal behavior with serious consequences, resulting in losses to the public treasury of 872 million Vietnamese *dong* (about US$60,000). Dao Thi Hoai Thu, former chief of the accounting section at IMS, was sentenced to three years imprisonment for intentional violation of economic management with serious consequences (Sidel 2004).

In June 2001 the director of another registered labor export company was arrested for cheating US$54,000 from 23 people "after promising to find work for them in South Korea." In September 2001, 29 Vietnamese workers abandoned by a Vietnamese labor export company in Brazil begged for help from the Vietnamese government, living hand to mouth in a Brazilian city. Criminal charges were later brought against the labor export company that, in collaboration with local authorities and police, had charged each of the 29 workers US$7,500 in fees in order to work abroad. The company had obtained three-month non-working tourist visas for them to Brazil although the labor contracts required five year visas, then abandoned the workers in Brazil. It appears that the workers eventually were repatriated to Vietnam (Sidel 2004).

In December 2001 another labor export company director was detained and indicted in December 2001 on charges of defrauding workers who wanted to go to South Korea, opening training classes and collecting US$5,000–6,000 per worker – a total of US$93,000 from eighteen workers – without arranging for any work in Korea (Vietnamnet 2001). In November 2002, an official at a state-owned labor export company, Ciepico, was sentenced to death for defrauding 97 workers of US$450,000 and then failing to arrange for work as promised in Taiwan and South Korea. Two accomplices were sentenced to life imprisonment and to a nine-year prison term (Agence France Presse 2002; Global Standards 2003).

In May 2003, four individuals – including three from labor export companies and one from a state organization – were indicted and arrested for defrauding Vietnamese workers who wanted to go to Malaysia (Vietnamnet 2003b). In June 2003, police in Ho Chi Minh City (Saigon) broke up and detained a labor smuggling ring that was sending unauthorized workers to Malaysia on tourist visas rather than the work visas required by the Malaysian authorities, some carrying false identification papers. The workers had been required by unscrupulous labor exporters to pay US$1,500–2,000 each to go abroad plus US$550–675 in Vietnamese currency (Vietnamnet 2003c). In August 2003, Hanoi police detained two people on charges of defrauding workers in labor export to South Korea. The police seized about US$15,000 in Vietnamese and US currency as well as identification papers and passports. Those detained reportedly had charged US$6,000 per person for spurious promises of work in South Korea (Vietnamnet 2003d).

In Taiwan, numerous abuses of Vietnamese workers were reported, including the deaths of two Vietnamese workers in July 2004 due to the negligence of their Taiwanese employer. The Taiwanese authorities banned several dozen Vietnamese labor exporters after repeated disputes over Vietnamese workers leaving their jobs and shifting to illegal work, and the Vietnamese authorities sought to reduce export of workers to Taiwan in 2004 and 2005 in response to these problems by cutting worker departures and reducing the number of authorized labor exporters (Taiwan Migrants Forum 2003; Asian Labour News 2003; Vietnam News Agency 2004a).

In January 2004, a Vietnamese woman was arrested in Hanoi for organizing the trafficking of local women "aged around 15" into China, and the press announced that she would be prosecuted for child trafficking (ABC Radio 2004). In April 2004, a Ho Chi Minh City (Saigon) court sentenced defendant Tran Huu Hoang to eight years in prison for illegally sending Vietnamese workers to Taiwan. Hoang originally worked for a labor export company, but went off on his own and defrauded eleven workers of US$2,700 apiece with promises of labor in Taiwan. Instead he arranged tourist visas to Taiwan at an additional cost of US$1,180 for each worker. Hoang's Taiwanese accomplice was sentenced to only forty days imprisonment in Taiwan – a sharp comparison to the severe penalty meted out in Vietnam under Vietnamese law (Vietnam News Agency 2004b).

A rapid increase in labor demand in Malaysia in 2001 and 2002 resulted in tens of thousands of workers being sent to Malaysia in 2002 and 2003. Inevitably the heavy demand led to unscrupulous labor exporters in Vietnam taking advantage of workers and weaknesses in the regulatory system, including a rapid expansion in approvals of labor export companies permitted to send workers to Malaysia, intended to take advantage of the market opportunities available there. The forms of those abuses varied: some involved defrauding of workers without sending them abroad; others involved sending workers to Malaysia (or other countries) on tourist visas (the so-called "job tours"), then abandoning them; still others involved arranging low-paying or dangerous jobs.

Some of the Vietnamese workers in Malaysia lost their jobs when the Malaysian construction industry sharply contracted in 2004 as the price of steel rose and credit dried up. Others left the jobs arranged for them in violation of Malaysian law and their contracts. There were extensive reports of Vietnamese workers being detained and, in some cases, caned under Malaysian law for being present in Malaysia without valid labor authorization, as well as of poor working conditions in Malaysia (Saigon Times Daily 2002a; 2002b, 2002c; 2002d; 2003;Vietnam Investment Review 2002b; 2002c; 2003e).

DAFEL and the Ministry of Labor worked with the key labor export companies sending workers to Malaysia to bring them home on multiple flights from Malaysia. A number of the Vietnamese workers who were displaced from jobs in Malaysia have demanded compensation for their losses (Vietnam Investment Review 2003e; Saigon Times Daily 2003).

THE REVISION OF THE LABOR CODE

The next step in strengthening protection for export laborers and strengthening management of the rapidly growing export labor system was a much-needed revision of Vietnam's Labor Code. That long-debated revised Labor Code was adopted by the National Assembly on April 1, 2002,[2] and provided several significantly enhanced and detailed provisions for the rights of export workers. In addition to a number of provisions on labor contracts and bargaining, the new Code notably brought detailed rights and obligations of labor export enterprises and workers from earlier implementing regulations into the main Labor Code for the first time.

In general terms, the 2002 Labor Code brought specific provisions on export labor from the Code's Implementing Regulations (where they had been placed prior to 2002) into the main text of the Labor Code, and strengthened the text. In specific terms, the new 2002 Labor Code strengthened the licensing requirements for labor export companies (Art. 135), strengthened at least the textual force of export laborers' rights to include information, training, contractual, consular and judicial protection and other rights (Art. 135a), and prohibited illegal recruitment and required compensation for illegal acts against export workers (Art. 135b).

The rights and obligations detailed in the 2002 Labor Code are substantially more detailed than those in the 1994 Labor Code, particularly with respect to the rights and obligations of labor export enterprises, the rights and obligations of export laborers, and against unlawful and fraudulent export labor recruitment. The 1994 Labor Code had only dealt with export labor in a cursory and general fashion, requiring permits for labor service companies, allowing them to receive fees, and providing some textual rights to workers.

113

The export worker rights defined in the 2002 Labor Code were similar but more detailed than those provided in earlier legislation, and they were now part of the main Labor Code, rather than cast off into the subsidiary Implementing Regulations. Export workers were granted (in some cases regranted) rights to have information, training, to "complain, denounce or initiate an action to the authorized body of the State of Vietnam or of the foreign country against breaches of the labour export enterprise and the foreign employers" and "to receive compensation for damage caused by breaches of the contract by the enterprise" (Labor Code 2002, Art. 135a). The obligations were also detailed – to "enter into and perform the contract correctly," "to comply with the law of Vietnam and the law of the foreign country, and to respect the customs and traditions of the foreign country," "to pay fees for labor export," and "to pay compensation for damage caused by breaches of the contract" (Labor Code 2002, Art. 135a). Mechanisms for enforcement were provided, including mediation and eventually the right to sue in administrative courts.

The Vietnamese government has proceeded to "make detailed provisions on training of export labour, on organization and management of workers abroad, and on establishment, management and use of the [newly established] labour export assistance fund," as required under Article 135b of the 2002 Labor Code. In July 2003 the government issued a detailed *Decree No. 81/2003/ND-CP on Detailed Provisions and Guidance for the Implementation of the Labor Code with respect to Vietnamese Laborers Overseas* (July 17, 2003) (Decree 81 2003).

Decree No. 81 (2003) on labor export governs export labor enterprises, the channels for Vietnamese working abroad, registration of contracts, government management of labor export, specific provisions on the granting and withdrawal of licenses to labor export enterprises, rights and obligations of labor export enterprises, procedures for sending workers abroad, rights and obligations of export laborers, the fund for labor export support, responsibilities of the Ministry of Labor and Social Affairs, other ministries and government agencies, dispute resolution, and dealing with violations. It imposed substantial duties on Vietnamese laborers working abroad, but also gave them certain rights, and it imposed duties and privileges on labor export companies as well. For example, labor export companies were required to refund fees paid by laborers if the workers were not sent abroad within six months of selection. Laborers were entitled (Art. 18) to accurate information on working conditions and contracts; to training and orientation; and to the protection of law, both Vietnamese and foreign (Decree 81 2003, Art. 18).

In turn Decree No. 81 on Export Labor was followed with a detailed *Circular No. 22 on Detailed Provisions and Guidance for the Implementation of the Labor Code with respect to Vietnamese Laborers Overseas* (Circular 22 2003). Circular 22 provides even more detailed procedures and specifications for certain aspects of the labor export process, including granting licenses to labor export enterprises, affiliates of labor export enterprises, labor export contracts and their registration, recruitment of export laborers, training of export laborers, administration of labor export, commendation and sanctions, and implementation of the labor export regime. With particular reference to the rights of Vietnamese workers overseas, Circular 22 provides detailed rules for the recruitment of workers in Vietnam – a controversial area that spawned many unscrupulous practices in earlier years. It prohibits labor export companies from recruiting through brokers or collecting recruitment fees; requires detailed information on available jobs overseas to be made available to workers and local governments; reserves ten percent of labor export slots for demobilized soldiers, poor workers, and other favored groups; and requires labor export companies to protect the rights of Vietnamese workers abroad (Circular 22 2003).

TEXT AND IMPLEMENTATION IN VIETNAMESE LAW

The 2002 amendments to the Labor Code and the 2003 implementing documents were clearly intended to address those elements of the Daewoosa case that are amenable to regulation in the home (sending) country for export labor: detailing the rights and obligations of both workers and the labor export companies that send them abroad, and delineating the role of the government and labor export companies in protecting workers' rights, including the roles of the Ministry of Labor, Ministry of Foreign Affairs and other government agencies. The strengths of the 2002 Labor Code and the 2003 implementing regulations (Decree 81 and Circular 22) are in the specificities of their provisions, including explicit provision of rights of workers and duties for labor export companies and government agencies, provisions for decertifying labor export companies, and provisions for resolution of disputes that allow use of both mediation and judicial processes. Thus the text of law is considerably stronger and more detailed than when the Daewoosa events occurred.

It is now a matter of implementation and enforcement, and the Vietnamese authorities are taking some steps in those directions as well. These implementation and enforcement steps include indictment, detention, arrest, prosecution, imprisonment and, on at least several occasions, execution of illegal labor exporters and human traffickers (as detailed earlier in this report from publicly available sources, and necessarily incomplete), and considerably more active work by government authorities (including the Department for Administration of Foreign Employed Labor, the Ministry of Labor, and the Ministry of Foreign Affairs) to assist or relocate workers in locations where Vietnamese export workers have encountered a variety of problems, including Malaysia, Taiwan, and Korea (Sidel 2004). The next step for Vietnam, which it recognizes as important, is to enable these detailed provisions to be enforced and implemented on a regular and consistent basis. It has begun that process, through charging and convicting illegal labor exporters and human traffickers, and undertaking programs with domestic and foreign organizations to improve enforcement and implementation.

Vietnam is in the midst of a long and complex transition from a scene in which the law in practice often continues to serve largely to protect the economic interests of private and government authorities, backed by police and local officials and an illegal but ubiquitous system of loan sharking and extortion, in extracting profits at every stage of the labor export process. It will take years for the legal system to effectively and consistently enforce protections for export laborers. But two key beginnings have been made: the drafting of the new Labor Code and its detailed, implementing regulations (discussed above), and an initial series of prosecutions of illegal labor exporters and human traffickers. When those proved to be still insufficient, the government drafted and the National Assembly approved in mid-2006 a new law on labor export intended to provide yet further textual protections.

But in Vietnam a busy process of drafting laws and regulations results in valuable text that in many cases seeks and purports to protect the rights of those less favored in Vietnam's rapid process of marketization and economic growth. And it must be stated clearly: the intent behind that rights-protecting text is usually genuine, not false or fraudulent. An admirable ethos of social justice continues to imbue the work of many Vietnamese Party and government officials, despite widespread and growing gaps under Vietnam's rapidly growing market system, corruption and other significant problems.

Vietnam will need to continue to work both on strengthening the legal framework for protecting export laborers' rights and, particularly, on the implementation and enforcement of that framework and its provisions. This is complicated by the economic goals of labor export companies and the government agencies that generally own or invest in them, as well as others in Vietnam with an economic interest in the labor export process – local governments and their officials; police; banks and loan sharks; and others. In particular, it will be necessary to strengthen both framework and implementation so that export workers have direct and straightforward access to the judicial system (through administrative and labor courts) to redress their complaints and to win civil judgments as well as administrative judgments against state entities and labor export companies.

These problems represent the key issues in the next stage of Vietnam's legal reform process. Vietnam's legal reforms have shown clearly their ability to promote economic development, commercial transactions, and flexibility for business enterprises. To date Vietnam's legal reform have not shown sufficient strength in protecting rights. But the 2002 amendments to the Vietnamese Labor Code, the detailed implementing regulations on labor export issued since then, and increased implementation and enforcement by the Vietnamese authorities indicate that, while law provides opportunities for significant oppression, opportunities for progress, for a different role for economic law, are also present as well. The years ahead will tell which of these forces wins the battle for economic law in Vietnam.

Exploitation of export laborers is an issue in China as well, where the Party and government are faced with the similar contradictory challenges of providing employment, generating revenue, and protecting workers' rights. In China the press, trade unions, and occasionally, ad hoc workers' organizations have had some success in publicizing and advocating for the rights of export laborers who are mistreated either by the Chinese organizers of labor overseas, or by the overseas employers. These developments in China indicate that a gradually strengthened role for civil society institutions may help to protect workers' rights under economic law that has contradictory purposes, perhaps aiding in redressing the balance of textual law that can easily become unbalanced by official leaning toward the side of employers, labor export companies, and workers' "duties" – and away from rights (Chan and Norlund 1998; Chan, Kerkvliet and Unger 1999). Similarly, around Asia, civil society organizations have arisen to publicize problems in transnational labor, mirrored by the emergence of non-governmental organizations working on the issue in Taiwan and other locations. If economic law – as in the case of labor export from Vietnam – textually supports both duties and rights, but is often implemented to enforce duties while leaving rights unprotected, the availability of a strengthened judiciary, press, and civil society organizations may help to readjust this balance. Without those institutions playing a greater role, even the positive changes in economic law to enhance the rights of export laborers on paper may come to naught in practice.

NOTES

1. Of the Vietnamese Party and government agencies involved in the Daewoosa matter, the Ministry of Foreign Affairs appears to have played the most consistently positive role in seeking to protect the rights of the Vietnamese workers on Samoa (Vietnam Labor Watch 2001). See also the press release issued by the Vietnamese Embassy in Washington on December 6, 2000, "Embassy requests safety protection for Vietnamese workers" (reprinted at Vietnam Labor Watch 2001, 14).
2. Several other translations and texts of the 2002 Labor Code are available from other sources. I refer to this as the 2002 Labor Code because it was adopted in 2002, though it went into effect on January 1, 2003.

CHAPTER 5

LAW, THE PRESS, AND POLICE MURDER: THE TRIAL OF LT. NGUYEN TUNG DUONG

How is official misconduct – official acts that violate the law – discovered and punished in Vietnam? This is an important issue for the legitimacy of the legal system, and, more broadly, the legitimacy of the Vietnamese Party and state. This chapter goes back to an earlier era in Vietnamese legal reform to explore the dynamics of response to official misconduct – here, police murder – by exploring the legal responses to the killing of a young civilian in Hanoi in the early 1990s. By looking at this individual but well-known case, we may be able to understand the treatment of official misconduct as well as some of the dynamics between law and an increasingly active press at that point in the reform process.

My goal here is to explore one instance – albeit a famous instance – in which official misconduct demanded redress, and the ways in which the Vietnamese written media sought to respond to a variety of conflicting signals from reporters, editors, audiences, and the various sectors of the political, security and legal apparatus in covering a well-known murder case in Hanoi. In this case, at least for some of the Vietnamese newspapers discussed here, editorial life existed in a complex and shifting state between autonomy and censorship, a state in which the highly complex informal politics of response to state, security and legal officials and to the public (rather than slavish response to intensive external guidance from the state) played a major role in press coverage (Palmos 1995; Tho 1992; Hiebert 1992; Heng 1992; Templer 1999; Thai 1996; Asia Watch 1987; Asia Watch 1993).

One way in which some Vietnamese media have sought to convert the politics of direct external guidance into a politics of response to multiple, sometimes conflicting, internal and external signals is through specialization, and the creation of flexible spheres for more autonomous reporting – primarily of social, economic, cultural and legal affairs. In doing so they have accepted the retention of Party and government limits on the reporting of political events, both at the central and local levels, and on the activities of Vietnam's small group of dissidents. They have implicitly stayed away from such reporting on political and dissident matters and have sometimes reduced political coverage considerably. Thus a series of national and local newspapers have, in effect, been granted greater autonomy to report – sometimes in controversial or lurid detail – on a wide variety of social, legal and other topics.

Thus a number of newspapers have both implicitly been granted and have reached out to seize more autonomy in reporting on crime and corruption, including arbitrary action and corrupt behavior by the police and other authorities. The increased reporting on legal issues – including some violations of law by police and other authorities – has advantages both for the press and for a Party and government seeking to legitimize a carefully controlled strengthening of legal frameworks. And so, in a number of cases the Vietnamese press, usually portrayed as subservient to and heavily controlled by the Party apparatus, has taken the lead in exposing criminal behavior by police and other authorities, forcing legal and political institutions into punishing wrongdoers. And in a number of such cases the press has exposed and re-exposed wrongdoers in a more energetic manner than legal, Party or government authorities might have foreseen or wished, utilizing some new-found autonomy to bolster their claims to represent public opinion, and at times putting heavy pressure on courts and prosecutors to resolve cases in accordance with the newspapers' views of events. All this flies in the face of a certain western perception, still strong in 2005 and 2006, that the Vietnamese newspaper media are entirely controlled by the Party and state.

A DEATH AT TET

Nguyen Viet Phuong was a young Vietnamese man who was born and died amidst violence in a city many now regard as one of Asia's most peaceful. At Tet 1993 he was 21, born during the Christmas bombing of 1972, on a day when American B-52s swept over Hanoi. His paternal great-grandfather, grandfather and maternal grandfather had been recognized by the state as martyrs in the resistance to the French. Phuong was a child of Hanoi, growing up in Ba Dinh district close to the city center. He went to primary and middle school at district schools and graduated from the Phan Dinh Phung Middle School in 1991. Like many Hanoi youth of his generation, he did not go on to college. In his case, the local press reported later, that was because "his family was poor, his mother was chronically ill" (Phu nu Thu do 1993a).

So, like thousands of other Hanoi youth, literate but poorly trained, Nguyen Viet Phuong went off to a tenuous kind of work in Hanoi's new market economy. In October 1992 Phuong was hired as a temporary employee, "to work on a contract," in the northern office of a Japanese, Hong Kong and Vietnamese joint venture company. "He worked on transport, banking, delivery, collecting funds, paying for goods" – largely unskilled service work, but a lucky job for a relatively few young people in the new market economy. He was fortunate to be in an office and out on the streets, and not in a factory.

We know far less about Nguyen Tung Duong, who was executed in 1996 as a result of his encounter on the Chuong Duong Bridge in Hanoi with Nguyen Viet Phuong at Tet 1993. Duong was a police lieutenant (*trung uy*), age 35 in 1993, a nearly two-decade veteran of Hanoi police work serving in the Hoan Kiem district of the Hanoi traffic police (*giao thong canh sat*). He was married and had two sons (Phu nu Thu do 1993a).

Nguyen Viet Phuong's work for his company often took him over the Chuong Duong Bridge from central Hanoi toward the suburban, industrial, fast growing Gia Lam District. On January 29, 1993, at the end of the annual Tet holiday and the beginning of the new year, Phuong's superior received 50 million *dong* in cash (about US$5,000 at the 1993 rate of exchange) in payment for goods. In the early 1990s, such cash was often forwarded to Ho Chi Minh City for purchases or investment rather than being placed in Hanoi banks. Phuong and his boss put the money in a small black satchel so that it could be taken over to the far end of Gia Lam Bridge for onward delivery to Ho Chi Minh City via a transport plane from suburban Gia Lam Airport. At about 7:00 pm on January 29 Phuong set out east toward the bridge on his motorcycle, the cash in the satchel, his two thighs pressing the satchel against the motorcycle to keep it safe. As Phuong set off his boss called out to him, "Come back quickly for the end of Tet, lad" (Phu nu Thu do 1993a).

Traffic on the bridge was very light on the holiday night, and the weather was piercingly cold. At about 7:30pm Phuong turned onto Chuong Duong Bridge, heading east toward Gia Lam. Several moments later two other young men riding their motorcycles over the bridge in the same direction heard three cries of "thief, thief, thief!" They looked over and saw two men standing by motorcycles, one leaning over the bridge railing onto the automobile roadway from the motorcycle path. The observers reached and tried to help Phuong, who was bleeding heavily. One of them asked the other man, Lt. Duong, if he had fired his weapon. The answer seemed to be no, then yes. Phuong was taken off to the emergency room of the Viet-Duc (Vietnamese-German) hospital in central Hanoi. He died on the way to the emergency room, and his father and boss found his body there later that night (Phu nu Thu do 1993a; Dai Doan ket 1993a, 1993b).

Even after two years, three court hearings, at least three formal investigations and a review by Vietnam's Supreme People's Court, the events on the Chuong Duong Bridge that night remained blurred. The police officer, Lt. Duong, maintained almost until his execution that he had merely stopped Phuong for the common traffic violation of operating a motorcycle in an automobile lane. He said Phuong had objected, the two had exchanged words, then scuffled, Phuong had reached for Duong's gun and the gun had gone off as it was in Phuong's hand.

But witnesses, forensic specialists and Phuong's family would spell out a conflicting narrative – that Lt. Duong knew Phuong from his many trips across the bridge, knew that he carried money and goods, waved him down for a traffic violation in order to rob him, attempted that robbery, and shot Phuong when Phuong resisted. The conflict over those versions of the facts would electrify Hanoi for the next two years, propel two newspapers into a national spotlight for demanding justice in the case and punishment for the police officer, bring thousands of Hanoians onto the streets and some into violent clashes with police, and result in one of Vietnam's first publicly admitted executions in over ten years.

The death of Nguyen Viet Phuong case immediately came under the jurisdiction of police investigators attached to the Hanoi Public Security Bureau. After several months of investigation, the police group released a report on March 3 asserting that Lt. Duong had waved down Phuong on the bridge "while carrying out his traffic control duties," and Phuong refused to stop, but sped up and moved into the automobile lane. Then, according to the investigators, Duong again demanded that Phuong stop, when he did they quarreled on the bridge. Duong's gun went off as they scuffled, and Phuong was hit by two bullets and died on the road to the emergency room (Phu nu Thu do 1993a).

The police investigators transferred the case file to the Hanoi People's Procuracy with the recommendation that Duong be charged with a violation of Article 103 of the *Criminal Code of the Socialist Republic of Vietnam,* which penalized "endangering a person's life or health while on official duty" and carried a punishment of imprisonment of between one and five years, or three to fifteen years "in serious circumstances" (Criminal Code 1989; also see Quigley 1988).

"WHY DID DEATH COME TO THIS YOUTH, WHO REGULARLY CARRIED BUNDLES OF MONEY ACROSS THE BRIDGE?" – THE NEWSPAPERS ENTER THE FRAY

The death of Nguyen Viet Phuong and the role of Lt. Duong were first reported in detail in two newspapers based in Hanoi, *Phu nu Thu do* (*Women of the Capital*) and *Dai Doan ket* (*Great Unity*), in May and June 1993. Each assigned a team of reporters to investigate Phuong's death. But it was the release of the police investigation report and the police recommendation that Duong be charged only with the lesser offence of causing a death while on official duty – denying the robbery elements, and rejecting a murder charge – that sparked *Dai Doan ket* and *Phu nu Thu do* into taking up the case as a *cause célèbre,* devoting significant resources to their investigations by reporters, dealing with the authorities, and publishing extensively on the matter.

It was no accident that *Phu nu Thu do* and *Dai Doan ket* were among the most active in reporting the story. *Dai Doan ket* is the newspaper of the Vietnamese Fatherland Front, the Party-led umbrella organization of intellectuals, scientists, religious and cultural figures, and a group accustomed both to lively debate and, beginning in the late 1980s, to increasingly seeking to push the government on social, intellectual, and legal issues. *Phu nut Thu do* was widely read by women in and around Hanoi, and had made its mark by reporting more forthrightly than other periodicals on corruption, mistreatment of women and the ways in which women were not fully sharing in the new prosperity of the market economy (Nga 1995).

From the beginning, both newspapers knew the power of their words and the issues at stake. As *Phu nu Thu do* wrote in early May of 1993, "Nguyen Tung Duong is presently in custody, public opinion awaits how he will be tried. We hope that Duong will be tried on a correct charge even though the criminal is a police officer, in order to set an example and so the people can trust the law" (Phu nu Thu do 1993a).

Dai Doan ket and *Phu nu Thu do* took up the case vigorously at the end of May and the beginning of June, shortly after the police investigation report and recommendation were made public. *Dai Doan ket* began by confirming the stories of the two witnesses on the bridge, and added the perspectives of Phuong's father and his boss, who had searched for him on the night of his death. Police officers on the bridge and at the Hoan Kiem district station denied to Phuong's boss and his father that any untoward accidents or other events had taken place that evening. Only when the father and employer went to the Viet-Duc Hospital did they learn that Phuong had died (Dai Doan ket 1993a).

Dai Doan ket also swiftly criticized the police investigation report, claiming that Phuong had been shot not during a quarrel but with his arms raised. The newspaper relied on its own interpretation of physical evidence, the position of the two men, the position of the motorcycles and the firing of the second shot. And the newspaper directly challenged the lesser charge filed by the Hanoi police.

> There are public security officials who have told us that Phuong was shot and killed ... because he resisted. But does it make sense that tens of thousands of people cross the bridge every day, and no one else is shot, only Phuong? The reasons ... are not sufficient. The inquiry must be more complete, and perhaps it must be "Why did death come to this youth, who regularly carried bundles of money across the bridge?"
>
> (Dai Doan ket 1993a)

"YOU SHOULD ACCEPT SOME MONEY"

Dai Doan ket and Phuong's family upped the stakes in mid-June, when *Dai Doan ket* front-paged a letter from Phuong's father reviewing the physical evidence and raising a number of questions about police procedure and the investigation. Phuong's father also recounted a conversation with one of the investigators in which the police official indicated, only fifteen days into the case, that Duong would be sentenced to two years in prison for the death. But the more serious allegations were to come. According to Phuong's father,

> Mr. Yet [the procurator] ... said: "I think you should accept some money and you should not waste your energies with any more requests. We have come to a conclusion and whatever level this goes to it will stop with that conclusion. In any case your son is still dead. I will ask Duong's family to come in." And as expected, Duong's family members came in to bargain and said to me that if I write a paper suggesting that

prosecution be foregone and requesting that Duong be released, then the Duong family would give me 30 million dong [about US$3,000 at the official 1993 rate of exchange].

(Dai Doan ket 1993b)

Phuong's father then laid down the gauntlet for the legal and political authorities. He requested formal reinvestigation of the case. He asked that if the facts were as he and others believed them to be, that Duong be tried for murder under Article 101 of the Criminal Code, not the lesser Article 103 charge "endangering a person's life or health while on official duty" that the police investigators had recommended (Dai Doan ket 1993b).[1]

In the ensuing summer of 1993, *Dai Doan ket* and *Phu nu Thu do* published a barrage of reports and contributions criticizing the actions of the police investigators and prosecutors, delving into the physical evidence of the case, and demanding that Lt. Duong be tried for murder. Some of these articles were written by newspaper correspondents. But others – some often written in significant detail and in legal terms – were signed by citizens as varied as a high school student in Hanoi (Phu nu Thu do 1993b), a judge or staff member at the Central Military Court (quoting from a 1984 Council of Ministers decision on use of firearms by police) (Phu nu Thu do 1993b), a Hanoi mother (Phu nu Thu do 1993b), a representative of a group of retired cadres (Dai Doan ket 1993d), a reprint of a formal complaint by a Hanoi store-owner with knowledge of the case charging that the Hanoi prosecutor had tried to intimidate him (Dai Doan ket 1993b), a group of readers from Nha Trang in Khanh Hoa Province (Dai Doan ket 1993d), a large number of female readers from Vong La village outside Hanoi (Dai Doan ket 1993e), and additional articles by journalists from *Dai Doan ket* and *Phu nu Thu do* (Dai Doan ket 1993d, 1993e).

Under the continuing barrage of the press, public opinion, and perhaps, political decisions, the Supreme People's Procuracy took over investigation of the case in August 1993, and Nguyen Viet Phuong's body was exhumed and transferred to the Procuracy for further examination (Dai Doan ket 1994a). Sharp criticism of police and prosecutorial handling of the case, and continued demands that Duong be tried for murder, continued unabated in the newspapers throughout the fall and winter of 1993 and early 1994. In conformity with the emerging pattern of widespread anger (and newspaper strategy), writers included a *Dai Doan ket* editorial team (Dai Doan ket 1993d), Phuong's former boss at the joint venture company, with a testimonial to Phuong's character (Phu nu Thu do 1993e), and a famous actor and director (Dai Doan ket 1993e), as well as a beatific article on the original witnesses to Phuong's death (Dai Doan ket 1993f).

"WHICH CRIME NGUYEN TUNG DUONG COMMITTED IS NOW THE CRUX OF THE MATTER"

By now the din was so intense that it was difficult to deny that Duong was guilty of something, and it was too late to sweep the matter under the rug or to pay off Viet Phuong's family. A report from a Supreme People's Procuracy meeting in August 1993 put the matter bluntly.

> [T]he participants all agreed that Duong must shoulder the entire responsibility for the death of Nguyen Viet Phuong. That Duong com-mitted a crime – this no one denied. But what offence in the Criminal Code did Duong commit? Our nation is currently building itself into a state ruled by law, and thus if we wish to indict accused A for crime X, there must be sufficient evidence, scientific evidence. The issue of which crime Nguyen Tung Duong committed is now the crux of the matter, and the investigation organs under the Supreme People's Procuracy will have to answer that before public opinion."
>
> (Phu nu Thu do 1993e)

The key issue remained whether Duong's encounter with Viet Phuong was part of an official duty under Article 103 of the Criminal Code (a lesser crime with lesser punishment), or whether it was part of a robbery attempt and thus outside any official duties. If the encounter was outside the scope of his duties, it was generally agreed that the shooting and death that occurred incident to the non-official stop and the robbery were prosecutable as homicide under Article 101 of the Criminal Code (Dai Doan ket 1993c). Lt. Duong was transferred from Hoa Lo Prison in central Hanoi, where he had been under the control of local Hanoi authorities, to another deten-tion facility under the control of the Hanoi military region (Dai Doan ket 1994b).

As the end of 1993 drew near, another *Dai Doan ket* report closed on an optimistic note.

> We hope that with their serious and objective work the Investigations Directorate … will shortly uncover the truth in this complicated case, establishing a basis for Nguyen Tung Duong to be tried in the courts on

the correct charge for that which he brought about, ensuring the strict and clear character of the law, and the consolidation of the trust of the people.
(Dai Doan ket 1993g)

The national prosecutorial team responded with a conciliatory state-ment in late November, perhaps reflecting the somewhat more civil relationship that *Dai Doan ket* seemed to have with national prosecu-tors than with the Hanoi police investigators and local prosecutors. The Deputy Procurator-General in charge of the case asked for patience and for time while the Investigations Directorate came to conclusions on a "very complicated" case in which "only the accused and the victim were on the scene when the events occurred and the victim died on the way to the hospital" and "witnesses arrived after the events occurred" (Dai Doan ket 1993h).

By January 1994, as the national Procuracy neared a decision on a charge against Duong and prepared to move into the indictment (*truy to*) and trial (*xet xu*) stages of the case, the newspapers became active once again. The pressure on the Supreme People's Procuracy to amend the charge to murder was intense, and in January 1994 *Dai Doan ket* published what it called a "draft" of the conclusions of the investiga-tion. The draft report recommended elevating the charge from "endan-gering a person's life or health while on official duty" (Article 103 of the Criminal Code) to murder (Article 101). The factual question remained whether Duong's scuffle with Viet Phuong leading to Phuong's death was within the scope of official duties. But Duong, of course, was not cooperating with that process of altering the charges – he continued to maintain that he had fought with Viet Phuong, his gun had gone off, and that he knew nothing of the purse containing 50 million *dong* that Phuong was carrying (Dai Doan ket 1994a).

"OFFICIAL DUTIES" OR "MOTIVATED BY ABASING PURPOSES"?

By now the public discussion, which may have mirrored and influenced internal discussion in legal and political institutions, had turned to a parsing of the murder statute that Duong looked increasingly likely to face. *Dai Doan ket* pointed out that Article 101(1)(a) of the Criminal Code's murder section, murder "motivated by abasing purposes with a view to committing or concealing another offence" carried the possi-bility of life imprisonment or the death sentence, whereas two other

127

potential murder sub-sections (Article 101(1)(b) and (c)) stipulated imprisonment for between five and twenty years.[2] Duong's refusal to acknowledge that he had been attempting to rob Viet Phuong, and the difficulty in showing robbery as the purpose (the other offense Duong might have been trying to conceal that could lead to the higher murder count), began to make it more likely that Duong might be charged with a lesser homicide count than a charge that might bring a long prison sentence, life imprisonment or death. But *Dai Doan ket* continued to believe that robbery had been the motivation for Duong's stop, and it continued to push for the more serious murder charge (Dai Doan ket 1994a).

On January 28, 1994, a year short of a day after Duong killed Phuong, the Investigations Directorate of the Supreme People's Procuracy submitted its report on the investigation of the events on the bridge. Based on a re-examination of physical evidence by its own investigators and a senior military pathologist, the witnesses' statements and Duong's own changing statements and admissions, the Investigations Directorate concluded that Duong should be indicted for murder under Article 101 of the Criminal Code. The report "refuted" Duong's claim that Phuong had been reaching for his gun, they had struggled, and the gun had gone off (Dai Doan ket 1994c).

"PUBLIC OPINION AWAITS THE INDICTMENT"

But in a move crucial to the development of the case, the Investigations Directorate did not decide whether Duong was attempting to rob Viet Phuong, leaving open the possibility of the lesser charge and lesser sentence that was later to infuriate citizens throughout Hanoi. After reviewing the summary of evidence itself, including Phuong's shout of "thief, thief, save me!" *Dai Doan ket*'s conclusion was clear:

> Justice will only occur if Nguyen Tung Duong is indicted under section (1), subsection (a) of Article 101 of the Criminal Code (motivated by abasing purposes with a view to committing or concealing another offense). Public opinion now awaits the indictment by the Procuracy and investigation institutions.
>
> (Dai Doan ket 1994b)

The decision on which murder charge to use, however, reverted to the Hanoi prosecutorial authorities after the investigation report from the national procuracy was complete. And in February 1994 Hanoi local prosecutors once again infuriated public opinion by indicting Duong not on the "abasing purposes ... concealing another offence" murder charge, but on the lesser murder charge contained in Article 101 of the Criminal Code that provided for imprisonment upon conviction of between five and twenty years, rather than a longer sentence, life imprisonment, or death (Dai Doan ket 1994b, 1994d).

"HE WAS KILLED BECAUSE HE SPOKE THE TRUTH: THIEF, THIEF . . . ."

The public and media reaction was immediate. Now openly organized by the Women's Union, a group of women in Phuc Xa village outside Hanoi wrote angrily to *Phu nu Thu do*, which front-paged their comments: "[I]f the lad Phuong had not been carrying a purse of money on his motorcycle then perhaps he would not have been killed. He was killed because he spoke the truth: thief, thief ... and Duong had to shoot him so that he would not live on to say the truth, that Duong was a thief." Phuong's family spoke up harshly as well, also in *Phu nu Thu do*, denouncing the decision of the Hanoi prosecutor to indict Duong on the lesser murder charge (Phu nu Thu do 1994a, 1994b).

The trial was set for May 12 and 13, and eagerly anticipated throughout Hanoi. In the days before court convened *Dai Doan ket* and other newspapers applied heavy, sarcastic pressure on the court to answer remaining questions about the purse and Duong's motivations and actions on the bridge. "Duong himself admitted and the witnesses also confirmed that after Duong shot Phuong, the money purse found its way from Phuong's motorcycle to Duong's motorcycle. A chance phenomenon, or an inevitable one?" (Dai Doan ket 1994d).

"HALFWAY DOWN THE ROAD, THE BURDEN SNAPS"

The trial of Lt. Duong was held on May 12, 13 and 14, 1994 before a Hanoi people's court judicial panel of two judges and three lay people's assessors, closely watched by Viet Phuong's family, Duong's family, police colleagues of Duong's, journalists, higher court and prosecution officials and spectators – all within the courtroom – and more than a thousand crowded outside on Hai Ba Trung Street in central Hanoi (Phu nu Thu do 1994c). "It may be," *Phu nu Thu do* noted, "that never in the history of the Hanoi Court has there occurred a trial of this scale."

The prosecutors made clear that they wanted Duong to be convicted and imprisoned for the longest possible sentence, twenty years, on the lesser murder charge. On the third day of the trial, "halfway down the road," as *Dai Doan ket* would later term it, and faced with an still unclear record and sharply conflicting statements by the participants, the chief trial judge issued a formal decision returning the case file to the Hanoi People's Procuracy "for supplemental investigation to clarify the motive and purposes of Nguyen Tung Duong in committing the murder" (Phu nu Thu do 1994d).

Newspaper reactions were ambivalent – *Phu nu Thu do* applauded the general view that Duong had indeed committed some form of murder, the new evidence presented, and the professional behavior of the participants, but called it "unfortunate" that the investigation remained open sixteen months after Phuong had died (Phu nu Thu do 1994c). *Dai Doan ket* also applauded the fact that there was "no contrary view" to the assertion that Duong had committed some form of murder. But it also took a darker, more conspiratorial view of the decision to proceed with the trial with a record so unclear.

> Public opinion has been full of doubts (*thac mac*), and questions have been asked: why, when it felt that the file contained so many unclear points, did the Hanoi Court still put the case up for trial? Why didn't [the Court] return the file to the Procuracy for truly thorough preparation before beginning the trial?... Really difficult to understand!

"Halfway down the road, the burden snaps" (*nua duong dut ganh*) was the sardonic headline to the *Dai Doan ket* coverage, a commentary on a weak court under intense pressure from more powerful forces within its walls and outside its building (Dai Doan ket 1994e).

"THERE WILL ONLY BE ONE TRUTH, THERE WILL ONLY BE ONE TRUTH"

In the days following the retransfer of the case to the procuracy for additional investigation, *Phu nu Thu do* and *Dai Doan ket* kept up pressure for a trial and conviction. Each sought to publicize the detailed findings of the military forensic team, which it viewed as insufficiently incorporated into the prosecutor's arguments. *Dai Doan ket* again denounced the errors and biases in the original investigation, tying those mistakes to the shortcomings in the current trial, and it provided a forum for one of the trial judges to explain the decision to send the case back for reinvestigation. In a particularly harsh commentary, *Phu nu Thu do* asked why some of the witnesses' statements in court had been different from some of their earlier statements. "There will only be one truth," a wrathful *Phu nu Thu do* warned and repeated, as it called upon the court and prosecutors to caution the witnesses – particularly Lt. Duong's witnesses – to testify truthfully in court (Phu nu Thu do 1994d, 1994e, 1994f, 1994g; Dai Doan ket 1994f).

In August 1994, *Phu nu Thu do* and other newspapers published the results of the court-ordered reinvestigation by the prosecutors. The Procuracy again stated that the evidence was insufficiently clear to determine whether Duong had been attempting to rob Phuong, in effect pushing the decision back to the Hanoi court. *Phu nu Thu do* published a number of angry letters on the delay and the investigators' report (Phu nu Thu do 1994i). Its own response was righteous fury:

> Over a long time, the 'Chuong Duong bridge case' has become a thermometer, measuring the trust of the people in the objectivity and the spirit of justice and enlightenment of the institutions defending the law ... . The fundamental issue is not whether to judge heavily or leniently, but that we do not know which crime was committed, and that it has not been investigated clearly. And thus when the institutions of law are unable to indicate what police officer Nguyen Tung Duong's motivations were when he committed murder, then that is a debt that society has a right to demand.
>
> (Phu nu Thu do 1994h)

"CENTRAL INSTITUTIONS CONTRIBUTED MANY VIEWS"

By this point, pressure was becoming intense on the Hanoi local pro-secutors to amend its original indictment to increase the severity of the charge (and potential punishment) against Duong. After resisting that for months, the situation suddenly changed in late September of 1993. *Dai Doan ket* explained why:

> We have learned that after the file was transferred to the Hanoi Procuracy [after the reinvestigation at the central level], and before the indictment was released, Central institutions responsible for protec-tion of law [in the Central Committee of the Vietnamese Communist Party] contributed many views.

And on September 15, 1994, the Hanoi People's Procuracy issued Indictment no. 636, charging Nguyen Tung Duong under Article 101, section (1), sub-section (g) of the Criminal Code (murder constituting a case of hooliganism). In this way no robbery indictment was included and the prosecutors sidestepped the robbery issue, but under this framework of punishment the accused could be forced to bear the highest level of punishment available under the Criminal Code (Dai Doan ket 1994g).

"JUSTICE FOR THE LIVING AND JUSTICE FOR THE DEAD"

With the logjam broken, and Duong now charged with a crime that could bring a higher sentence, the trial proceeded more smoothly and the court had more confidence in the decision to be rendered. But, apparently fearful of backsliding, the newspapers did not let up the pressure. In the week before Duong's trial reconvened on October 19, *Dai Doan ket* reviewed the evidence for robbery and murder and headed its coverage "There must be justice for the living and justice for the dead!" (Dai Doan ket 1994h).

On October 19, 1994, Nguyen Tung Duong's trial reconvened. Once again the courtroom was packed, and now more than 10,000 listened outside. Again the prosecutors, Lt. Duong's lawyer and the lawyer for Phuong's family spoke, and Duong was questioned again. On October 20, during interrogation by the judges, Duong said that the gun had been in his hand (rather than Phuong's) when it went off, and that it had gone off by accident. That account was challenged in great detail by the chief military forensic specialist, called in by the Supreme People's Procuracy to work specially on the case. After extensive argument by the prosecutors and lawyers for Duong and for Phuong's family, Duong was convicted of murder "motivated by abasing purposes with a view to committing or concealing another offence," the robbery of Nguyen Viet Phuong, and sentenced to death (Ha Noi moi 1994; Phu nu Thu do 1994j).

"THE JUDGMENT OF THE COURT WAS NOT DUE TO PUBLIC OPINION"

Whether by design or legal analysis, the court convicted Duong of the precise charge – and mandated the precise sentence – that *Dai Doan ket*, *Phu nu Thu do* and other newspapers had demanded. The President of the Hanoi People's Court tried to end the matter with a clear statement: "Nguyen Tung Duong committed murder in order to appropriate the assets of the victim; he committed the crime with a clear motive and purpose, determined to carry that out to the end." But beyond the legal analysis there were strong defensive elements in the judgment as well. While admitting the complications of the case and the great interest it had aroused, the court vigorously denied that public opinion or the press had played any role in its decision.

> The Hanoi Court tried the case of Nguyen Tung Duong under conditions in which public opinion in society on the case was very complex; that fact served all the more to make the Court abide by the law seriously and strictly. The judgment of the Court was not due to public opinion, but had to follow the law . . . to defend justice for society and justice for each person before the law.
>
> (Dai Doan ket 1994j)

The newspapers that had taken up the Duong case greeted the sentence with triumph, full of praise for the judges. *Phu nu Thu do* even front-paged a story bold bannered "When the death sentence against Nguyen Tung Duong will be carried out." Domestic press coverage dramatically expanded into mainstream outlets such as *Lao Dong* (*Labor*), the trade union newspaper, as well as other local Hanoi newspapers, and a number of newspapers directly run by the Party (Phu nu Thu do 1994k, 1994l; Dai Doan ket 1994i, 1994k).

"AND WHAT IF NGUYEN TUNG DUONG'S TWO SONS LOST THEIR FATHER?" – THE BATTLE IS JOINED

For the first time, now, Lt. Duong began to have his media defenders as well, newspapers that had been largely silent for the entire long legal process. Police and Ministry of Interior newspapers such as *An ninh Thu do* (*Capital Security*) now ran long stories, virtually all disagreeing with the verdict and sentence (An ninh Thu do 1994a, 1994b, 1994c, 1994d).

An ninh Thu do used the same methods to defend Duong as *Dai Doan ket* and *Phu nu Thu do* had utilized to express popular anger toward Duong and the Hanoi prosecutors. It published letters and short articles by a Hanoi high school student, a Hanoi mother writing on behalf of a group of mothers in her neighborhood, a doctor at Hanoi's Thang Long Hospital, also writing on behalf of a group of his colleagues, a retired cadre in Hanoi's Kim Lien Distract, a female artist, writing on behalf of other performers at the Youth Drama Troupe, and a soldier's wife (all An ninh Thu do 1994d); all criticizing the severity of the sentence or the evidence for the specific crime for which Duong had been judged.

During the two-month period between Duong's conviction on October 21, 1994 and his appeal hearing in mid-December, *Dai Doan ket* and *Phu nu Thu do* continued to run articles on the case, defending the verdict and sentence, seeking to set the stage for a rejection of Duong's appeal, reporting by name on which officials had delayed investigation and judgment for nearly two years, and now directly warning the legal authorities of the newspapers' own power and that of public opinion (Dai Doan Ket 1994j; Phu nu Thu do 1994m).

The intensity of the press battle was dictated by the appeal schedule. Under the Criminal Procedure Code, Duong had a limited period from the date of his sentence to appeal. So the window for "public opinion" to make itself felt – whether *Dai Doan ket* and *Phu nu Thu do*'s public opinion, or the security newspapers' public opinion, was short indeed. And with the widespread perception that public opinion and the press had indeed influenced the first trial, neither side was taking any chances.

Lt. Duong indeed appealed the judgment and sentence, and the Supreme Court scheduled the appellate hearing in the case for December 13 through 15, 1994. Thousands gathered outside the stately French colonial courthouse housing the appellate tribunal as the appellate hearing began underway, and the tribunal's proceedings were broadcast over loudspeakers. On December 13 clashes broke out between angry members of the crowd concerned that the appellate tribunal would weaken the final verdict, and police guarding the courthouse. Rocks were thrown from the crowd, and "police were seen charging the crowd of several thousand using batons and shields that give off blue sparks and electric shocks," although it was unclear who had attacked whom first (Agence France Presse 1994a, 1994b, 1994c; The Economist 1995; Kyodo News Service 1994).

On December 15, 1994 the Supreme Court appellate tribunal approved the verdict of the Hanoi court, noting that the case had "caused bad political and social consequences." Once again the judgment was covered in the domestic press, both by *Dai Doan ket* and *Phu nu Thu do* and also by other national newspapers that had not earlier given priority to the Duong case (Phu nu Thu do 1994n; Dai Doan ket 1994l, 1994m). Triumph was once again the theme of the *Dai Doan ket* and *Phu nu Thu do* coverage; *Phu nu Thu do* termed the ruling "welcomed by the people as a verdict on the correct person, for the correct crime, and correct under the law" (Phu nu Thu do 1995a). But the coverage was neither as prominent nor as exultatory as after the October hearing, and more often now relegated to inside pages than beginning on the front page.

Following the decision by the Supreme Court tribunal upholding the death sentence and the violence during that appellate hearing, press coverage dropped away quickly. But careful efforts were underway to interpret the results in official ways, to placate Hanoi and national police forces that were angry over the treatment of their lieutenant and their forces – and perhaps their inability to control the result of the case – and to make peace between the legal institutions that had been brought into conflict during the Duong case.

For its part, *Dai Doan ket* was cooperative in that reconciliation effort. A senior national prosecutor explained in the newspaper in late December 1994 that the Nguyen Tung Duong case was an example of the positive role of public opinion in cooperation with the state in the struggle against crime (Dai Doan ket 1994l). Nor was the incident indicative of a general problem of police corruption, stated the president of the appellate tribunal in the Duong case under a front-paged banner headline in *Dai Doan ket* the next week. "The Nguyen Tung Duong phenomenon was particular, and it cannot dim the great feats of arms and sacrifices of the people's public security over the past fifty years" (Dai Doan ket 1994m).

There was little coverage in early 1995, when Duong's formal appeal for clemency was lodged with then-President Le Duc Anh under the provisions of Vietnam's Criminal Procedure Law. The Office of the President requested opinions on the clemency petition from the President of the Supreme Court and the Procurator-General of the Supreme People's Procuracy.

President Le Duc Anh issued Decision no. 333/CTN on February 27, 1995. rejecting Nguyen Tung Duong's appeal for clemency (*don xin an giam*) following a recommendation by the President of the Supreme Court and the Procurator-General that clemency not be granted (Phu nu Thu do 1995a; Dai Doan ket 1995b). On the same day, the Chief Judge of the Hanoi People's Court issued a decision to enforce the appellate court's judgment, in accordance with the Criminal Procedure Code, and establishing a judgment execution committee for the case. That committee included the Chief Judge of the Hanoi People's Court, the Chief of the Enforcement Division of the Hanoi

People's Procuracy, the Deputy Commander of the Hanoi Police, and "representatives of some related institutions" (Dai Doan ket 1995b).

Pursuant to that decision, and after detailed preparations were undertaken, the judgment execution committee met at 3:00 a.m. on the morning of March 5, 1995 to carry out the sentence at Cau Nga, the execution ground for Hanoi located in adjacent Ha Tay province. *Dai Doan ket, Phu nu Thu do* and other media reported the execution in detail, in what Amnesty International later called "[t]he first official confirmation of a death sentence having been carried out since 1985" (Bui Cong Ly 1995; Dai Doan ket 1995b; Agence France Presse 1995; Amnesty International 1996).

After hundreds of column inches on the case over two years, *Dai Doan ket* finished its coverage in sparse terms that seemed to come from an official text: "In accordance with the convict's wishes, Nguyen Tung Duong met with his family before the sentence was carried out. The sentence of death against Nguyen Tung Duong was carried out swiftly and in an orderly fashion, in accordance with law, and was completed at 4:30 on the morning of March 5, 1995" (Dai Doan ket 1995b).

But *Ha Noi moi* (*New Hanoi*), the Hanoi Party newspaper not earlier associated with extensive coverage of the Duong case, provided a much more detailed report on the execution – and probably the most detailed coverage ever publicly issued on an execution in Vietnam. While the *Dai Doan ket* and other reports read like brief wire service digests of an official government release, the reporting of the *Ha Noi moi* journalist, Bui Cong Ly ("Justice Bui"), implied presence at the execution itself:

> On the morning of March 5, at the Hanoi prison, Nguyen Tung Duong was escorted from his cell to the judgment execution committee to complete final procedural formalities. The ... committee included representatives of three institutions: the city court, procuracy, and public security. Those participating as witnesses and supervisors of the final procedural formalities also included representatives of other institutions: the Hanoi prison, criminalistics technicians, archival personnel to identify the prisoner, central forensic specialists, and local government personnel on location at the prison.
>
> Then the technicians from the archival institution identified the prisoner, by taking fingerprints of Nguyen Tung Duong at the site; those were examined by the criminalistics technical experts and a comparison was done on the spot, under a magnifying glass, between the fingerprints taken there and the fingerprints in Nguyen Tung Duong's archived file. It was then announced that the results confirmed

that the person against whom sentence was to be carried out today was Nguyen Tung Duong.

Before the judgment execution committee, Nguyen Tung Duong was directly read the decision of the President rejecting the appeal for clemency from the death sentence and the decision of the President of the municipal People's Court on carrying out the judgment. Then he signed the record of proceedings, and met with family members before going to the execution ground.

At the Cau Nga execution ground, the execution committee issued the order to execute Nguyen Tung Duong. When the firing was completed the forensic physicians carried out an examination of the convict's corpse, and then signed the report to confirm: Nguyen Tung Duong was dead.

The judgment was carried out in conformity with procedural formalities, carefully, accurately and safely.

(Bui Cong Ly 1995)

Newspaper coverage ceased almost completely after Duong's final appeal was denied and while President Le Duc Anh considered his clemency petition. One exception was an acerbic, sly, truculent summary in a *Dai Doan ket* wrap-up article on "Ten cases that caused the worst public reaction (*tai tieng*) in 1994," published just before Duong's execution. *Dai Doan ket* defiantly gave the people and the press some credit for justice in the case of Nguyen Tung Duong.

The case of Nguyen Tung Duong committing murder on the Chuong Duong Bridge has caused an uproar in public opinion within society and in the newspapers throughout the past two years. It caused the worst reactions about the Hanoi traffic police during 1994. The case took three hearings and took very extensive labor and time. Many people have said that if this case had occurred in a different place, where the people's standards of intellect and culture (*dan tri*) had not yet been familiar with law, and without the unusually active efforts of the press, the case also would have been concluded at the first hearing.

(Dai Doan ket 1995a)

But not all agreed that the press had helped reach a just result. A staff member at the Institute of Strategic Studies under the Ministry of Defense strongly stated the contrary view, angrily endorsing acerbic comments on the role of the press in the Nguyen Tung Duong case made by a senior Hanoi judge.

I am in strong agreement with the views expressed by Mr. Pham Quang Liem, Deputy Chief Judge of the Criminal Tribunal of the Hanoi

137

People's Court, when he answered journalists' questions in *An ninh Thu do*: the purpose of every trial is to be accurate with respect to persons and to be accurate with respect to crime. Press institutions are not trial institutions. Debating the case of a defendant is not the function of newspapers and radio. We should not bring in freedom of the press in order to conduct psychological incitement utilizing matters that are contrary to the truth.

(An ninh Thu do 1994a, 1994b)

And so newspaper coverage of the death of Nguyen Viet Phuong, and the trials and execution of Nguyen Tung Duong ended about as abruptly as the deaths themselves occurred.

What does the coverage of this case teach us? One lesson is that despite the wealth of coverage, we still know little about the internal processes and pressures under which Vietnamese editors and journalists work when confronted with complex social issues in which there is intense public interest. In this case, for example, it is clear that *Dai Doan Ket* and *Phu nu Thu do* perceived that they were relatively free (until the end of the trial) to pursue the case. And it is reasonably clear that the security newspapers, including *An ninh Thu do* remained under more restricted publication restrictions until the final stages of the matter.

Why are those pressures applied and signals communicated in specific cases? How are they applied and communicated, both to newspapers and then within them? Both issues require further research. What is clear is that under certain circumstances Vietnamese newspapers do feel a certain flexibility to pursue the punishment of certain individuals in power – and, at least in this case, they pursued that punishment vigorously. Complex cases like this certainly do not mean that the Vietnamese press is "free" in any sense, for obviously it is not. But such cases introduce significant complexity into the discussion, a complexity that belies and provides texture to the usual perception that the Vietnamese press is completely directed, controlled and dominated in its daily, article-by-article work by the political structure in which it seeks to work.

The Vietnamese written press has been effectively strategic in choosing arenas for reporting in which the Party and state have, at least in formal terms, promised more autonomy than in the past. Law is a clear example of both the increased autonomy promised (though not always delivered), and the ways in which the written media has sought to bootstrap onto those formal expressions of autonomy. When the

Vietnamese press treats law as a somewhat separate sphere of social life and reports on it in more aggressive and autonomous ways than is possible with political spheres that have not been granted enhanced (albeit formal) autonomy, the arena itself becomes a shield for the press. Freedom of the press itself could not, at least under current circumstances, serve as nearly such a powerful shield for press activity as reporting on law or analogous arenas of a now more separate social life in Vietnam.

Ten years after Nguyen Tung Duong was executed, the killing on the bridge and the execution of the policeman still stir emotions in Hanoi. For some, it represents the first time that the press flexed its muscles for justice, and among the first occasions in Vietnam when a police murder was punished. For others, the Duong case represents a trial by the media, in which a weak judicial system was unable to withstand the pressure of public opinion whipped up by two powerful newspapers. To this day in Hanoi there are some who believe that Nguyen Tung Duong knew that young Phuong was carrying cash, stopped him to rob him of it, and killed him in the process. And there are others who, just as passionately, believe that Phuong's death was an unfortunate accident hyped by a newly energized press.

In the years since Phuong and Duong's deaths, both the press and the judiciary have become more powerful. The Vietnamese media – particularly newspapers – now regularly engage in exposes and investigations like the Duong case, though often in areas other than police killings. Officials have come to respect the power of the press – again, especially the newspapers – and a wider range of newspapers has joined the investigative and reporting fray. But the judiciary has become at least somewhat more confident as well. There are legal scholars and knowledgeable observers in Hanoi who watch the growing power and confidence of the Vietnamese press, the willingness of newspapers to take different sides and argue, often with each other, the more slowly growing confidence of the judiciary, and particularly the emerging role of defense lawyers, who weigh all of these factors and believe that Lt. Duong might not be convicted of the same crime today, and might well not be sentenced to death. For them, as all sides have grown in confidence and capacity, and as defense lawyers have emerged as a powerful force in the trial process when they were not in 1995, a more nuanced result might be reached today.

Of course, we can never know. The death of Nguyen Viet Phuong and the execution of Nguyen Tung Duong were markers in the development of both a more robust press and a more confident legal system, though the press continues to outstrip the judiciary in confidence and, many would say, capacity. In that sense the execution of Nguyen Tung Duong was a stepping stone toward a more just legal system and a more autonomous civil society in Vietnam, though to this day it is difficult to know whether, in the end, justice was truly done.

NOTES

1. In the same issue, *Dai Doan ket* published a long letter from a retired Army lieutenant colonel also demanding reinvestigation and appropriate prosecution of the case, vigorously raising the question of prosecution under the full murder statute, and demanding that the Supreme People's Procuracy and Supreme People's Court intervene directly in the case (Dai Doan Ket 1993b).
2. Article 101(2) provides: "If the offense is committed in circumstances other than those set in paragraph 1 of this article, or there are no extenuating circumstances, the offender shall be subject to a term of imprisonment of between five and twenty years."

CHAPTER 6

LAW AND THE REGULATION OF CIVIL SOCIETY: NONPROFIT ORGANIZATIONS, PHILANTHROPY, GRASSROOTS ORGANIZATIONS, AND THE STATE

The key principles underlying the post-1986 reform of Vietnamese law and the legal system include a strong role for the state and an instrumentalist concept of law as serving state interests and priorities, and a notion of rights as state-granted rather than emanating from concepts of natural rights. State attitudes toward citizen-initiated social activity, expressed through law and political policy, have ranged from repressive to ambivalent in the past to sometimes encouraging today in certain arenas. The state and Party's regulation of the emerging Vietnamese nonprofit and voluntary sector illustrates these issues at work, and how state and Party responses have changed in the nearly twenty years since the *doi moi* process began.

In recent years, Vietnam's emerging and diversifying voluntary sector, including a wide range of organizations that are closely related to or dominated by the Party or state, has expanded rapidly to fulfill social needs from which the Vietnamese state is retreating and to play other roles in Vietnamese society. The emerging voluntary sector, broadly defined, now includes Party-related mass organizations, business, trade and professional associations, policy research groups, social activist and social service groups, religious groups, clans, charities, private and semi-private universities, social and charitable funds, and other institutions.

The state has sought to encourage the growth of social organizations, at least partly to compensate for the inability of the state to keep pace with social needs in the reform period. At the same time, the state retains management and control over the sector at a level more detailed and specific than in many other countries. That management and control is exercised through a regulatory structure that subjects voluntary groups to the "dual management" of both state ministries and a national Ministry of Home Affairs at the national level, and other means detailed in this chapter. Beyond those important measures, the state's punitive efforts are concentrated on a very small number of organizations that are perceived to be political challenges. For the vast majority of the thousands of formal and informal organizations now active throughout the country, the Vietnamese state generally acquiesces in and even encourages their day-to-day activities, while retaining a detailed regulatory structure and making clear that the state and Party remain generally in control of the pace and direction of growth in nonprofit activity.

This mutually enforcing balance between state encouragement and control of the voluntary sector is a key facet of the history of Party and state attitudes toward the voluntary sector. In 1946, during a period of alliance between Ho Chi Minh's revolutionary forces and other political groups, Ho's coalition government promulgated a statute that both permitted and fairly strictly regulated the development of voluntary organizations. Under that 1946 statute, the state held the primary role in authorizing voluntary groups, was the sole grantor of rights to them, and retained continuing control and authority over them. This pattern would be repeated in later legislation (Sidel 1997a).

After years of fighting against the French, the victory at Dien Bien Phu in 1954, the retaking of Hanoi, and several years of Party rule, 1956 and 1957 saw rapid land reform along a Chinese model and growing resistance in intellectual and political circles to increasing Party authoritarianism. In late 1956, Vietnam experienced its own version of the Chinese "Hundred Flowers Movement," an outpouring (at least within relatively narrow circles of intellectuals) of demands for tolerance and gradual democratization.

When the Vietnamese Hundred Flowers was shattered by the Party in late 1956 and early 1957, reformist magazines and newspapers were closed and discussions were stopped, dozens of intellectuals and cultural figures were imprisoned and emergent civil activity was severely curtailed. In mid-1957, the Party promulgated new regulations on associations that severely limited rights to assemble and the ability of civic organizations to form, reflecting rapidly tightened policies at this time of tension. Although Vietnamese social and civic life was to change dramatically in the next several decades, and particularly after the *doi moi* era began in the mid-1980s, the 1957 law and regulations on associations have not yet been abrogated and remain in effect, at least until a new Law on Associations is adopted by the National Assembly (Law on Associations 1957; Decision 258 1957).

Between 1957 and the mid-1980s, decades of war being followed by a decade of intense poverty, social organizations other than directly controlled Party mass organizations and labor unions had no significant role in Vietnamese society. But after wars, a long period of Stalinist economic, political and social policies, and the beginning of rapid economic reform and social change in the mid-1980s, the role, number and variety of Vietnamese social organizations of various types has now expanded rapidly, of course in a process still controlled and managed by the Communist Party (Mulla and Boothroyd 1993; Beaulieu 1994; Giao 1994; Kerkvliet and Marr 1994; Marr 1994; Sidel 1997a; Gray 1999; Kerkvliet 2001; Pedersen 2002; Wischermann 2002; Kerkvliet et al 2005; Civicus 2006; on southern developments, see Oanh 1998, 2002).

These changes in society and in Party and state policy required legal specification. Three years after the *doi moi* process took hold in 1986, the Vietnamese Party and government issued new policy documents in 1989 encouraging the growth of a social organizational sector within broad limits set by the state and continuing political controls. The restrictive 1957 law and regulations remained in force, but the 1989 policy documents were a political attempt, through administrative documents, to balance state encouragement of at least some voluntary activity with continued close control (Instructions 1 1989).

Eighteen months later, the pendulum swung back a bit. Between January 1989 and mid-1990, the Party and government apparatus had become considerably more concerned about the activism and growing political role of some voluntary groups, as well as its increasing inability to keep track of the growing number and range of such organizations. Prominent among such groups was the Club of Former Resistance Fighters, who demanded better conditions for veterans and began to take their demands into the political realm. A government document issued in June 1990 (once again, formally implementing the 1957 law and regulations, which remained on the books), sought once again to stiffen some controls on social organizations. Like the 1957 Law and Regulations, and the 1989 Instruction on Mass Organizations, the 1990 document re-emphasized a process of approval (*cho phep*) for associations and other social organizations rather than moving toward a registration (*dang ky*) system that might require less state intervention (Instructions 202 1990; Sidel 1997a).

UP FROM AMBIGUITY: THE 1992 SCIENCE AND TECHNOLOGY CIRCULAR AND THE OPENING OF CHANNELS

The early 1990s were a period of rapid growth in policy research institutes, social service and social activist organizations, new and voluntary cooperatives, and other forms of voluntary organizations. Their increasing diversity also had one important commonality: virtually all operated publicly without formally registering with the state, and, in most cases, were largely satisfied with that ambiguous legal status.

But in January and November 1992, the relatively liberal Ministry of Science, Technology and the Environment opened a more flexible window, an avenue for some social organizations to seek a fully legalized, formal, state-recognized and registered status. Seeking at least rhetorically to encourage and motivate scientific talent, raise funds for basic and applied science and technology research, and help scientists remain in the basic and applied sector, the Ministry promulgated regulations endorsing and encouraging organizations promoting scientific and technological innovation and exchange. A number of urban voluntary organizations, including some of the most important policy research, social service and social activist organizations then operating, understood the legalization that was possible through the relatively flexible and welcoming window provided by the 1992 Science and Technology Regulations, and they registered with the Ministry under those Regulations (Decree 35 1992; Ministry of Science and Technology 1993).

The 1992 Science and Technology Decree provided a measure of legitimacy to a number of voluntary organizations. It also gave them some measure of protection through affiliation with the powerful science, technology and environment system within the government. That was an affiliation not only in bureaucratic terms but also, at least to some degree, in ideological and even political terms as well. Policy research as well as some social activist and social service groups now put on the mantle of science and technology, and they did so willingly and intentionally. There was little that could provide more political protection than the science and technology arena that had been declared, for so long in Soviet and Vietnamese practice, to be both technical and non-political.

Groups such as the Center for Gender, Family and Environment in Development in Hanoi and the Social Development Consulting Group in Ho Chi Minh City registered or found legitimacy under the rubric of the 1992 Science and Technology Decree. And throughout the 1990s, the Science and Technology Decree was regularly cited throughout urban Vietnam as important support for the formation of new civil organizations. Although control was still sought and retained, the pendulum continued to swing gradually toward encouragement and flexibility in the several years after the 1992 decree was promulgated. Hundreds of new voluntary groups were formed, including many voluntary agricultural cooperatives to replace the involuntary or mobilized cooperatives formed during the period of central planning in the countryside.

There is some evidence that the drafters of the 1992 Decree understood the sea-change they were effecting, the space they were opening. For "the first time," wrote Vu Cao Dam, a key drafter of Decree 35, "a new democratic idea was found in a State document on science and technology: that the State acknowledges the 'right' (*quyen*) of 'citizens,' instead of the commonly used term 'permission' (*cho phep*) in earlier legal documents" to organize science and technology activities and social organizations. On Decree 35, Professor Dam continues,

> the traditional conception that the State is the superior body 'granting permission' to carry out science and technology activities that was commonly found in official documents was replaced by a democratic spirit, that recognized the 'right' of each individual and social organization to carry out science and technology activities ... Second, those primarily responsible for drafting the Decree were successful in disguising implicit provisions, so that even though the Decree provides that individuals and social organizations 'must' register with state organizations when they wish to establish social organizations ... in reality it ... grants each citizen the 'right' ... to develop broad forms of science and technology service and research organizations, abolishing ... the right of bureaucratic 'examination and approval' of the administrative system, limiting the administrative function to approving the 'registration' form supplied by citizens. The result, as we all know, is that today it is difficult to be able to count precisely how many science and technology research, training and service organizations were established by citizens and social organizations through the spirit of Decree 35/HDBT. And so the terms "35 Center" and "35 Institute" appeared .... As we reflect on it today, the Decree was issued under the limited framework of an administrative system, but it really played the role of a *democratic charter for science.*
>
> (Dam 2002)

Decree 35 certainly did embody these principles and reforms. The language may still seem state-driven to western interpretation, but it had new meaning in Vietnam: "All state institutions, military units, economic organizations, social organizations and each citizen have the right (*quyen*) to organize and undertake science and technology activities," according to Article 1. And, under Article 15, "science and technology organizations that are ... established at the provincial or municipal level, or by collectives or individuals, must register (*dang ky*) their activities [and not, as in an earlier draft, "apply for approval"] at the provincial or municipal science and technology office (or commission)" (Decree 35 1992).

FORMAL RECOGNITION IN THE CIVIL CODE

The 1992 Decree on Science and Technology was a watershed for the Vietnamese associational sector, particularly the intellectual and professional sector based in the cities. But it was, in fact, what Vietnamese legislators and scholars sometimes call an "under-law," a legal document issued by one ministry and not applicable throughout the country by all government authorities. Further recognition in the form of a full national law was given to the expanding social organization sector in 1995, when the Civil Code of the Socialist Republic of Vietnam was adopted by the National Assembly. The Civil Code formally recognized economic and social organizations, social and charitable foundations (funds), and other voluntary groups as legal entities, and under certain situations absolved members of such organizations from personal liability (including seizure of assets) "for carrying out civil tasks of the social organisation or social/ professional organisation" (Civil Code 1995, Art. 114). Similar stipulations were made for social and charitable funds, when funds are "managed, used and disposed of in accordance with the stipulations of law and in accordance with the purpose of operation of the fund as stipulated by its statute" (Civil Code 1995, Art. 115). In the mid-1990s, Vietnam was more familiar with the work of associations and other social organizations than the work of foundations and other social funds, and the Party and state may well have been concerned with an influx of overseas Vietnamese funds. This may partly account for the stronger limitations placed on the activities of social and charitable funds, a residual concern for their activities in a rapidly changing nation.

Of course hundreds or thousands of social organizations of various types had existed during the ten-year period of reform preceding the

146

promulgation of the Civil Code – the Code certainly did not initiate the emergence of the sector. But the recognition of legal personality was important, and at the level of national legislation rather than ministerial regulation. The Code sought to remove still significant legal, economic and political obstacles to participation in the voluntary sector, in part by enabling voluntary groups to pursue bank loans with greater ease and flexibility, for example, and it sought to protect members' personal assets from risk due to losses or to negligence of members acting in their organizational roles. Finally, by recognizing social and professional organizations and funds in a key piece of national legislation, the Code opened the door both to facilitating and restrictive implementing legislation at the national, ministerial and provincial levels, a chapter in the tale of social organizations in Vietnam that would play out over the next decade.

THE SPECIAL PROBLEMS OF VOLUNTARY AGRICULTURAL COOPERATIVES

The evolution and problems faced by a particular kind of citizens' organization – voluntary agricultural cooperatives – illustrate some of the complexities faced by social organizations in the Vietnamese reform process. In March 1996, a new statute governing and encouraging agricultural cooperatives, the Law on Cooperatives (*Luat Hop tac xa*) was adopted, reflecting a new stage in Party and state attitudes toward the agricultural cooperative sector. Rural cooperatives were originally a means toward rapid Chinese-style collectivization in the 1950s, and in many areas of the Democratic Republic of Vietnam they were not, or not entirely, voluntary. These state-mandated, state-organized units were among the first victims of the *doi moi* era that began in 1986, although they also appear to have weakened during a series of prominent if not entirely authorized, rural reform experiments going back to the early 1980s.

In the late 1980s, many state-organized agricultural cooperatives were weakened, dismantled, or fell into ruin when peasants deserted them. Some did survive, however, and in the face of individualized, household agriculture peasants in several areas formed voluntary production, irrigation, marketing and other cooperatives. The fate of the older cooperatives in a period of transition to the market, and the emergence of newer kinds of voluntary cooperatives, caught the eye of policymakers and policy researchers in the early 1990s (Vinh and

Nhan 1994). By 1995 the prominent Vietnamese agricultural scientist Dao The Tuan and his research team had completed the first full-scale survey of agricultural cooperatization under market conditions since the *doi moi* era began (Dao The Tuan 1995; see also CIEM 1996).

Professor Tuan and his colleagues found some vibrant, active cooperatives, and many others in deep decline. The causes of this were complex, but cooperatives in decline had often encountered some or all of the following problems: reluctance of local authorities to deal with "unofficial" or "unrecognized" citizens' organizations and to issue the necessary permits for them to borrow from state-run banks; significant difficulties negotiating loans from state banks; significant problems in negotiating repayment periods that fit appropriately with planting, harvesting and marketing seasons; insufficient rotating capital; local cadres with low technical, managerial and business skills; shortages of seeds, pesticides and other agricultural commodities; difficulties in transferring newer technologies to the peasants; highly volatile, rapidly shifting, prices and availability of agricultural production commodities; difficulties in finding stable sales markets for agricultural commodities; reliable transport; and reliable payment; and overly high taxation policies, particularly at the local level (Dao The Tuan 1995).

The 1995 Civil Code began the legal process of providing some more support to the cooperative sector. This was after a lengthy period of decline, and then state neglect, as the peasants reformed cooperatives at their own initiative at the local level and in at least some localities. The legal status and personality of larger cooperatives was explicitly recognized in the new Civil Code. After considerable debate about how to treat smaller and more informal cooperatives, the National Assembly decided to recognize that smaller cooperatives "are subjects in civil relations" and may achieve full legal personality – enabling them to enter into contracts and loans – through registration with, and approval by, state institutions (Civil Code 1995, Art. 120; see also Ministry of Justice 1995; Law on Cooperatives 1996).

This debate over the status and powers of smaller cooperatives typified the decades-long conflict over state recognition of various kinds of social organization, and the mixing of caution toward and encouragement of the voluntary sector. Some drafters reflected the more cautious side of this discussion, seeking to exclude smaller cooperatives from legal personality and from the scope of the Civil Code, on the grounds that they were "a simple kind of organization, unstable, lacking in solidity." Other drafters favored a more inclusive and encouraging approach, and they were backed by citizens and many National Assembly members:

> Although they are a simple form of organization, they constitute an indispensable need, and they have developed naturally from the needs and for the benefit of working people themselves in the process of development, as they expand production and business, foster the strength of communities ... and help each other to resolve problems in production and in life.
>
> (Ministry of Justice 1995)

THE LONG ROAD TOWARD A LAW ON ASSOCIATIONS IN VIETNAM

In the state regulation of the associational and social organization sector, as in many other legislative fields, there are often multiple regulatory efforts underway in a number of sectors of the government at the same time. Thus even while the Civil Code was in draft, and the Law on Cooperatives in preparation, a separate drafting group in Hanoi began work in the early 1990s on a law to replace the more restrictive 1957 regulations on associations. Those efforts to draft a national Law on Associations became bogged down in the late 1990s over a range of difficult issues in state management, registration, coverage, and other problems. The Party and state released other legal documents that sought to strengthen another complex aspect of state-society relations – enhancing citizens' participation in the work of the state, particularly in the rural areas (Regulations on Democracy in Communes 1998 and 2003).

Both in the 1990s, and since the drafting process to formulate a Law on Associations was reinitiated in 2000/2001, drafters have sought a law to replace the 1957 associational regulations that maintains state control and knowledge of the associational sector and to clarify an increasingly confused environment, while also providing encouragement to a range of associations and other social organizations that fulfill Party- and state-favored goals. From the beginning of the drafting of the Law on Associations (*Luat ve Hoi*), it has been understood that the new law will continue to require the registration and approval of voluntary organizations of various kinds, as well as continuing controls on activities, reporting requirements, financial affairs and other important areas to impose some discipline – or at least give the state the ability to

149

impose some order – on this burgeoning sector. But the process has been long, subject to debate on complex and politically sensitive issues, and in recent years has been sharply affected by the growing power of national business, trade and professional associations.

Among the issues that emerged in the late 1990s was the tax treatment of associations and the emerging voluntary sector. In the mid-1990s Vietnamese voluntary organizations generally, if informally, understood that domestic voluntary organizations were not required to pay domestic corporate income (or business) tax (*thue doanh thu*) or profit tax (*thue loi thac*), two of the basic tax mandates applicable to the for-profit business sector. The relatively simple basis for this informal exemption was that social organizations were not business enterprises, since the two major business taxes in question were applicable to business enterprises only. A relatively narrow and more formal exemption from income and profit tax was provided to domestic companies and science and technology organizations (*to chuc khoa hoc ky thuat*) that invested in science and technology research or undertook contracts for the development of science and technology (Joint Circular 1992). But for many years the tax-collecting Ministry of Finance has been reluctant to further formalize such exemptions, much less provide positive tax incentives for charitable donations and for nonprofit groups.

The growing complexity of the associational sector and of the relationships between multiple regulators – the early Government Commission for Organization and Personnel (GCOP), now the Ministry of Home Affairs, and others – have consistently stymied the completion of the Law on Associations. In the meantime, individual decrees and regulations have been used to regulate parts of the associational sector that have developed particularly quickly, that were subject to little formal state regulation in the past, and that have caused regulatory headaches for the state.

REGULATING THE EXPANDING ARRAY OF SOCIAL AND CHARITABLE FUNDS

One of those areas has been the proliferation of "funds" (sometimes termed "foundations") for a variety of social, charitable, artistic and cultural, educational and other activities. The gathering of financial assets to assist in such endeavors had been generally sanctioned by the 1995 Civil Code, but not in specific terms. The growth of funds prompted the state to seek a more detailed regulatory environment that both encouraged the raising and use of charitable funds while maintaining some control over their structure and processes and some differentiation from for-profit activities.

While earlier legislation had begun to deal with associations, clubs and other such entities, no legislation had governed the rapid emergence of social and charitable funds after those entities had been recognized in the 1995 Civil Code. The government began to remedy that gap in 1999 with the promulgation of a decree regulating the organization and operation of social and charity funds. The 1999 Decree on Social and Charity Funds decree reflected the government's cautious encouragement of private charitable funding. It sought to limit fund operation to nonprofit purposes, to prevent them from drawing on government assets except for charitable activities, and to promote openness in their operations. State control – or at least the option of state control – was maintained by a requirement – as in all previous legislation on the topic – that funds be approved by a government agency, including three members who would carry legal responsibility for the fund's activities. The people's committees of provinces and centrally-administered municipalities were authorized to approve funds, with downward approval permitted to lower units (Decree 177 1999).

Funds were permitted to absorb both foreign and domestic donations, for receipt of foreign donations was an important goal of this legalization process. The decree required that each fund be governed by a "fund management board" and by designated staff. And a sort of inspectorate, the "fund control board," was required in each organization as well, a requirement that originated in early legislation and that the Ministry of Home Affairs would seek to carry forward into the Law on Associations.

Perhaps most importantly, the concept of dual governance was maintained: funds were subject both to state finance authorities and to "professional management of their operations by ... specialized [state] management agencies" (Decree 177 1999, Art. 16). The regulations also, of course, gave the state the authority to dissolve or suspend funds in its broad discretion "when it has seriously violated laws or infringed upon the State's and/or people's interests." Funds may be suspended for an even broader array of reasons, also maintaining exceptionally broad state discretion and authority. Administrative, civil and criminal sanctions are available to enforce this state authority (Phuc 2002).

The question of investment of fund assets was partly skirted in these early regulations. The Decree stipulated that funds may use revenue that includes "interest on deposits and other lawful revenues." Utilization of funds was limited to "financial support for programs and projects for humanitarian and charity purposes, [and] promoting ... cultural, sport, scientific and social development." Spending on "management activities" was limited to five percent of fund revenue (Decree 177 1999, Art. 14). These general provisions on social and charitable funds were recodified in the 2004 Civil Code.

THE DECREE ON THE ORGANIZATION, OPERATION AND MANAGEMENT OF ASSOCIATIONS AND IMPLEMENTING REGULATIONS

As the drafting of a Law on Associations continued to drag on for over a decade, the Vietnamese authorities decided in 2001/2002 to promulgate a decree governing the organization and management of associations both to govern the burgeoning sector and to preview and test the approaches and provisions that might be utilized in a full law. Decree 88 on the Management of Associations, promulgated by the government in July 2003 on the basis of drafting undertaken by the Ministry of Home Affairs, provided the new framework for associational activities – and has helped to create growing conflict between the control orientation of the ministry and the increasingly strong efforts of national associations to maintain distance from government ministries (Decree 88 2003).

The 2003 Decree on Associations, like all earlier legislation, explicitly excluded the mass organizations under the Party from its scope. These organizations – the Vietnam Fatherland Front, Labor Confederation, Ho Chi Minh Communist Youth League, Vietnam Peasants Association, Vietnam War Veterans Association, and the Vietnam Women's Union – have long been governed directly by the Party and by their own statutes. The Party and state are considerably less concerned about managing the few but important mass organizations than the thousands of emerging associations and social organizations, though increasingly powerful national associations now complain openly of the special treatment accorded to the traditional mass organizations. The 2003 Decree on Associations defined associations broadly as "voluntary organizations of citizens, Vietnamese organizations of the same professions, the same avocations, the same gender, with the common purpose of gathering and uniting their members, conducting regular activities, seeking to protect the legitimate rights and interests of their members, supporting each other in effective activities, contributing to the nation's economic and social development, which are organized and conduct their activities in accordance with this Decree and other relevant legal documents."

Under the Decree, various kinds of associations may be established with the approval of state agencies at the local, provincial or national level. They must not have "purposes or activities that violate the law," a broad term that retains flexibility and discretion for state action, and they must have charters and designated offices to enable the state to find and regulate them. Specific requirements for associational charters are provided.

These reasonably stringent establishment and registration requirements have not been substantially weakened from previous legislation or in practice. But in a concession to demands from the associational sector, the establishment requirements have been paired with a requirement, long urged by officials in social organizations and some government officials, that the examining state agencies must issue receipts for such applications, reply to the petition if it is "complete" and "lawful" within sixty days, and provide "clear reasons" if the application is denied. In turn activists and more liberal officials failed to include a provision providing for automatic approval of associational applications if a decision is not communicated within the sixty-day time period, or a right to judicial appeal of administrative decisions. This complex drafting was a form of compromise that retains the approval (cho phep) system rather than moving toward a less discretionary registration system, but with at least a minor bow to the concerns of the associational sector.

At each stage the opportunity for state control is maintained under the 2003 Decree on Associations. Associations must have a "mobilization committee for establishing the association" that is subject to state approval, must hold a founding meeting with contents stipulated by the decree and subject to state approval, report on the results of that founding meeting within thirty days, and have their charters approved by relevant state agencies. State agencies retain the power to approve establishment, divide or separate associations, and merge, consolidate or dissolve them. The Ministry of Home Affairs would seek to retain all of these provisions at the next stage, the drafting of the formal Law on Associations; in turn many in the associational sector would seek to weaken some of these management and control mechanisms.

Under the 2003 Decree, associations are permitted, among other rights, to provide information on their goals and purposes, represent their members and protect their interests, organize and coordinate membership activities, provide "advice and criticism on matters within the association's scope of activities," contribute their views on drafts of laws and regulations, to raise funds, including from "business or services in accordance with the provisions of law" to provide funding for operations, and to receive "lawful support" from organizations and individuals at home and abroad. They are obligated, among other provisions, to submit to management by relevant state agencies, report on congresses, changes in officers, establishment of offices in other localities, file annual reports on organization and activities, submit to inspection and audit by relevant state agencies, "maintain funds received for the association's activities in accordance with the provisions of their Charters, and they may not disburse [such funds] to members," and make annual financial reports to the stipulated state agencies. Other provisions provide detailed rules on the division, separation, merger, consolidation and dissolution of associations, with a focus on ensuring that associational assets do not end up in the pockets of individuals.

The 2003 Decree on Associations reaffirms the primary role of the Ministry of Home Affairs in exercising "uniform management with respect to associations throughout the country." Ministries and other state agencies play a substantial management role as well in connection with the professional work of associations, part of the dual management structure that causes increasingly restive attitudes among national associations. Violations of the decree are subject to administrative, civil and criminal sanctions depending on the type of violation and its severity.

Six months after Decree 88 was promulgated, the Ministry of Home Affairs issued implementing regulations under the Decree. The implementing regulations provided detail on such issues as the number of members required for the "mobilization committee for establishing the association"; the required contents of the applications to found an association; dual regulation of associations by state and provincial agencies with specific line responsibility in areas of associational specialization (i.e. state health agencies providing professional management of health associations); the required number of signatures necessary to establish associations at each level; and cumbersome procedures for the approval of associational charters (Circular 1 2004).

TOWARD A LAW ON ASSOCIATIONS

The 2003 Decree on Associations was promulgated both to provide some order in the burgeoning world of Vietnamese associations and to serve as an experiment for the future drafting and promulgation of a national Law on Associations (*Luat ve Hoi*). Drafting of the Law on Associations gathered steam once again in 2002 and 2003. In 2003, the Legislative Work Commission of the National Assembly convened a symposium on comparative experience in drafting nonprofit (associational) law with the Vietnam Association for the Handicapped, attended by members of the drafting committee for the Law on Associations and a senior officer of the National Assembly. This was one of a number of research and drafting meetings that accelerated in 2003, 2004, and 2005.

In a review of this stage of the drafting process, the National Assembly pointed out that

> although [the Law on Associations] had been included in the legislative work programme ... for the Ninth Session of the National Assembly (1995), up until now we have not yet promulgated any law that details the formation of associations – which is one of the fundamental rights of citizens provided in the Constitution. We might say that this is a difficult law ... Moreover, the ... development of associations and social organizations in Vietnam is very complex [in keeping with] the level of social development. So new factors in the sphere of associations and social organizations continue to appear.

The meeting re-emphasized the importance of developing a Law on Associations and its relationship to other pending legislation, with a dual emphasis on "affirming the role of the Party as laid down in Article 4 of the Constitution," "ensuring citizens' rights to form association, and fostering citizens' democratic and creative spirit." One delaying factor in the law has been the drafters' (and National Assembly's) desire to enact a detailed law that "does not require [frequent] amendments of guidance and implementation documents ... consistent with the new policy on lawmaking of the National Assembly of Vietnam."

The discussion also came to "broad unity" on the "principle of nondistribution of assets within associations and social organizations, and that such a non-benefit principle must be emphasized in the future drafting of the Law on Associations. There was general agreement that the future Law should include professional, social, funding, clubs, charitable and other such organizations, but not political, religious or trade union groups, and perhaps not the six major mass organizations that have traditionally reported to and been governed directly by the Vietnamese Communist Party.

After a lengthy process of drafting a Law on Associations to govern the formation, management, supervision, operations, internal structure, funding and other aspects of the work of Vietnamese associations and other social organizations, the eighth draft of the Law on Associations (*Luat ve Hoi*) was released by the Office of the Government in Hanoi in December 2005 for comment, setting off a firestorm of reaction from national associations representing intellectuals and business sectors. But the bitter debate on the Law on Associations has earlier roots that are important to identify.

Decree 88 on Associations (2003) had been regarded by the Vietnamese associational sector as unnecessarily restrictive and limiting, both in its dual management and control structure and in the related difficulty of effecting approval and registration through line ministries and the Ministry of Home Affairs. At the same time, however, business, professional and intellectual associations were pushing for legal verification of their status and the status of hundreds of associations around Vietnam.

After numerous discussions and eight drafts, what emerged was a draft law that retained many of the most criticized elements of Decree 88 and earlier drafts. These included the retention of the dual management and control structure of line ministries and the Ministry of Home Affairs; a complex, lengthy, two stage system for the formation of associations and other social organizations that was now termed "registration" rather than "approval" (*cho phep*) but retained most of the characteristics of the 1957 and 2003 approval systems. Six key Party-related mass organizations were also excluded from the Law, prompting fierce calls from other national associations for equal treatment and the inclusion of the mass organizations in the draft Law.

Several key questions emerged for discussion on the official draft Law on Associations. First, how would the state "manage" or "administer" the associational sector under the framework of the new Law on Associations? The draft Law and its successors provided for a sort of dual management structure in which (for associations at the national level), the Home Ministry would manage the sector in terms of organization on behalf of the government, and government "ministries and ministerial-level agencies shall be responsible for . . . state management of the activities of associations operating in the sectors for which such ministries are responsible." (At the provincial level, the draft Law provided for management of the association sector by the People's Committees of provinces and directly-administered municipalities.)

This dual management formulation at the national level (management of associations by both the Ministry of Home Affairs and ministries) has produced substantial controversy in the national associational sector, which understands the need for Home Ministry administration but disagrees on the role of line ministries. For its part, the Home Ministry prefers to maintain a role for the ministries, but indicates that the role envisioned is somewhat different from the "*bo chu quan*" or "ministry-in-charge" relationship of the past. For its part, the Vietnamese Union of Science and Technology Associations (VUSTA) and other national associations disagree that the new formulation is, in substance, different from the past, but merely a rerendering in legal terms, and they are concerned that the formulation, if maintained in the final law as adopted, would reinvigorate their subordinate relationship to government ministries that has been fading in recent years.

A second key debate raged on the "scope" of the Law – and, in particular, whether six key Vietnamese mass organizations will be subject to the Law on Associations, or outside its scope. These six organizations are the Vietnam Fatherland Front, Vietnam Labor Confederation, Ho Chi Minh Communist Youth League, Vietnam Farmers Association, Vietnam War Veterans Association, and the Vietnam Women's Union. The Home Ministry was prepared to bring this issue to the National Assembly for discussion on two alternatives: excluding the six mass organizations from the scope and coverage of the Law, or including five of them with the exception of the Fatherland Front.[1]

KEY REMAINING ISSUES FOR A LAW ON ASSOCIATIONS

There have been a number of other issues and debates in the drafting of a Law on Associations for Vietnam. The draft Law on Associations provides for *registration of associations* through a complex multi-staged process that largely tracks the complex procedure that has been utilized in the 2003 Decree 88 on Associations. That highly cumbersome process that requires at least two submissions by the association to the relevant state authority and at least two approvals by the relevant state authority, and could take more than 180 days to form an association through all of these steps. And the official draft law provided few guidelines or limitations on discretion of the relevant state authority in rejecting an application or at other points in the exercise of state discretion, nor an opportunity to appeal or to seek judicial resolution of such complaints. Nor does the draft Law provide effective guidelines or limitations on the exercise of state discretion in the application process, other than requiring an application receipt and providing time limits for state action. This cumbersome and discretionary process, and the continued reliance on approval mechanisms even if now termed registration, caused substantial opposition from national associations and other social organizations. They demanded a single system of state management under the Ministry of Home Affairs, and a simplified formation and registration process that did not cede as much approval authority to that Ministry and line ministries.

Geographic restrictions on registration of associations have also proven a problem. The draft Law on Associations, like earlier regulation and earlier legislation in China, provides that an association may "not have a ... main field of operation with other associations ... legally established in the same local territory," a highly restrictive provision that discourages multiple associations to serve the people and social development (and to compete with each other to provide good services or other activities).

Government management of associations remains a key division point between the government and the associational sector, and even within the government as well. The official draft Law provides that in addition to the Ministry of Home Affairs overall management of associations on behalf of the government, line ministries and agencies will also exercise control of associations within their work domains. This dual management and control structure replicates earlier legal structures, including the oft-criticized 2003 Decree on Associations. It has been strongly criticized by national associations and other commentators, and stoutly defended by the Ministry of Home Affairs as necessary for the management of the sector. In 2006 and 2007 it remained a key controversy in completing the Law on Associations.

The prohibited purposes and activities of associations is another point of division. The draft Law on Associations defines "prohibited activities" very broadly and in ways that give significant, largely unfettered discretion in interpretation and enforcement. In language similar to the 2003 Decree 88 on Associations, the draft Law prohibits "illegal activities which jeopardize the legitimate interest of organizations, individuals and communities, and the great unity of the entire people, [or which] violate national security [or] social order and safety" (Art. 8); prohibits associational names that "conflict with the national tradition, culture, and ethical and moral practices" (Art. 11); and includes a further broad prohibition on "illegal activities which jeopardize the great unity of the entire people of Viet Nam [or] national security [or] social order," subject to criminal or administrative sanctions.

The associational sector criticized such provisions as overbroad, internally contradictory and confusing. And they appear to allow no opportunity to challenge state decisions, either in the administrative or judicial realm. And one might therefore expect the dueling draft prepared by specialists associated with the Vietnamese Union of Science and Technology Associations to prohibit a narrower range of activities and to provide for less state discretion in applying such principles. Yet the VUSTA draft also gave the state broad discretion to prohibit associational purposes and activities. In a tactical concession to the Party and state, the alternative draft tracks the relatively broad formulation of organizations and acts that the state may prohibit contained in the 1966 Convention on Social and Political Rights, arguably even providing for greater state discretion in this area.

The draft Law permitted associations to conduct (in one translation) "advocacy on its objectives" or, in a perhaps more accurate translation of the Vietnamese text, "to publicize the objectives of the association." This limited scope for *advocacy and participation in public affairs* has been criticized by opponents of the draft law, and the alternative draft provides a broader scope for such work.

A significant problem in many nonprofit law drafting processes is whether the state allows associations and other nonprofits to engage in income producing activities – and, if income producing activities are allowed, what kinds are allowed. For example, must income producing activities be related to the nonprofit mission of the association? The draft Law on Associations is vague on this issue, an increasingly important concern for social organizations in Vietnam as they struggle to raise revenue for their work. The draft Law permits associations to engage in "raising funds from membership fees and other sources of revenue in accordance with the law" and speaks of "legitimate revenues gained from the Association's activities" (Arts. 39, 55, 56). It remains unclear, even in the eighth draft, whether associations are allowed to engage in revenue producing activities, and, if so, of what kinds. The alternative VUSTA draft was somewhat more flexible, though still vague, in treatment of income. This issue is complicated because the draft Law also contemplates that associations can establish "affiliated legal entities" (*phap nhan thuoc hoi*) (Art. 37). But it is not clear whether such entities are intended primarily to produce revenue (regardless of their legal form), rather than providing services or associational activities. If so, there is a very significant danger that associations will be formed primarily to take advantage of the formation of "affiliated legal entities" that will produce revenue under an associational "umbrella," thereby, in effect, providing an advantaged "cover" for business activities. This has occurred in a number of other countries.

The draft Law on Associations virtually ignored the tax issues that become increasingly important for nonprofit sector development as national prosperity increases, focusing instead on issues of registration and governance. This is consistent with early drafting in a number of other developing countries (Irish et al 2004). The late 2005 submission draft of the Law on Associations provided only that "those associations that work for humanitarian and charity purposes or for public interest shall enjoy preferential tax rates according to the Law" (Art. 57). The alternative VUSTA draft was slightly more specific, and introduces the concept of special privileges for public benefit organizations.

Issues such as minimum capital requirements or norms for associations are used in some nations to restrict sector entry by nonprofits. And in some countries nonprofits are required to spend a minimum proportion of their assets or income each year on their social or charitable activities, are permitted to invest in only limited investment vehicles (i.e. cash and state bonds), and are restricted in the use of their investment returns. Often there are restrictions on fundraising by domestic nonprofit organizations. The official draft Law on Associations did not impose minimum capital requirements on associations and other organizations, nor did it require them to spend a minimum portion of their assets or income on charitable activities, nor does it limit investment vehicles. The draft Law recognized "donation[s] from domestic and foreign individuals and organizations" as a key source of revenue for associations, and does not restrict that fundraising in the Law. But other Vietnamese regulations detail a range of approval requirements for fundraising from foreign sources, and the alternative VUSTA draft is considerably more flexible on permitted fundraising (Sidel and Vasavakul 2006).

In recent years, governance and accountability have emerged as key issues in state-nonprofit relations. The governance issues – sometimes detailed in nonprofit codes, sometimes in other legislation – include: statutory requirements for organizational governance such as the duties and meetings of the governing board; criteria or requirements for management, and approval of specific organizational activities; regulations on personal benefit to board members or employees; and rules on the handling of violations of internal or external governance requirements by administrative agencies or the courts.

Accountability issues center on the question of to whom associations are accountable – the government, society, their members, their donors, or others? Are tax returns or other government filings required for all organizations, or certain organizations with a certain minimum turnover or donations? Are there special accountability requirements for associations dealing in foreign funds? Must government filings, annual reports or other organizational reports be disclosed to the public or published? And are there well-understood, consistent accounting standards applicable to associations? Finally, nonprofit or associational self-regulation has emerged as a significant point of attention in recent years, including the use of codes of conduct, accreditation ranking or rating systems, or other self-disciplinary systems – to protect the sector from increasing state regulation, to improve standards and professionalism in the sector, or for mixed or other purposes. In a number of countries governments are now actively supporting, encouraging or partnering in such self-regulation initiatives.

The official draft Law on Associations provided a reasonably complete set of basic requirements for associations' charters (bylaws), and for basic governance requirements that cover the organizational structure (consisting of the general meeting, management board, inspectorate board and other bodies defined by the association's charter); very limited meeting requirements; elections of officers and board members; voting; duties and responsibilities of the board and chairperson and inspectorate board; limited reporting responsibilities; and the rights and duties of associations.

The draft Law generally stipulated that associations must operate on a "not-for-profit" basis, and "not-for-profit" is defined as "not to work for profit in order to distribute among the members of the Association." But the draft Law was insufficiently clear that leaders or members of associations are not permitted to derive personal benefits from their roles in associations, and insufficiently defines personal benefit, which may include compensation. There are dangers that if associations are permitted to carry out revenue producing activities, leaders or members may take a portion of those revenues as compensation, a form of commission-based compensation that can encourage associations to pursue revenue-producing activities over their mission-based activities. The alternative VUSTA draft did not go much further in restricting personal benefits and compensation.

Associations can be accountable to the state, to society, to their members, to donors, to others. Under the current draft Law, Vietnamese associations would be almost entirely accountable to the state, with very strong accountability mechanisms directed toward government – and relatively few methods of ensuring accountability toward society, members or donors. The Law's emphasis on "state administration" re-emphasized accountability toward the state, particularly the host of state approval requirements. There is brief mention of "openness" and "transparency" (*cong khai, minh bach*), which may imply broader accountability to the public, but no specifics. These are important principles of accountability to society and the public as well as to the state, but there are very few legal provisions in the draft Law that give any substantial force to the requirement of "openness" and "transparency" (Sidel and Vasavakul 2006)

The only forms of accountability to the public, members or donors were considerably more limited in the draft Law. Associations would be required to publish an announcement of their establishment in public newspapers (Art. 18), a very limited form of public accountability. Associations were required to hold membership meetings, but the draft Law did not seem to require that they be held each year, or that such meetings must be public. More serious accountability to members (as well as to society and donors) would require public annual meetings. An inspectorate board is contemplated, a beginning effort at accountability to members.

The draft Law provided for annual reports of associations, requiring that the association's annual report be open to members. But there appears to be no requirement that annual reports be available to the general public, as they should be. In some countries associations are even required to publish versions of their annual reports in the newspapers, or on the Internet, and Vietnam could reasonably require the same for larger associations and other nonprofits, as well as other forms of public, member and donor accountability. The draft Law did not provide for accounting standards in any way, stipulating only that associations "shall be subject to the relevant regulations on accounting" (Art. 38(10)); and that "the Government shall provide specific regulations on financial policy of associations" (Art. 57(2)). And there appeared to be no provisions for handling violations of accountability requirements in the draft Law, particularly those few accountability requirements that imply accountability to society, members, and donors (Sidel and Vasavakul 2006).

In mid-December 2005, this debate reached a point previously unknown in modern Vietnamese legislative history, when a team of specialists convened and supported by the Vietnamese Union of Science and Technology Associations drafted their own alternative Law on Associations in response to the difficulty in forcing changes in the official draft. That alternative bill reached its fifth draft by mid-January 2006; it was the first time in modern Vietnamese history that opposition to a government-drafted law had reached a level that a "rebellious" alternative law was presented for discussion.

The VUSTA alternative draft provided alternative approaches on virtually every question under debate. The alternative draft would provide a simplified procedure for forming and registering associations that is much closer to a registration (*dang ky*) model than an approval (*cho phep*) model, and a single system of state management (Home Ministry at the national level; People's Committees at the level of provinces and below), with specified roles for state management; a reporting mechanism for associations; differentiates among associations (registered and unregistered; public benefit and not). The VUSTA draft also made specific provisions for the legal treatment of "unions" or "federations" of associations like VUSTA, would initiate a national register of associations, broaden the rights of associations, particularly relating to advocacy and participation in public affairs, introduced the concept of particular privileges for a category of public benefit organizations, and, in procedural terms, at multiple points in the draft provided more time limits for administrative action and greater opportunities to challenge administrative action (VUSTA 2006; Can 2006; Sidel and Vasavakul 2006).

FIGHTING FOR CIVIL SOCIETY?: THE CONFLICT OVER NONPROFIT LAW IN VIETNAM

The debate over the Vietnamese Law on Associations illuminates conflicts that have plagued the relationship between the state and the associational sector in both China and Vietnam. In China, the Party and state have managed these conflicts by retaining control through a variety of mechanisms – including dual management structures, approval mechanisms for a range of nonprofit activities, and other measures – while permitting the sector to expand rapidly to fulfill pressing needs in Chinese society. In Vietnam, the rapidly emerging strength of the business, trade and professional sector, represented most clearly by the Vietnam Union of Scientific and Technological Associations (VUSTA) and the Vietnam Chamber of Commerce and Industry (VCCI), sparked a major conflict in late 2005 and 2006 over the extent and scope of governmental control over the emerging associational sector. That conflict went further, in legislative terms, than has occurred in China: in Vietnam, it resulted in the drafting of the alternative Law on Associations discussed in this chapter, and the threat to seek to bring that alternative draft law to the floor of Vietnam's National Assembly.

Like the debate on "motorbike constitutionalism," between Hanoi municipal officials and the owners of motorbikes in one of Vietnam's most prosperous cities, this is in part a conflict among elites. Here large and increasingly powerful associations representing Vietnam's business and intellectual elites seek to protect their autonomy from a state that attempts to use modes of management regarded as a legacy of the past – particularly the "dual management" of a Ministry of Home Affairs and a line ministry. The state's opponents here cannot be ignored, nor, like rural peasants or ethnic minorities, can they be suppressed in the interests of national policy. The Party and state need both centralized modes of control, but also the initiative and autonomy that business organizations and intellectuals bring to the reform process. All this comes together in the battle over the Law on Associations.

The results, however, will likely not be so momentous. As in China, Vietnam is likely to come to a compromise that allows for both a level of control that satisfies the Party and state, and a level of autonomy that temporarily satisfies powerful associational actors while allowing for some flexible expansion in the future. Of perhaps more import for the future – though little discussed in 2005 and 2006 – is how these debates and compromises may affect smaller and weaker community-based organizations that may seek to defend the economic and other rights of forces less powerful than large companies and Hanoi and Saigon-based intellectuals. If the result of the debates in 2005 and

2006 is that control is applied more flexibly to the large and powerful business and intellectual actors and more rigorously to less powerful community groups, then these battles may need to be fought again in the future.

NOTE

1. Religious organizations are also excluded from the scope and coverage of the draft Law, but this does not appear to have caused any significant comment or discussion.

CHAPTER 7

TESTING THE LIMITS OF ADVOCACY: THE EMERGENCE OF PUBLIC INTEREST LAW IN VIETNAM

There was no sympathy among the Vietnamese public for the godfather of Saigon, Truong Nam Cam. Nam Cam, whose name also means "Five Orange" in Vietnamese, was the most feared man in Ho Chi Minh City for over a decade – the chieftain of Saigon's largest organized crime enterprise and a murderer, extortionist, purveyor of forced prostitution and gambling, and corruptor of Vietnamese officials up to the highest levels of the Vietnamese Communist Party and government. Virtually without dissent, Vietnamese believed that the godfather of Saigon should be executed, and they believed that only corrupt protection from senior political officials had enabled him to remain in power so long.

But during Nam Cam's 2003 trial in Saigon, and even after several years of increasingly active defense representation of criminal clients, private lawyers hired by several prominent defendants surprised the court and the prosecution with their energetic and sometimes defiant arguments for their clients. They argued that the prosecution had not proven key elements of its case against both gang members and allegedly corrupted high officials. And they demanded that the traditionally powerful state prosecution service withdraw or reduce some of the charges, or that the traditionally weak court find defendants not guilty, in a trial in which judicial independence had been perceived to have been compromised from the beginning.

Angry prosecutors, unaccustomed to zealous representation in such high profile cases or challenges to their authority, retaliated by threatening criminal sanctions or disbarment against the lawyers. The

Vietnamese press, blanketing the most prominent trial in modern Vietnamese history but well aware of its foregone conclusions, leapt on the lawyers' activism as one of the few new developments in the case. Faced with active and favorable press coverage, prosecutors eventually backed down from their threats of sanction against the defense lawyers. The main defendants represented by active counsel were still convicted, but in several cases received reduced sentences at least partly as a result of their representation. And, perhaps most importantly, a new vision for lawyering continued to make inroads into Vietnamese law and public perception – the lawyer as an active force in representation, not merely the agent of dominant prosecutors and weak judges (Quang and Steiner 2005; Quang 2007).

Active client representation in prominent criminal cases, as well as the emergence of lawyering for the public interest, the strengthening of legal aid services, a new focus on increased access to justice for Vietnam's poor, rural peasants, and minorities, and the fitful emergence of clinical law programs are aspects of a shift underway in Vietnamese law now two decades after Vietnam's reforms began and the Vietnamese Communist Party began a long and cautious process of raising the profile of law in Vietnamese society. Lawyers and legal scholars in Vietnam have not settled on a term for these developments – public interest law; access to justice; law and social justice; law and social equality. But these concerns are clearly increasing in activity and prominence, as they are in China.

A number of factors help account for the rise, albeit a cautious rise, of public interest law and activist lawyering in Vietnam over the past several years. Law has become increasingly complex – a dizzying array of thousands of legal documents in dozens of forms have been enacted, promulgated, revised or released in the last two decades, by agencies that range from the Communist Party and Vietnam's legislature, the National Assembly, all the way down to townships at the village level. Much of this law is exceptionally difficult to understand – layered rapidly on earlier documents, often in both complex and highly general language – and difficult to access. Legal information sources have been improved in recent years, including a strengthened national gazette and online legal information services, but they are generally available only to legal professionals and still, at times, only in major cities. Access to justice is more and more difficult and expensive as law itself multiplies in complexity.

In substantive terms, there has perhaps never been a greater public need for zealous legal defense in Vietnam. Though prosperity has come to many in Vietnam and the nation is largely stable, peasants in the countryside lose their land to officials and developers; citizens are swindled by criminals working in concert with officials; shoddy products explode and leak; citizens object to administrative decisions made by government officials and now have legal processes through which to voice some of those objections; and corruption is, by all reports, truly omnipresent in Vietnamese everyday life at every level of government and economic and social activity. Vietnamese citizens need legal representation as never before – whether they are objecting to governmental or private action, or seeking to defend themselves against legal charges.

The new public interest law in Vietnam is emerging cautiously and with clear political limits. A legal aid system intended to help poor citizens, war veterans and their families, national minorities and others to access an increasingly complex legal system has taken shape and is now active in Hanoi, Ho Chi Minh City, and most of Vietnam's provinces. A few foreign aid donors – major contributors to the reform of the Vietnamese legal system over the past two decades – have belatedly begun to work on the substantial problem of access to justice that many Vietnamese citizens face, and to struggle to find programmatic means to address this difficult issue. Activist lawyers represent high officials accused of corruption and other crimes, poor defendants, occasionally political and religious dissidents. And these activist lawyers have even sought to establish an independent group to defend innocents already convicted and take part in other controversial cases. Vietnamese law schools are very gradually becoming interested in public interest law, and in some cases seeking to establish clinical programs or establish "law clubs" that help rural residents assert their rights.

For the most part, these developments have been unrelated to the prominent activities of foreign donors, who have long played a substantial role in Vietnam's economic reforms. The donors – led by the United Nations Development Programme (UNDP), the Swedish International Development Agency (SIDA), the Danish International Development Agency (DANIDA), other donors, and in recent years, the US Agency for International Development – have long over-emphasized structural and institutional assistance to Vietnam's law-related ministries and national legislature, and in more recent years the harmonization of Vietnamese law with international standards to meet the requirements of the US–Vietnam Bilateral Trade Agreement and the entry criteria for the

World Trade Organization. In both these capacity-building and legal harmonization activities, donors have substantially emphasized economic law, generally at the insistence of Vietnamese leaders and central institutions, to assist Vietnam in its transition to a market economy and integration with regional and international markets. With several occasional and notable exceptions, the donors have largely deferred the rising issues of access to justice and the need for law to protect the public interest and individual rights in a system characterized by rapid marketizing change and extensive corruption.

The result is two fold. On one side we can see unbalanced legal reform driven by urban officials based in Hanoi and Ho Chi Minh City and generously funded by foreign donors that focuses almost entirely on institutional development and formal processes of lawmaking and adjudication at the central level; and the harmonization of economic law with international norms. But a new phenomenon is emerging: legal reform without donors and watched by a sometimes nervous Party and government, most prominently characterized by activist lawyers, along with a growing legal aid system that has potential to become somewhat more activist while remaining under state control. This new phenomenon – the cautious and controlled rise of public interest law in Vietnam – is fueled and motivated by a growing understanding that the new legal system under construction in Vietnam may be effectively serving central institutional needs and economic integration, but is increasingly failing to provide access to justice and legal services for Vietnam's poor and weaker sectors of the population. This chapter analyzes those developments in six areas – legal aid; activist lawyering and zealous representation; the organization of public interest lawyers and the state's response; clinical legal education; access to justice; and the role of legal reformers in legislative development.

LEGAL AID

Legal aid in Vietnam has its origins in and is tied to the Party and state, but has recorded some initial successes. From the beginning, the Party and state have conferred multiple and sometimes overlapping responsibilities on legal aid. Legal aid is intended to help citizens with their increasing entanglements in civil, economic, and criminal law, to provide legal representation in a host of cases, and, in some cases to help in the protection of rights vis-à-vis other private parties or the state. At the same time legal aid was also intended to help "propagate" and explain the law, undertake mass legal education, and spread legal literacy. And all this work was intended primarily to benefit some of the most vulnerable groups in Vietnamese society, groups without significant representation or hope for private legal representation, including the war wounded and the families of dead soldiers, ethnic minorities, the rural and urban poor, elderly single people, the disabled, and domestic violence and trafficking victims.

These overlapping, at times even conflicting responsibilities have led to difficulties in building and expanding a legal aid system. But some impressive basic work has been accomplished under the leadership of the National Legal Aid Agency in the Ministry of Justice. Beginning in 1997, the Ministry of Justice and local justice bureaus began to develop a network of legal aid centers and activities throughout Vietnam (Decision 734 1997; Binh Dinh Legal Aid Centre 2003; Legal Documents on Legal Aid 2003). By late 2004, the legal aid system had extended from the National Legal Aid Agency in Hanoi to provincial legal aid centers in each of Vietnam's 64 provincial and metropolitan centers (Bao Phap Luat 2004), and, at least in some form over 800 local centers. Despite this impressive development in seven years, Vietnam's national legal aid director terms legal aid "still far from the grassroots" and there is a widespread sense that citizens closest to the grassroots are not yet being fully served (NOVIB 2004).

By the end of 2002, legal aid workers had assisted in 81,973 cases at the provincial level and 673 cases at the national level, and in that year the National Legal Aid Agency founded a pilot legal aid program targeted at women. By the end of 2003, the National Legal Aid Agency had assisted in some 1,013 cases, and the provincial centers in 125,025 more. Toward the end of 2004, the legal aid system had assisted in over 400,000 cases (Bao Phap Luat 2004). The expansion of legal aid is the most impressive program in securing access to justice in Vietnam since the reform era began.

But, as is the case in virtually all such programs to provide legal services, significant problems remain. They include:

Difficulties in outreach to specially targeted groups and the work conditions for legal aid lawyers and offices

The original 1997 statute establishing the legal aid system and all policy documents since have stipulated that legal aid was intended to emphasize service to war wounded and the families of dead soldiers, ethnic minorities, the rural and urban poor, elderly single people, the disabled, and domestic violence and trafficking victims. But in Vietnam as elsewhere, serving those target groups has often been complex and difficult. In 2002, for example, the Vietnamese Peasants Association estimated that 90 percent of Vietnamese peasants need some form of legal assistance. "The system of legal aid has not yet taken shape in a broad network, and it does not yet widely and deeply reflect the strata" of Vietnamese society, partly because "the authorized staff of legal aid centers is limited, and they are short of funds for activities." And where government institutions do not handle peasants' complaints effectively and in a timely manner, and the government has not explained the law effectively, "that can lead to long . . . legal disputes" (VnExpress 2002c).

The well-organized network of legal aid offices appears to end largely at the provincial level. Nearly 800 local offices have also been set up, but they are plagued by lack of support from local Party and state institutions, and a shortage of personnel, facilities, materials, and access (Bao Phap Luat 2004). In many cases, private lawyers who might support legal aid are not present at the rural grassroots level, and younger graduates will not practice at the local level. And – again a problem not limited to Vietnam – Vietnamese legal aid lawyers are paid little, often making only a quarter or less of their private counterparts (VnExpress 2004g).

Interference with legal aid lawyers

Restrictive judicial and lawyers regulations limit the ability of legal aid attorneys to represent their clients in court and to have access to clients in prison. As with private defense lawyers, legal aid lawyers have often been prevented from meeting clients upon arrest, taking part in cases during the investigation (pre-charge) phase; accessing investigatory documents or indictments; having access to clients at various stages of litigation; interviewing witnesses; presenting evidence in court; and other limitations. The legal aid authorities hope that the new Law on Legal Aid will help resolve some of these difficulties by specifying some of the rights of legal aid attorneys – and legal aid lawyers should also benefit to some degree from the specification of lawyers rights that is expected to emerge in the forthcoming Law on Lawyers.

The peril of bountiful donors?

Welcome and hearty assistance from foreign donors for legal aid has strengthened the National Legal Aid Agency in the central Ministry of

Justice in Hanoi as well as some provincial legal aid centers and some local legal aid offices. This assistance, the first major work explicitly to focus on access to justice in Vietnam by the international donor community, has been led by the Danish International Development Agency (DANIDA, also working through the Danish Institute for Human Rights); NOVIB (Oxfam Netherlands); the Swedish International Development Agency (SIDA); and the Swiss Agency for Development and Cooperation (SDC). Donor work is certainly welcomed – and it is important that the donors work on issues of social justice and access to justice – but donor support has also contributed to unequal development of legal aid services around the country.

For foreign donors, legal aid was the first and primary method available for addressing issues of rights protection and access to justice in the late 1990s and throughout this decade thus far, devoting tens of millions of dollars to the development of legal aid in Vietnam. As a result, foreign donors may have made funds available in amounts that may have exceeded capacity to absorb, and perhaps without sufficient coordination. Some improvement in that chaotic foreign funding process began in the early part of this decade, when the National Legal Aid Agency and its key donors met and formed a joint framework agreement on donor support for legal aid in Vietnam.

But more importantly, the opening of legal aid as virtually the sole channel for foreign donor interest in rights and access to justice, and the unavailability of other, non-governmental channels for the most part, has resulted in effective Party and state control over foreign donor interest in rights and access to justice. The result has been little or no donor investment in other ways of protecting rights and ensuring access to justice, such as work with law schools; support for public interest law nongovernmental organizations or firms; support for groups of citizens challenging state or private decisions; or other means of addressing rights and access to justice. Legal aid is certainly worthy of support, but it is only one piece of a broad-based approach to rights protection and access to justice. It should certainly not be the only donor window for work on these issues. But for too long support for legal aid has been the foreign donor community's only investment in rights protection and access to justice, leading to complacency in the donor community, an exaggerated sense of the importance of legal aid and of its successes in Vietnam, and highly effective Party and state control over the channeling of donor flows for particular sorts of state-dominated approaches to rights and access to justice.

THE ROAD AHEAD FOR LEGAL AID

The hopes of Party, government, and lawyers for a resolution of some of these difficult issues rest at least partly in the emergence of the Law on Legal Aid, which went into effect on January 1, 2007. It is not unique to Vietnam to misplace hopes for resolving political, bureaucratic, budgetary and other problems in a statutory document, though it is a particularly common feature in the Vietnamese legal reform landscape. But commentaries in the Vietnamese press by knowledgeable legal aid officials and others regularly reflect hope that the Law can help address lack of access to courts; interference by prosecutors and judges; lack of staff, facilities, and budgets for legal aid; the responsibilities and benefits to be accorded to a new form of "legal aid attorney" that does not exist under current regulation; and even the need to more effectively serve its target populations (Bao Phap Luat 2004). Yet those issues may not be directly susceptible to legislative solution, and in fact the Law on Legal Aid may only be able to establish a policy framework for addressing these problems. That is by itself no small accomplishment, and perhaps further progress can be made from there.

But these solutions do not address the key, long-term issue facing Party- and state-sponsored legal aid in Vietnam. Can legal aid effectively fulfill all its Party- and state-assigned tasks – to explain and propagate law and mediation; to represent clients in a wide range of actions involving private parties and the state; and, in certain cases, directly to challenge the state in representing the rights of clients against Party and state institutions? The current balance appears weighted heavily toward education and advice rather than toward direct rights protection, a result of over-tasking, under-resourcing, substantial public need, and perhaps Party and state intent.

Rights protection in Vietnam often appears to have a state-oriented purpose, which effectively means protection of the state in addition to, or rather than, the protection of individual rights. According to Minister of Justice Uong Chu Luu and the Director of the National Legal Aid Agency, Ta Thi Minh Ly, legal aid should not only help to "protect the lawful rights and interests of the poor and other [social] policy priority groups, and ensure justice for each stratum" of society. "[I]t is not only the people who gain, but the state also benefits substantially, for when people have understood the law then the phenomenon of

'indiscriminate' complaints is reduced, and defendants ... do not continue to mindlessly appeal their cases" (Bao Phap Luat 2004).

The complexity of the legal aid system and the issues surroun-
ding it led the Party to issue a document titled *Viewpoints of the
Party on Legal Aid Work* in September 2005 (Communist Party 2005a).
In commentary signed by the Deputy Secretary of the Party group
for internal affairs in the Party Central Committee – a senior and
centrally-placed official – the Party reiterated in strong terms that "legal
aid is first and foremost the duty of Party organizations and state agencies," and that Party and state officials must "overcome the passive
thinking of depending on social organizations, elected officials or an
ideology of patronage in which aid work is done by oneself ... 'kind-
hearted,' 'humanitarian' assistance." Closely related is a second point
firmly reiterated by the Party – that "political stability" must be ensured
in legal aid work. Legal aid must "not run counter to the Party's line and
policies." And the Party explained in strong terms: "In some places, there
is a phenomenon of abusing democracy and complaints; some dissatisfied
or negative elements have dragged and aroused the people to struggle ...
with authorities in provocation over some 'hot points' to create political
disorder, weaken political and economic stability, and depart from the
Party's leadership" (Communist Party 2005a).

Yet, the Party also wrote, within these political boundaries legal aid
must also be "socialized" – which means that in addition to the primary
responsibility that Party and state offices have for legal aid, aid work
also "must be developed ... in political, social, professional organizations and in other forms ... in order for legal aid work to have the
highest effectiveness." Finally, the Party called for a renewed emphasis
on the original targets of legal aid – the "poor, other [social] policy
priority groups, compatriots in inland, remote regions, and compatriots
from minority nationalities" (Communist Party 2005a).

In 2006 and 2007, after a decade of rapid growth in legal aid, numerous
successes had been won and some problems remained. Vietnam's
legal aid agencies are more often the publicists and popularizers of
state law rather than the protectors of citizens' rights against powerful
private or state interests. So key questions will remain about the will of
the state to allow, and the ability of Vietnam's dedicated legal aid
practitioners to undertake, rights protection that would truly mark
them as public interest legal organizations. Truly zealous rights protection may be impossible in a legal aid system tasked with such contradictory responsibilities.

These contradictions, between serving state policy and assertively protecting citizens in their relationships with the state and private interests, certainly appear in other Vietnamese institutions that are equally tasked with contradictory duties.[1] If legal aid is unresponsive in the arena of rights protection, other individuals and lawyers will step up to provide those services. We already see evidence of that, as activist private lawyers have emerged outside the legal aid realm to defend clients' rights and asserting claims against the state outside the realm of legal aid, and even seeking to form a private public interest law organization to pursue such rights and claims.

LAWYERS AND THE LIMITS OF ADVOCACY

Perhaps it was inevitable that Vietnam's private bar would emerge as the primary challenger to the power of the Party, prosecutors and courts in the Vietnamese legal system, if only because no other significant force for advocacy has ever emerged. The seeds for the emergence of lawyer voices began in the early 1990s, when the state formally re-recognized the existence and functions of a private bar, including some limited representational rights in criminal and civil matters. But testing the limits of advocacy was not the task of Vietnam's lawyers in the first years of their activities, nor was zealous advocacy initially encouraged by the Ministry of Justice, the regulator of Vietnamese lawyers, and by the powerful, state-sponsored lawyers associations that license and manage the professional activities of lawyers.

Active defense representation seems to have developed rather slowly in Vietnam after the *doi moi* reforms began in 1986. As Quang and Steiner and other authors have pointed out, lawyers remained under relatively strict state and bar association control throughout the remainder of the 1980s and through the 1990s, primarily through the 1987 Ordinance on Lawyer Organization. The 2001 revised Ordinance on Lawyer Organization began to liberalize a wide array of restrictions on lawyers by widening the array of practice options (now including partnerships and limited forms of cooperation with foreign attorney as well as independent practice). An important Party document on legal reform issued in 2001 made general reference to the relatively new theme of "democratic adversarial proceeding" (*tranh tung dan chu*), though as Quang and Steiner point out this concept was neither defined in the Party document nor provision made for its implementation (Quang and Steiner 2005; Quang 2007).

One key line of division has been between lawyers and state prosecutors. Legal privilege and custom have long favored the prosecutors: in the early years of the resumption of defense practice, for example, lawyers had no right to participate in the investigation stage of criminal cases, and often could only meet with clients if police and prosecutors agreed. Defense lawyers have encountered serious difficulties in interviewing and representing clients (particularly at investigation stages); obtaining documents; interviewing witnesses, and a host of other areas. For years, according to Vietnamese lawyers, prosecutors in court sat at the level of judges while defense counsel sat below them, at the level of their clients. Police and the judiciary perpetuated these inequalities and mistreatment. It is little surprise that lawyers were among those seeking to limit the role and power of the procuracy during the 2001 Constitutional amendment debates on the public prosecutors.

But advances for lawyers have been made. The 2003 revision of the Criminal Procedure Code provided defense lawyers with the right to meet with clients during criminal investigations and represent those clients during investigation stages (Quang and Steiner 2005; Quang 2007). And increasingly lawyers became more active in representation at trial as well, sometimes challenging evidence and occasionally complaining that police used force or torture in obtaining confessions.

Even in the late 1990s and the early years of this decade there were inklings of change – more substantial representation of criminal and civil parties; objections to limits on representation; calls for the revision of the primary statute governing lawyers; and increasingly discussions with lawyers' associations on the appropriate role of the profession. Particularly assertive private lawyers stepped up the intensity of their representation of officials and family members accused of corruption, fraud and other crimes. In 1999, the assertive representation of one of Saigon's most prominent industrialists, Tang Minh Phung, and several associates on corruption and fraud charges involving hundreds of millions of dollars was the first time that increasingly zealous representation is said to have broken into public perceptions (Gainsborough 2003a; 2003b). Despite the active representation in that case, Phung and three others were sentenced to death in 1999 and executed in 2003. But it was in Vietnam's single most prominent legal proceeding since the reform process began in the mid-1980s, the trial of the godfather of Saigon, Nam Cam, and over 150 of his co-defendants, that advocacy by lawyers emerged as a significant force.

THE ASSERTION OF ADVOCACY AND ITS LIMITS IN
THE CASE OF THE "GODFATHER OF SAIGON"

For two decades Truong Van Cam (Nam Cam) ruled much of Saigon, though the casual western or even Vietnamese visitor would not have known it. He headed a large crime family that ran a significant portion of the prostitution, drugs and illegal gambling in the city, and was regarded as responsible for a range of murders and beatings of opponents in Saigon and beyond. He was also reputed to have corrupted senior Party, police, prosecutorial and judicial personnel in Saigon and perhaps all the way to Hanoi.[2]

In late 2001, Hanoi cracked down on Nam Cam, the only true challenge to Party authority in Saigon. Cam and over 150 of his colleagues were arrested, including senior legal officials from Saigon and Hanoi that included the deputy chief state prosecutor based in Hanoi, a Deputy Minister of Police, one of Vietnam's leading journalists, and over a dozen other law enforcement or media personnel. They were all brought to trial in 2003 on various charges that included charges of murder, assault, bribery, extortion, promoting prostitution, various drug crimes, promoting illegal gambling, organizing illegal emigration, various abuse of power counts, and a host of other charges.

Some of the defendants in the Nam Cam trial were so notorious that, despite the funds available to them, few lawyers would represent them. Several Saigon lawyers, for example, refused to represent Nam Cam, and eventually the senior Saigon attorney Nguyen Dang Trung was appointed. A number of the defendants in the Nam Cam trial hired private lawyers, but the most skilled and aggressive of them were quickly reserved by the most powerful, wealthy and well-connected of the Nam Cam trial defendants. Deputy chief state prosecutor Pham Si Chien hired Nguyen Van Hien and Pham Hong Hai; Vice Minister of Public Security Bui Quoc Huy hired Ngo Van Thuy; and the former head of Vietnam Radio and leading journalist Tran Mai Hanh hired Dang Van Luan; the names of these lawyers have become well-known for their active representation, both during and after the Nam Cam case (Quang 2007).

Although active representation had begun to appear in cases before Nam Cam, some of the lawyers in this case surprised the court and the prosecution with their energetic, even defiant arguments for their clients. Arguing that the prosecution had not proven elements of its case against both gang members and allegedly corrupted high officials, the attorneys demanded that the traditionally powerful state prosecution service withdraw or reduce some of the charges, or that the traditionally weak court find defendants not guilty, in a trial in which judicial independence had likely been compromised from the beginning (Quang and Steiner 2005; Quang 2007). Among the most zealous advocates was Dang Van Luan, who represented the prominent journalist Mai Van Hanh. Hanh had served as Director-General of Vietnam Radio, editor-in-chief of one of the nation's most prominent journalism magazines, and a member of the Central Committee of the Vietnamese Communist Party – among the most senior political positions in the Party apparatus. In his defense of Hanh, Luan angered prosecutors by claiming that prosecutors had misread the law and, more damagingly, had "staged a play" about his client – in particular, that they had "arranged statements" between witnesses that were then used to implicate Hanh. Luan's defense prompted retaliation – the prosecutors alleged that he had violated Vietnam's Criminal Procedure Law, and issued a formal document to higher level Hanoi and Ho Chi Minh City prosecutors requesting formal charges against him (Quang and Steiner 2005).

Partly because of the narrow ambit of activity to which lawyers have been limited in Vietnam, this was one of the first times that prosecutors had sought formal charges against a defense lawyer because of active client representation.[3] Stunned and furious prosecutors, unaccustomed to zealous representation in high profile cases and generally unaccustomed to challenges to their authority, retaliated by threatening criminal sanctions or disbarment against the lawyers. The Vietnamese press, blanketing the most prominent trial in modern Vietnamese history but well aware of its foregone conclusions, leapt on the lawyers' activism. Faced with active and favorable press coverage, prosecutors eventually backed down from the threatened charges against the defense lawyers.

In addition to Luan's active defense of the journalist Tran Mai Hanh, a number of other attorneys mounted vigorous representations of their clients in the Nam Cam case. In particular, the prominent lawyers for two other high-ranking defendants – deputy chief state prosecutor Pham Si Chien, and Vice Minister of Public Security Bui Quoc Huy – sought to discredit investigators and prosecutors and their evidence and arguments. Although most of the prosecutorial wrath was directed at Dang Van Luan's representation of the journalist Hanh, the prosecutors also attacked these other attorneys as well.

The main defendants represented by active counsel in the Nam Cam trial were still convicted, but in several cases received reduced senten- ces at least partly as a result of their representation. And perhaps most importantly, a new vision for lawyering continued to advance in Vietnamese public perception – the lawyer as an active force in representation, not merely the agent of dominant prosecutors and weak judges.

ADVOCACY ON THE OFFENSIVE AGAIN: THE "CASHEW GROVE" MURDER CASE

Assertive representation continued to expand in the years after Nam Cam. But in 2004 and 2005 another major case focused professional and public attention on active defense representation, now not involv- ing major corruption, or gangland leaders, but the defense of poor peasants against prosecutorial attempts to convict them for the murder of a poor peasant woman in a cashew grove in southern Vietnam. The "Cashew Grove" (vuon dieu) case became a legend throughout the country as it has moved up and down the Vietnamese judiciary for twelve years, each time with appellate courts refusing to follow lower court convictions in the murder and sending the case back and back again for re-investigation.[4]

The peasant woman Duong Thi My was going through a divorce from her husband in the spring of 1993 when she was brutally murdered in a cashew grove near her home in the village of Ham Tan, in Binh Thuan province in southern Vietnam. Her mutilated and partly decomposed body was discovered about two days later with multiple knife wounds. Two suspects – a local official and his wife – were detained and then released for lack of evidence. The case languished for nearly five years, until a former resident of the village and convicted murderer, Huynh Van Nen, told prosecutors that he had had a hand in the killing and knew others who had also participated. Nen was the brother-in-law of the woman who had been originally detained in the case, and after reopening the investigation the police asserted that they had found witnesses to a letter supposedly written by the murdered woman to the village official proposing an assignation on the evening of the murder in the cashew grove.

The story became even more complicated from here. The police allegedly found, and prosecutors asserted, that Nguyen Thi Nhung, the wife of the village leader who was supposedly having some sort of affair with the murdered woman, had gathered up her family to confront the woman. Nhung's brother-in-law, police informant and convicted murderer Huynh Van Nen, allegedly named eight other family members involved in the murder, including five of Nhung's brothers and sisters, her two under-age children, and even her husband.

In this complex scenario, and with a combination of witnesses and some material evidence, the Binh Thuan prosecutors went to trial in March of 2001 in the district people's court in Binh Thuan province, where the murder occurred, and obtained a conviction against numerous family members. The defendants appealed, and in April 2002 an appellate court reversed their convictions, returning the case for reinvestigation to the police and prosecutors. After reinvestigation, the prosecutors once again brought homicide and related charges against five of Nhung's brothers and sisters at the Binh Thuan People's Court in August 2004, and once again obtained convictions. By this point, the case had already begun to receive extensive news coverage, and word of the appellate reversal of convictions in a homicide case – still quite rare in Vietnam – had reached reformist lawyers in Hanoi and Saigon. At the second trial the defendants' original volunteer lawyer was replaced by two of Vietnam's most assertive lawyers, Pham Hong Hai and Tran Vu Hai.

Tran Vu Hai is a prominent Hanoi business lawyer who studied law in Hanoi and Europe and has handled the representation of prominent defendants and public interest clients since the late 1990s. Perceived to be a somewhat flamboyant figure in Hanoi legal circles, he has served a term on the Hanoi People's Council and has advocated strongly reformist positions on business, commercial and public law issues, including private enterprise reform, the legal problems faced by small and medium sized businesses, and the reform of contract law, and greater powers for administrative courts.[5] He had also spoken in favor of stronger governmental efforts to provide housing for Hanoi's poor. In 2005, as further discussed below, Hai sought to organize Vietnam's first formal group of lawyers to handle public interest cases, "For Justice," an attempt that was viewed with some alarm in Party and government circles and shut down by the Hanoi Bar Association.

Pham Hong Hai's path to public interest lawyering is different than Tran Vu Hai. He studied law in the Soviet Union in the 1980s, then was a scholar in criminal law before turning to criminal defense in some of Vietnam's most controversial and high-profile cases. In the 1990s, Hai rose to head the Center for Criminal Law Research at Vietnam's most well-known legal research center, the Institute of State and Law in the Vietnamese Academy of Social Sciences, where he was an active participant in drafting and debates on the revision of the Vietnamese Criminal Code and an active scholar. In the late 1990s Hai left the academic world to practice criminal law, taking up representation of defendants in a series of Vietnam's most prominent criminal cases, including Nam Cam as well as Cashew Grove and the Ministry of Trade case discussed below. He served as Vice Chair of the Haiphong Lawyers Association and in October 2005 was elected Chairman of the Hanoi Bar Association, after the previous chair failed to be re-elected in the wake of the aborted attempt by Tran Vu Hai and his colleagues to found "For Justice," the first public interest law group.

The Cashew Grove defense geared up once Tran Vu Hai and Pham Hong Hai joined the effort. At the second trial the prosecution sought to show that one of the defendants had confessed openly and sincerely and on video; the defendant's daughter also confirmed details of the killing; and sought to rebut claims of violent interrogation and other malfeasance by the original police investigator, a man named Cao Van Hung. The defendants' new lawyers presented evidence from the original police informant denying his prior statements, as well as evidence indicating that the defendant who had supposedly committed the murder had not been in the area at the time of the murder. The defendants' lawyers went still further, arguing that police investigator Hung had excluded important documents and interviews from the case file, seeking to manipulate the case against these five defendants, and mistreated the defendants through physical abuse, solitary confinement, and deprivation of food. The defense challenged the prosecution's interpretation of the physical evidence and its failure to preserve important evidence. In the end, the defense portrayed the lead police investigator as incompetent, abusive and corrupt, and the prosecution portrayed the investigator's errors as minor and deplorable but not systematic and fatal to the government's case and attacked the allegation of mistreatment of the defendants. The Binh Thuan court re-convicted the defendants, finding the evidence sufficient and the allegation of mistreatment and investigator misbehavior both unproven and insufficient to overturn the weight of the evidence.

Rarely in a modern Vietnamese case – even in the Nam Cam case – had defense attorneys attacked a prosecution's case so vigorously and comprehensively. In August 2004 Pham Hong Hai and Tran Vu Hai went further, filing a formal complaint with the head office of the state prosecutor in Hanoi, the national police ministry, and three provincial law enforcement offices against the original investigator in the case, Cao Van Hung. Hung fought back, filing his own complaint with the Central Committee of the Vietnamese Communist Party in Hanoi, the National Assembly, Ministry of Justice, Ministry of Public Security and other agencies against the defense lawyers for defamation and humiliation.

Once again the defendants appealed from their conviction. At the second appeal hearing, the defendants produced witnesses allegedly confirming that the state's primary informant, Huynh Van Nen, had indeed been working far from the site of the murder on the night it occurred, and eliciting testimony on the physical evidence from the Institute of Criminal Sciences in Saigon and a senior scientist in the Institute of Forensic Medicine in the Ministry of Public Security in Hanoi. The appellate court overruled the verdict, calling the evidence weak and inconsistent, and directed the Binh Thuan authorities to re-investigate the case from the beginning with the assistance of the Ministry of Public Security in Hanoi. In late 2005 that re-investigation was underway, but the original family defendants had been released from prison in Binh Thuan Province and many familiar with the case assumed that no one could now be convicted for the murders. By late 2005, the national Judicial Academy in Hanoi had convened a significant workshop on the Cashew Grove case, for it implicated so many of the problems in modern Vietnamese legal reform – the role of and limitations imposed on defense lawyers; prosecutorial and police over-reaching and mistreatment, and a range of other problems.

The Nam Cam and Cashew Grove cases are two especially prominent examples of assertive representation by defense lawyers in cases of significant public interest. But this small band of lawyers has been involved in a wide range of other cases as well. For example, Pham Hong Hai – a key lawyer in both Nam Cam and Cashew Grove, and the new Chairman of the Hanoi Bar Association after the "For Justice" matter, as discussed below – has represented corruption defendants since at least 2001. His clients include the alleged murderer of a prominent journalist, a defendant in a major corruption case involving bribery and embezzlement of government development funds in a major road building project in a poor mountainous district, his assertive representation for deputy chief state prosecutor Pham Si Chien in the Nam Cam trial, and other matters. And in one of the most prominent recent corruption cases, Pham Hong Hai represented Vice Minister of

Trade Mai Van Dau in 2004–2005 when Dau and others were accused of selling licenses to engage in garment trade with the United States and other countries (Vietnamnet 2004b).

Different from the representation of prominent criminal defendants who are gangsters (Nam Cam) or government officials (Vice Minister of Trade Mai Van Dau or procurator Pham Si Chien), and different from the representation of ordinary citizens caught up in extraordinary cases (Cashew Grove), is the representation of political and religious defendants. In several cases, recently most notably the trial of Mennonite pastors in Saigon, private attorneys have stepped forward to provide criminal representation in sensitive political and religious cases. Here the motivations of the lawyers involved are even more difficult to parse, for the entrepreneurship of appearing in high profile cases would seem less at work here, in matters about which the Vietnamese authorities and press generally remain silent until a verdict is rendered. Here too there may be a certain legitimization in the world of lawyers, if perhaps not the world of clients and of the press, based on the growing sense that all defendants deserve some counsel, and that standing up to the government is a positive attribute for attorneys. And the authorities do not seem to object, for defense lawyers in prominent religious and political cases play the same sort of legitimizing role for the criminal process and the legal system as in high profile non-political cases – or at least the Party and government likely hope.

FROM CLIENT REPRESENTATION TO COLLECTIVE ACTION FOR SOCIAL JUSTICE: SEEKING TO ESTABLISH VIETNAM'S FIRST PUBLIC INTEREST LAW GROUP

In the spring of 2004, Tran Vu Hai and some of his colleagues took their individual client representation, *pro bono* work and policy advocacy a step further, gathering a group of like-minded lawyers that proposed to form and run Vietnam's first public interest law group. The group called itself *For Justice* (*Vi cong ly*), drafted a ten-point *quy che* (articles) and submitted the articles to the Hanoi Bar Association for registration and approval because most of the members were also members of the Bar Association and Vietnamese law requires formally organized groups to be registered and approved (Vietnamnet 2004a).

The purpose of the group was clear. As Hai told the Vietnamese press, "These days many judgments are legally enforceable but ... clearly violate procedural law or have serious errors in the application of law ... so that the Supreme People's Procuracy and the Supreme People's Court have been petitioned many times for resolution. We will gather together those judgments and present them to the responsible institutions for consideration and handling." A prominent Vietnamese news site put it somewhat more diplomatically: "The goal of the project is to contribute to creating favorable conditions for the activities of lawyers in undertaking their responsibilities to protect the lawful rights and interests of Vietnamese individuals and organizations" (VnExpress 2004d).

The For Justice group was led by eight prominent Hanoi lawyers, most of the younger generation and most in charge of their own small firms. But they also migrated across generations in an alliance-building move that may have worried the authorities: apart from the founders, the initial participants' list also listed at least two senior legal officials, the Chairman of the Vietnam International Arbitration Center, Tran Minh Chi, and a Vice Chairman of the Vietnam Lawyers Association, former Supreme Court Chief Justice Trinh Hong Duong (VnExpress 2004e).

The authorities had tolerated a number of attorneys' *pro bono* representations, the prominent work by some defending high-level corruption and criminal defendants, the gradual migration into public policy, first pro-reform and pro-government, then increasingly critical of reform failures (such as Hai's comments on housing in Hanoi for the poor), and even the beginnings of some increasingly energetic representation of political and religious dissidents whose trials were clearly an utter sham. But a proposal formally to gather lawyers together in a registered organization to press for the redress of erroneous judgments – and the evident welcome it received from at least some lawyers in Hanoi – sparked a response from the Hanoi Bar Association, and behind them even more powerful authorities. On May 4, 2004, a day before the For Justice group was scheduled to announce its formation at a meeting in Hanoi, the Hanoi Bar Association formally issued a document barring the formation of the For Justice group and ordering that the group "immediately cease unlawful operations, in order to avoid unfortunate consequences" (VnExpress 2004e). The decision noted that "the organization and activities of the project initiative of the group 'For Justice' violate the law" (VnExpress 2004f).

The Hanoi Bar Association based its decision to bar the group on the Ordinance for the Regulation of Lawyers, claiming that only lawyers' offices and partnerships were permitted, that the Lawyers Ordinance permits lawyers only to engaged in "litigation, advising, and services," and that "other activities are a violation of law." The Chairman of the Hanoi Bar Association said that "there is no realm for collecting the views of lawyers to present suggestions to authorized institutions for resolution. The formation of the group 'For Justice' is really an organization, and speaking precisely an unlawful organization" (VnExpress 2004e).

The same afternoon the Hanoi Bar Association barred the formation of For Justice, four of its lawyer-members, led by Tran Vu Hai, issued a response calling their application "normal" and "consistent with the provisions of law." They cited Article 274 of the 2004 Criminal Procedure Code, which provides that "Every citizen has the right to uncover violations of law in judicial cases and decisions that have entered into legal force, and to report to persons in authority to protest in accordance with the relevant regulations." And they cited Article 53 of the Vietnamese Constitution of 1992, providing that "citizens have the right to make proposals to state institutions . . .." In early May the matter was left with the Bar Association's disapproval document; the Association was still studying the problem and its Chairman was threatening to discipline or expel bar members "who participate in this group" (VnExpress 2004e).[6]

In response – now faced with potentially serious consequences – the For Justice group did not announce its formation and turned the planned ceremony into a (lawful) discussion with people interested in the lawyers' activities (VnExpress 2004f). Three of the eight original founders decided not to attend the May 5 event, and withdrew from the group (VnExpress 2004h). But other founders remained both careful and defiant. "The group has not been established, but the [Bar] Association has announced that it must immediately cease its activities violating the law. This doesn't make any sense." And the Chairman of the Bar Association was "mistaken" when he cited the law to demonstrate that the establishment of For Justice violated its provisions. The group met with the leadership of the Hanoi Bar Association to discuss For Justice for the first time on the afternoon of May 9; "before that," noted one prominent news website, "each major contact had been through formal documents although they are all very close to each other in Hanoi" (VnExpress 2004f).

The For Justice group reconsidered its situation over the next several days. On May 10, one of the organizers told the press that in the face of strong Bar Association and political opposition the group would "temporarily" cease both its attempts to register and its activities. But there was no apology, and no backing down on the principles involved. "We are lawyers who are well-acquainted with the law. The formation of the group does not violate the law." The purposes of the group – to "gather the views of lawyers on cases that violate the law, and then to make suggestions to responsible institutions that have jurisdiction" are clearly in line with the authorized and encouraged role of lawyers. "But the crux of the issue is that in the past lawyers did this work in their own names, and now they are acting with and in the name of an organization called 'For Justice'" (VnExpress 2004f).

The next day, Tran Vu Hai and four other founders met with the leadership of the Bar Association that afternoon for more than two hours, when the Chairman again reiterated that the formation of For Justice violated the law by working outside the permitted arenas of litigation, advice, and services and demanded a cessation of activities. This time the group agreed to comply, noting that if state institutions gave approval, they would open activities in an appropriate form. The news website that covered this controversy noted dryly: "Of course, in an exchange with VnExpress, Chairman Ty noted that: 'The Ministry of Justice has agreed with the Association's way of resolving this'" (VnExpress 2004g, 2004h; Vietnamnet 2004a).

A day later, Tran Vu Hai met with the Vietnam News Service to discuss the For Justice episode. He reiterated the group's goal of raising cases of incorrect verdicts and injustices, defended the role of lawyers in gathering information on such cases to improve the administration of justice. He sharply denied that the group qualified as either an organization or an association, which would bring it within restrictive registration regulations, and potentially increase penalties for gathering together in violation of relevant regulations. In a withering sentence intended to draw unfavorable comparisons with Vietnam's frequent model in political restriction and economic reform, Hai noted that "in China, 250 law offices" had gathered together to provide support to individuals and organizations on legal needs and issues that "Chinese society was concerned about." Hai made his position clear – that if after discussions with the Ministry of Justice, the Office of the Government, and the Law Committee of the National Assembly it appeared that the group could go forward without dramatic change to its objectives and structure, he would favor going forward (Vietnamnet 2004a).

Over the next several weeks there was sharply negative reaction to the Bar Association's decision both within Vietnam and from the dissident community overseas, ever ready to find fault with the Hanoi leadership. Students, legal professionals and others wrote in support of For Justice's aims, though at least one observer thought the appropriation of the name "Justice" to be overreaching and unfair to others working in the legal system. "The goals of the 'For Justice' group are admirable," wrote one reader, "especially under current circumstances, when the trial work of the judicial and legal sector has many shortcomings and failures, and social justice has not yet been ensured." Another wrote that "if people's opinions were surveyed on this then certainly 90% would ... support the establishment of 'For Justice'."

But other readers agreed with the Bar Association's stance, calling the "concept [of 'For Justice'] good" but citing the potential for conflict of interest between For Justice lawyers and their membership in the Bar Association and questioning the need for a separate organization. Another also called the "goal admirable," but defended the interest of the government in examining and managing the formation of associations and warned that "if an association or group does not receive approval for formation from the [government] institution concerned, then its continued existence is unlawful. As the motivations and goals of this group must await the conclusions of the agencies concerned, the best would be that the group should terminate [activities] and dissolve before it's too late" (VnExpress 2004f, 2004g, 2004h).

Overseas, the For Justice episode was heavily covered by dissident and critical overseas Vietnamese websites and reaction was almost entirely favorable toward the group. An overseas Vietnamese website in Germany called the For Justice initiative "an extraordinary event for a system in transition between executive and judiciary." And numerous dissident websites reprinted a scathing commentary entitled "Who is for justice? And who is selling their conscience?" that excoriated the Hanoi Bar Association but rather inexplicably failed to discuss higher state and Party officials who, there is little doubt, played at least some role in the government and Bar Association's response to the Justice initiative.[7]

Several overlapping issues doomed For Justice. The authorities were concerned with lawyers moving from individual or loosely linked *pro bono* representation to a more formal grouping with a written charge. They were concerned with pressure on the prosecution and judiciary from highly skilled and motivated lawyers who would challenge incorrect verdicts and injustices that might well have been originally determined through political means. And they were very anxious about a shift in the role of lawyers, from technical agents to active proponents, from formal representatives to leaders in an adversarial process.

STRUGGLES WITHIN THE BAR

A number of these issues came to a head in the fall of 2005, when the 800-member Hanoi Bar Association held its triennial meeting and prepared to elect a new board of directors and chair. Reformist lawyers unhappy with the Association's resolution of the For Justice matter nominated two of the For Justice founders, the activist lawyer Tran Vu Hai and his associate Phan Huong Thuy, for seats on the Association's board of directors as two among 25 candidates for six director slots. The leadership of the Association – whether acting on its own or with direction from above – promptly removed the names of the two For Justice proponents from the candidates' list, ostensibly because of complaints received about them in the wake of the For Justice case. That removal from the candidate list in turn prompted a significant dispute when the Association's general meeting opened in mid-September. After discussion the two activist lawyers were returned to the candidate list, but were not elected.

But the conflict within the bar was not over. Although the For Justice leaders were not elected to the Association's board, there remained widespread dissatisfaction with the Association's leadership. And so the membership moved to elect one of the most senior of the reform-oriented lawyers, Pham Hong Hai, as Chair of the Hanoi Bar Association for a three year term beginning in 2005. Hai was the first non-Party member elected Chair of the Hanoi Bar Association, and had joined the Association, from Haiphong, only a month before his election. But he had long roots in Hanoi from his service in the Institute of State and Law, teaching at Hanoi's law schools, and work in several Hanoi law firms.

Upon his election Hai struck a conciliatory note. He spoke of the desire for change that his election symbolized, and of increasing the role of the Lawyers Association in reforming law and strengthening the status of lawyers, promised to seek "relative independence" from state control but to "conform to the law," and advocated strengthening the training of lawyers and cooperation with lawyers' groups throughout the country (Radio Free Asia 2005a, 2005b, 2005c; BBC 2005a, 2005b).

ACCESS TO JUSTICE: LEGAL RESEARCH AND PROGRAMS

Concern about access to justice began to strengthen in the Vietnamese legal community and the donor community in the mid to late 1990s. Both groups were concerned about increasing gaps in wealth, gaps in access to legal services, and use of the law against poor peasants and others. The relatively low capacity of the court system and its difficulty in picking out and resolving cases involving false charges and complex issues in the face of a powerful prosecution service contributed to this sense.

For the government and Party, access to legal services was the first and key issue to address. That was addressed through the legal aid agenda discussed earlier and an expansion of the training of lawyers and their roles. But the Party and government also sought to go further. The Comprehensive Legal Needs Assessment unveiled in 2003 reemphasized the growing concern for access to justice, noting that: "Essential for the achievement of each of [Vietnam's] goals is the delivery of a practical effective long term development strategy and action plan to strengthen Vietnam's legal system to the point where it supports sustained economic growth and development and, at the same time, provides access to justice for all members in the society" (Legal System Needs Assessment 2002). Other elements of the Needs Assessment stressed the need for strengthened access to legal documents, the courts, government agencies at all levels, legal services and legal aid, court decisions and judgments, and participation in governance.

Meanwhile donors were also beginning to work on access to justice after a decade of heavy emphasis on strengthening central legal institutions, lawmaking processes and quality, and economic law. Oxfam Hong Kong commissioned a research study in 1999 on access to justice and law for the poor (Sidel 1999). In the next several years the United Nations Development Programme – hitherto concerned almost entirely with capacity building in central legal institutions, lawmaking, and economic law – commissioned an important study on access to justice in Vietnam (UNDP 2004).

The UNDP study should have set off a wide array of useful programmatic activities, for it clearly indicated the seriousness of the access to justice issues in Vietnam. The study concluded that "the level of awareness of existing legal institutions for access to justice is relatively low … especially low with regard to the formal judicial institutions such as the courts and the procuracy, and supporting institutions such

as the legal aid centres and the grass-root[s] mediation groups."
Awareness of administrative institutions such as local governments
and the police was, on the other hand and not surprisingly, "relatively
high." And legal awareness differed dramatically by region and income,
"decreas[ing] with decreasing income levels, and ... lower ... in rural
and mountainous areas as compared with those living in urban areas"
(UNDP 2004).

Beyond awareness, the UNDP study also clearly indicated that access
to "legal information and institutions to protect their rights as citizens"
is also "low and uneven ... The level of access to legal institutions
seems to be consistent with the level of awareness. In other words ...
access to the court and the supporting institutions, such as the legal aid
centres, grass-root[s] mediation groups and lawyers, is lower than access
to the people's committees and the police" (UNDP 2004).

This places "significant responsibility on [police and administrative
institutions] to promote justice." And according to the study's authors,
"legal aid centres and the grass-root[s] mediation groups seem to be
underutilised – indicating that the institutions set in place to promote
access to justice for the poor and the disadvantaged groups are not
successful in reaching their target groups." Finally, "while ... cost [is] an
important factor influencing [people's] decision whether or not to seek
remedy for injustice, the survey suggests that people perceive the
impartiality of judges and clear laws supporting the case to be more
critical for justice to prevail" (UNDP 2004).

Low and uneven awareness and access leads to "relatively low" and
uneven confidence "that the legal institutions in place are effective in
protecting their rights." And "the level of confidence among those who
have accessed legal institutions and those who have not is quite similar,
suggesting that people's perceptions correspond with the real situation." Confidence perceptions were considerably higher among those
who had worked with legal aid centres and grass-roots mediation
groups, "suggest[ing] that these institutions suffer from an unwarranted
weak image among those who have not accessed their services" (UNDP
2004). And the study found an "important role accorded the people's
committees and the mass media," particularly compared to the courts
and other institutions, "seem[ing] to indicate that – in people's minds –
the administrative system and mass media are of significant importance
to access to justice at the local levels" (UNDP 2004).

For UNDP, the prescription was clear, and it was correct: "While
further development of the existing legal and judicial institutions is

important, strengthening people's access to justice is crucial. This includes increasing the level of legal awareness, as well as the level of access to and confidence in legal institutions in place. The survey suggests a need for increased outreach of legal institutions at the grass-roots level for a higher level of utilization, especially by the poor and people living in remote areas" (UNDP 2004). But the survey also suggested what UNDP called "the focus of continued reform."

> While other – less formal – mechanisms for access to justice require support and attention, continued efforts have to be made to reform the court system, as clearly stated by the Communist Party and the Government of Viet Nam. Certainly, an impartial, independent and competent court system, upon which people may rely ... when seeking justice, is crucial for a society promoting the rule of law, democracy and human rights.
>
> (UNDP 2004)

But the donor community has been slow to embrace extensive programming on access to justice, both because of a commitment to capacity building in legal institutions and, for some donors like the United States, a commitment to helping Vietnam harmonize its laws with international norms in connection with the US–Vietnam Bilateral Trade Agreement and Vietnam's entry into the World Trade Organization. Traditionally major legal reform donors such as Sweden, Denmark, Canada, the United Nations and the Asian Development Bank have been slow to move toward law programming that seeks to help redress some of the injustices of the Vietnamese reform process and the inadequacies of current legal structures in helping the poor assert their rights.

CLINICAL LEGAL EDUCATION

Another component of public interest law is the training of future lawyers using clinical methods that provide assistance to ordinary citizens, often those that cannot afford legal services, and train law students in legal skills and realities. But clinical legal education and legal education's engagement with access to justice has developed considerably more slowly in Vietnam than other aspects of public interest law – and considerably more slowly than clinical programs have developed in China.

At the policy level, moving from rote lectures and focus on law as text to a better mix of lecture and participatory learning and a focus on law in action are now clearly strongly recommended. The national Comprehensive Needs Assessment of Vietnam's Legal System Development, drafted over several years by Vietnamese legal institutions with the support of the United Nations and other funders, calls for the Vietnamese legal education sector to "[e]nsure that at least 70% of the studying time in the legal training programs by modern teaching methods (such as clinical education, teacher-student interchanges in class, problem solving method, simulations, rather than consisting entirely of the lecture method)" (Legal System Needs Assessment 2002, secs. 4.2.5.2.1; 3.3.1.12).

Over the next several years, the Legal Needs Assessment was transformed into a Legal System Development Strategy in a process chaired by the Ministry of Justice and involving all of the major Vietnamese legal and politico-legal institutions. That new Legal System Development Strategy, released in mid-2005, calls generally for reforms in legal education and the issue that "legal education ... still lag[s] behind practical demands," without specifically mentioning clinical legal education (Legal System Development Strategy 2005, introduction and sec. 2.4). The Judicial Reform Strategy also promulgated by the Party in June 2006 mentioned strengthening legal education but did not refer to clinical programs or instructing law students in the realities of the Vietnamese legal system (Judicial Reform Strategy 2005).

On the ground, there appears to be little significant activity yet underway in clinical legal education. A few law students may be active in the legal aid clinics promoted by the Ministry of Justice and by justice bureaus at the local level, and others volunteer. But organized clinical programs are in their infancy. Given the rapid development of clinical legal education in China, the almost complete absence of these programs in Vietnam is perhaps best explained by a lack of donor initiative. A few Vietnamese legal academics have attended clinical law conferences in Bangkok, Tokyo or elsewhere in the region, and eventually a few donors may become interested in this important area. In the absence of significant initiatives in clinical legal education, there are some other efforts underway. At the Faculty of Law at Vietnam National University in Hanoi, for example, faculty and students are working with communities in northern and central Vietnam to establish "law clubs" that help rural residents to understand law and their rights. Finland and American foreign aid are supporting this work with small grants.

THE CAUTIOUS RISE OF PUBLIC INTEREST LAW
AND ADVOCACY IN VIETNAM

This chapter is the first effort undertaken to introduce and analyze the emergence of public interest lawyering in Vietnam. It covers a range of episodes and actors – ranging from the state-sponsored (such as legal aid), to the activities of lawyers operating within bounds of recognized defense but pushing the boundaries of advocacy (such as the high profile representations of Nam Cam, Cashew Grove, and other cases), to attempts to move beyond defense, beyond representation, to organization of lawyers to petition for correction of incorrect verdicts. These episodes show a system that allows lawyers systematically more flexible roles and that has expanded the boundaries of advocacy while legitimizing criminal and judicial process. Where attorneys press too hard – where they move from individual advocacy and representation to collective action, the organization of a group to press for redress – the Party and state retain the authority to curb those activities. And, at least for now, the lawyers comply, for they too are tied to a system of licensure and observation in which the state continues to play the dominant role.

But these boundaries are expanding. In China, public interest lawyering was virtually unknown before the early 1990s. But in a decade and a half it has become a recognized force in the Chinese legal world – from combative public interest lawyers that represent beaten or overtaxed peasants, or those whose land or property has been forcibly taken away, to an increasingly active clinical legal community. The state has fought back against the most assertive of these advocates, particularly those who seek to represent peasants and their villages that have risen up in rebellion against corrupt cadres, armed thugs, excessive taxation, and the looting of land and property. But they are not disappearing from the Chinese scene, gathering more and more support as each year passes.

Likewise the boundaries are expanding in Vietnam, though later than in China. Before Nam Cam and Cashew Grove, it was virtually unknown for legal advocates in Vietnam to seek to sanction prosecutors, or vice versa. Before For Justice, collective action by public interest-minded counsel was unknown and untried. The next steps in this process of expanding the vocational and political boundaries of Vietnamese lawyers may not come in collective action, but in an expansion of defense and advocacy activities on the part of the poor, both urban and rural. Eventually, however, lawyers will find a way to engage in the sort of collective action that For Justice attempted and was prevented from undertaking, as the system continues to become more flexible. But that road forward in Vietnam, as in China, will not be easy.

NOTES

1. For example, the primary government organization tasked with protecting the rights of Vietnamese laborers working abroad, the Department for Administration of Foreign-Employed Labor (DAFEL), is also responsible for the contradictory tasks of increasing foreign currency earnings for Vietnam through sending labor abroad, and for reducing unemployment and strengthening worker skills through such foreign labor. See Sidel 2004 and Chapter 5.

2. The discussion of the Truong Van Cam case is based on extensive coverage in VnExpress and other Vietnamese media outlets from 2003–2005.

3. Other charges against lawyers are unrelated to client representation and directly related to alleged criminal violations committed directly by the lawyer involved. For example, a lawyer in Ho Chi Minh City, Nguyen Dinh Tu, was arrested and charged in September 23 with leading a trafficking ring that sent a number of poor women off on false pretenses for work in Taiwan and Hong Kong that did not exist. The women were allegedly cheated out of US $3,500–6,000 each; at least six were detailed in Hong Kong, and another 14 deported back to Vietnam. VnExpress 2003b; VnExpress 2003h. In another high profile lawyer discipline and criminal case, Saigon lawyer Le Bao Quoc was charged with extortion and attempting to bribe a case for 3 billion dong [about US$190,000] using funds requested and obtained from a client. Quoc was allegedly offered 2 billion dong [about US$120,000] by the opposing party to delay the execution of a judicial ruling that the opposing party return a parcel of land to Quoc's client. Vietnam News Briefs 2005; Vietnam News 2005; VnExpress 2005a.

4. The discussion of the Truong Van Cam case is based on extensive coverage in VnExpress and other Vietnamese media outlets from 2003–2005.

5. I have benefited from a discussion with Tran Vu Hai and from various articles on his and other lawyers' activities in the Vietnam Economic News, Saigon Times Daily, Vietnam Investment Review, VnExpress, Vietnamnet and other sources.

6. In a review of its work at the end of 2004 entitled "Twenty Years of Construction and Development," the Hanoi Bar Association noted briefly that "owing to timely and resolute intervention, various negative phenomena have been limited. Most noteworthy is that the group "project initiative for justice" ['For Justice'] was discovered and it was demanded that they stop so as to avoid serious consequences."

7. The German article is at Shcd.de. The "Who is for justice?" essay is available at www.lmvntd.org, gianghovunglen.tripod.com, www.vnn-news.com, www.lenduong.net, and other overseas outlets.

CHAPTER 8

DONORS, LAW AND SOCIAL JUSTICE IN VIETNAM: THE UNCERTAIN PROMISE

Since the early 1990s foreign assistance amounting to tens of millions of dollars has poured into Vietnam's legal sector to support legal reform. There can be little doubt of the well-meaning nature of this support: donors, both official and nongovernmental, have welcomed Vietnam's commitment to strengthening its legal system with enthusiastic and generous support aimed at enhancing the authority and capacity of law and legal institutions. There can be little doubt of the successes in that assistance, while there is also growing skepticism in many parts of the world about the utility and effects of legal assistance (Nang 1994; Bergling 1997; Rose 1998; Pedersen 2001; Salemink 2003). This chapter seeks to outline the scope and direction of foreign assistance to Vietnam's legal reforms in the era of *doi moi*, and to analyze the initial results and prioritization of those activities and directions for the future.[1]

These issues are of particular concern in socialist transitional states such as Vietnam and China, where legal reform has received significant donor support. Two vignettes from this volume may serve to illustrate some of the issues in this donor support – assistance that has ostensibly improved and "modernized" Vietnamese law, and strengthened and professionalized courts, prosecutors, police and justice officials.

MORE LAW, FEWER RIGHTS?

In late February 2003, in the largest case of criminal human trafficking and involuntary servitude brought in the United States since the Civil

War, the owner and manager of a large garment factory employing over 200 Vietnamese and Chinese workers in American Samoa was convicted of multiple criminal civil rights charges under US law in connection with the trafficking, beating, starving and other mistreatment of his workers from Vietnam and China.

Why is this case – discussed in considerably more detail in Chapter 4 of this volume – relevant in the discussion of donor support and the effects of legal reform? The Vietnamese workers mistreated in this case had been sent to the Samoan garment factory by two labor export companies in Vietnam, companies owned and controlled by the Vietnamese Ministry of Trade and the Vietnamese National Administration of Tourism. Those workers were accompanied by Vietnamese "supervisors" (one might term them overseers) from those state-owned labor export companies who participated in or observed the mistreatment of the Vietnamese workers. Loan sharks back in Vietnam enabled the workers to go abroad by providing capital for their fees at usurious rates, protected by local police and state authorities acting as local enforcers. In turn local police, security and state authorities enforced this system, threatening families of the Vietnamese workers who complained about their treatment overseas and holding families to their commitments to illegal loan sharks, including using threats of violence against them. These events – this system of labor export that resulted in a maiming, beatings, other mistreatment, and the largest US human trafficking case for more than a century, developed in part under the Vietnamese legislative and regulatory structure for export labor that has emerged in Vietnam over the past ten years under a legal reform process and labor and social welfare regime substantially supported by foreign donors, as well as under US law.

The Vietnamese export labor legal regime and the labor law regime from which it is derived is intended to earn export revenues for Vietnam, help reduce rampant unemployment, and, at least rhetorically, protect the rights of workers sent abroad. It is not entirely succeeding in that last, rights-protective goal, reflecting broader failures both in Vietnamese law and in donor support for the revamping of Vietnam's economic law system. That modernization and renovation of Vietnam's economic law has resulted in a system that is more detailed, more legal, arguably more regulated and, today, used with considerably more effectiveness by those within Vietnam with greater economic and political power and against those with less power. Under the new economic law regime, it was easy to enforce the duties of workers and very difficult for them to enforce their rights. The new legislation served ministries that wanted to increase export earnings for Vietnam and reduce domestic unemployment, labor export companies that sought profits for themselves and their ministry owners, procurers of labor in Vietnamese villages and cities, who sought individual profits, and the police and officials who worked with all of them, often also for a fee. The conviction of the factory owner in American Samoa should not blind us to the failings of legal protections in Vietnam, in which – at least in this case – more law resulted in greater opportunities for abuse, while giving workers few ways to effectively implement the general rights that legislation supposedly grants them. The labor export companies and supervisors and their overseas partners cited 1980s and 1990s regulations on labor export, and contracts signed by the workers that limited their opportunities for redress. In the arena of labor law and labor export, the picture that emerges from the Samoan debacle is one of more law, and fewer rights.

Nor, of course, should we ignore or excuse the failings of the American legal system in this case. By providing for lowered labor protections on Samoa and other territories, and greater incentives to ship into the US market, combined with reduced labor inspections in recent years, the United States too bears a substantial responsibility for the events on its territory. That we focus here on the meanings of this case for Vietnamese legal reform certainly does not excuse American failings.

LEGAL MODERNIZATION AND THE DIFFICULT COURSE FOR LAW'S AUTHORITY AND LEGITIMACY

At a minimum, the strengthening of law and legal structures through domestic efforts backed up by significant donor support should strengthen the authority and legitimacy of law and the legal system. Another scene from Vietnam illustrates the exceptional difficulties in enhancing law's legitimacy and authority, and the ambivalence of attempts in single party-dominated states to strengthen law's power, despite significant domestic and donor efforts.

For more than a decade, as described in Chapter 7, a gang leader named Truong Van Cam dominated a considerable part of Saigon (Ho Chi Minh City), Vietnam's commercial and business center. Known as the Godfather Nam Cam, he directed hundreds of gang members, ran scores of hotels, restaurants, casinos and other enterprises, extorted protection money from hundreds more establishments, and had opponents beaten and killed. He also corrupted dozens if not hundreds of Ho Chi Minh City police, prosecutors, city officials as well as national police, prosecutors, and political officials. After years as a key criminal boss of Ho Chi Minh City, with authority directly rivaling the Communist Party secretary and mayor of the city, Nam Cam was arrested and charged with murder, extortion and a range of other serious crimes in December of 2001 after intervention from central Party and state officials.

In the months that followed, investigators sent from Hanoi – for the local police and prosecutors could not be trusted – uncovered and charged or removed an increasingly senior array of officials with close links to Nam Cam. Among those who are alleged to have taken instructions from this gangster were at least two members of the Central Committee of the Vietnamese Communist Party, a national deputy prosecutor-general, several vice ministers of the interior (the ministry responsible for police and internal security in Vietnam), a leading journalist, a Vietnamese ambassador abroad, and others. Questions were even raised, and then squelched, about the role of a former prime minister.

The senior officials named and charged in the Nam Cam case were alleged to have used their influence to arrange Nam Cam's release from prison in the mid-1990s, support and protect his criminal enterprises, arrange positive news coverage or dampen negative reports, and provide information to the criminal enterprise. The extent of Nam Cam's criminal activities in Ho Chi Minh City was a matter of concern, but it was the management, manipulation and corruption of a host of senior officials that made clear how Cam had thoroughly corrupted the authority and legitimacy of law in Vietnam's largest city and commercial metropolis. Vietnamese police, local officials and senior national government and Party officials have always been subject to two masters, to divided authority – to the Communist Party, on one hand, and to the law on the other, with Party policy trumping law in the case of conflicts. Nam Cam took advantage of that divided loyalty, the Party's fundamental ambivalence about legal authority and legitimacy, and the resultant weakness in legal norms and enforcement, to suborn hundreds if not thousands of police, prosecutors, and local and national officials. He made them subordinate to his authority, to his criminal legitimacy in Saigon, rather than either the Party or law. When they had to make a choice, police, prosecutors, judges and officials obeyed him, not the law, and not the Party. Nam Cam utilized the weaknesses in law's power that result from that divided authority structure to bring senior officials under a third pole of authority – his own.

The godfather Nam Cam's long and successful challenge to the legitimacy and authority of law in Vietnam, and Vietnamese government ministries' and labor export companies' roles in the denial of rights to Vietnamese export laborers are but two examples of continuing issues in the Vietnamese legal system. Despite signal successes in legal reform in Vietnam in other areas, donors must reflect carefully on these and other failures – for they send a clear signal that their legal support in Vietnam is insufficient, and that legal reform may in fact be helping to produce structures and actors that are either oppressive or illegitimate.

There remains, in the minds of many donors and not a few Vietnamese, a fundamental misunderstanding of the early years of legal reform. These are regarded, for example, as the years of positive, effective regulation. But regulation for what? In the labor law field, for example, this was actually a period of effective deregulation of workers' rights (including the rights of export workers). The right to strike was severely restricted in the 1994 labor code, a derogation from an earlier social compact. Minimum wage guarantees went unenforced, then were reduced or even eviscerated by subsequent legislation and then further eviscerated by the lack of inflation protections (Labor Code 1994). In the series of labor export regulations promulgated throughout the 1990s by the Vietnamese government and its ministries, a rhetoric of protection for export laborers was balanced with a strong rhetoric of labor discipline. The implementers, state ministries that owned labor export companies, chose almost entirely to enforce discipline rather than rights. So it may be that, at least in certain important fields, the increase in regulation served disciplinary interests but did not serve the interests of rights. Rights, I would submit, have instead been effectively deregulated, a process in which the elaboration of law has served to eliminate rights.

THE IMPERFECT PROMISE OF DONOR-SUPPORTED LEGAL REFORM

Contrast these episodes, and the problems of rights protection and law's authority that they illustrate, with fifteen years of donor support for legal reform and the strengthening of the Vietnamese legal system.

That donor support that has provided tens of millions of dollars for legal system development in Vietnam; donors, Vietnamese institutions and senior legal and political officials generally regard that donor assistance as successful. The picture that emerges from the evaluation reports of donors and of the Vietnamese government is of a legal system gradually being strengthened, of the spread of law's legitimacy and authority. This picture is of the building of legal and governance institutions – the training of judges and prosecutors, the training of legislators, better operating procedures, computerized facilities, more detailed drafting of laws, better dissemination and even – a particularly daring claim in recent years – better implementation and enforcement, participation and access. In this picture – the picture from Hanoi, not from Samoa or the gang-controlled enterprises of Ho Chi Minh City, the *Rechtsstaat* of law is being built as the fundamental prerequisite for the building of a strong, autonomous, authoritative and legitimate legal system (Rose 1998).

We are left with the conundrum that donor support for Vietnamese law reform has had some success in the building of institutions – but that those institutions, and the law that underlies them, continue to lack the authority to serve and support the weaker and poorer sections of Vietnamese society. Instead, the picture that emerges from these cases and others is of a new Vietnamese law, built at least partly on a donor edifice, that is often being used to support exploitative market forces rather than to protect those harmed by such markets, that builds structures that are suborned by criminals, and that favors economic and bureaucratic elites over ordinary citizens.

LAW AND DEVELOPMENT AND THE CHANGING ROLES OF DONOR SUPPORT

How did we get to this state? Looking back, it is possible to identify five broad generations of efforts to mold and assist the legal systems of what we now call the developing world, including the transitional socialist countries. In the first generation of these efforts, Britain, the United States and other countries sought to shape and mold the legal systems of colonies and quasi-colonies, often finding and supporting local elites in those processes. In Asia, the shaping of colonial and quasi-colonial law took place in India, China, Thailand, the Philippines, and elsewhere in a process that has been well documented by scholars and donors.

That lengthy first stage of molding the legal systems of Asia entered a new phase, a second generation, after the Second World War, now in the name of development and modernization. Again, this story is well told by British, American, Indian and other scholars. In Asia, the creation of a Japanese constitution and reshaping of its legal system, and the modernization of the Taiwanese, Korean, Thai, Indonesian, South Vietnamese, and other systems, all relied to some degree on bilateral and private assistance. These efforts were increasingly supported by multilateral aid as the World Bank and the Asian Development Bank began to recognize the importance of law in the creating of modern market economies in Asia. This is the era we generally identify with "law and development" – a period focused on developing modern market economies and the state (often liberal in economic terms and authoritarian in political terms) that would support market development (Friedman 1969; Trubek and Galanter 1974; Merryman 1977; Seidman 1978; Gardner 1980). The Soviet Union was active in donor legal support as well, assisting the DRV and other countries in building the legal structures for socialist economic development as well. Socialist law and development activities in the Soviet period are a story that remains to be told by scholars, far less well-known than its western counterparts.

This second stage of donor support for market legal structures in Asia largely concluded in the early to mid-1970s amidst strong criticism of the practices and objectives of what came to be known as "law and development." This was a period of such intense criticism and political impact that today we can legitimately call the raging criticism of law and development in the early and mid-1970s the third stage of the law and development movement itself. This part of the story is also reasonably well-known. Along with other work, David Trubek and Marc Galanter's *Scholars in Self-Estrangement*, the iconic law review article from 1974 that today remains one of the most cited pieces of legal scholarship of our era, was a blow to the 1950s and 1960s law and development efforts that were intended to construct liberal law in the developing world (Trubek and Galanter 1974). Joined by other critics, the law and development movement as practiced through American foreign aid and private donors in the 1950s and 1960s could not flourish under the onslaught of criticism and the skittishness of donors.[2]

After the third stage, the intense criticism of law and development, donor support for law and development entered a period in the wilderness. From the mid-1970s to about 1990, what may be termed the fourth stage of law and development activities, many donors reduced or shied away from legal reform activities. In Asia the World Bank and the Asian Development Bank focused on infrastructure development and economic policymaking. Bilateral donors focused on similar activities. Even the private foundations, such as the Ford Foundation, retreated from previously strong support for law and development activities. This does not mean that a number of Asian countries were not themselves active in promoting economic law to develop controlled market economies, including structural improvements to courts and legal education. But those were conducted largely internally, for the most part away from donor support.

Of course little of this western history of law and development included the Democratic Republic of Vietnam. The United States was active in bringing legal structures and doctrines to south Vietnam in the 1960s as an additional layer on the French law that had earlier been imported. That story of legal importation to a state that was to disappear in 1975 has yet to be effectively told, nor can this volume undertake that task. And, of course, legal transplantation was carried out in North Vietnam, where Soviet specialists worked with Vietnamese counterparts in the 1950s and 1960s to formulate structures for courts, prosecutors, police and other institutions and to draft laws. Key elements of the Vietnamese legal structure that resonate throughout the country today (or plague it), are the product of the Soviet version of law and development, merged happily with Vietnamese Party doctrine: the strong instrumentalist role of the Party and its primary legal agents, the police and prosecutors; the weak, obedient role of the courts; a small group of legal intellectuals that had creative and innovative ideas but could not express them; and the primacy of politics over autonomous law (Sidel 1997; Gillespie 2002a, 2006).

It was perhaps only the transformation of the socialist world that could have truly breathed new life into the corpse of law and development, ushering in the fifth stage of donor activity in law and development and the mushrooming of donor legal support since about 1990. Yet this era did not begin with the fall of the Soviet Union in 1989, as is commonly assumed. Instead, western donor support for law and development, thrown into chaos and sharply reduced in the 1970s and early 1980s, at least partly as a result of the substantial progressive criticisms of its results in the developing world, came to life once again and found its re-legitimization in the early 1980s in China, the first of the Party-dominated states to move decisively toward the market.

The call for the transformation of socialist law was the donors' salvation from the law and development critique of the 1960s and early 1970s, the mechanism to return to the legal fray. China, the first socialist country to decide upon substantial marketizing reforms, led the way. At the request of Chinese officials, for example, the Ford Foundation re-entered the arena of substantial donor support for legal development in the early 1980s with extensive support for Chinese law schools, with an emphasis on elite institutions and on the training of younger faculty abroad. This was at least six years before donors re-entered the law and development field in other areas of the socialist world after the collapse of the Soviet Union and many of the ruling parties in central and eastern Europe (McClymont and Golub 2000).

What occurred in 1980s China, the re-entry point for donors in law and development in the new frontier for those activities – the transitional socialist world – was a truly careful balancing of interests and activities, a well thought out bargain. Determined to avoid both the mistakes and the criticism of early law and development efforts, and in measured but clear response to domestic Chinese policy, the Ford Foundation sought initially to support local capacity-building initiatives in legal education and scholarship rather than market economic law reform in the legislative and regulatory sphere. This programming decision derived in part from a strategic sense that focused Ford funding could have greater impact in law faculties, which would then in turn have substantial impact in other schools and in policy formulation. Another part of the calculus was Chinese power: in the legal arena, China's message to the Ford Foundation and the few other early donors was clear: donors may work in law to support the development of a trained cadre of legal scholars and policy specialists, but were not permitted to work explicitly on building a liberal democratic state. But China and Ford were able to work together on broadening the perspectives and capacity of China's new, elite legal intellectuals, a project directly endorsed within China, despite its dangers for the Chinese leadership as Chinese intellectuals began to argue for elements of a liberal state. And, for the Ford Foundation, this was a project considerably less likely to garner scathing attention from the lurking critics of law and development than a direct focus on the legal structures of a market economy might have elicited.

About five years later, in 1988 and 1989, Ford expanded its work in China to include support for strengthening court and legislative processes, with a focus on training and research. And within a few years other donors, including the United Nations and the World Bank, came into the Chinese picture as significant donors, working on the more traditional subjects of donor legal support: economic law reform in various areas, training of government lawyers – the kind of activities that had been significantly criticized in the 1970s, but were now acceptable, at least in a transforming socialist country (McClymont and Golub 2000).

By the 1990s, of course, this fifth generation of work in law and development had expanded far beyond China and indeed beyond the formerly socialist world. The construction of a liberal legalism in Asia and Latin American market states might have been criticized in the 1970s, but the transformation of socialist to market states in the legal sphere was considered a legitimate project in the 1990s. In turn that work in the socialist states re-legitimized a return to non-socialist states as well. By the early to mid-1990s law and development activities were flourishing once again in dozens of countries around the world (Carothers 1999; Alford 2000).

DONOR LEGAL ASSISTANCE TO VIETNAM

Thus the stage was set for donor assistance to legal reform and the strengthening of legal institutions in Vietnam, beginning in the early 1990s. The "new" law and development (Rose 1998) had already been legitimized in China since the mid-1980s, and in dozens of other countries in the late 1980s and early 1990s. Donor legal support in Vietnam was thus part of this new generation of law and development activities. These activities in Vietnam can be divided into two phases, the first from roughly 1990 to 2000, and the second beginning in about 2000.

THE INITIAL FOCUS ON ECONOMIC LAW
AND LAWYER RETRAINING

Donor legal support in Vietnam began on a small scale in the late 1980s, as Vietnam reopened gradually to the world after decades of war and autarkic economic policies. Multilateral donors led the way, especially the United Nations Development Programme (UNDP), the World Bank, and the Asian Development Bank (ADB), with bilateral donors either supporting multilateral efforts and, for a few bilateral donors, supplementing those efforts with similar initiatives of their own. As Carol Rose, John Gillespie and evaluation efforts from the Vietnamese government, UNDP and others have clearly shown, those earliest efforts focused squarely on the institutional arrangements for a market economy – the redrafting of banking, investment, labor and other economic law, and retraining of government lawyers and young and middle-aged officials on key elements of the market economy and aspects of international integration. The Asian Development Bank retrained Vietnamese lawyers; the World Bank provided advice on economic law redrafting and overseas training; Australian bilateral aid supported training for government legal officers in Melbourne and in Vietnam – among a host of examples (Sevastik 1997; Rose 1998; Gillespie 1999a; UNDP Matrix 2000).

By mutual agreement between a cautious Party and government of Vietnam and cautious donors, those efforts did not include direct work on the authority, legitimacy or, usually, the enforcement of law. Nor did they focus on rights and on those left behind in Vietnam's rapidly developing market economy, both those in poverty, and those left behind in their ability to assert their rights. The donor support consensus in place in the late 1980s and throughout most of the 1990s relied on the strengthening of institutions and laws to produce growth, more equality, and help lift Vietnam and the Vietnamese out of poverty.

FROM ECONOMIC LAW TO INSTITUTIONAL CAPACITY BUILDING

One set of activities went beyond economic law and its formulation – a series of activities conducted by UNDP and several other donors intended to support capacity building and strengthening of the Ministry of Justice as the government's point body for legislative redrafting, legal planning, and law reform. In a broadening transition from narrow support for economic law reforms to initial support for institutional strengthening, the transitional bridge was institutional strengthening for the Ministry of Justice and other government and legal institutions. Donor economic law activities continued with a wide range of ministries and other government bodies. But the first UNDP activities with the Ministry also began in 1992, when a foreign legal advisor was first posted to the Ministry's headquarters on Cat Linh Street in Hanoi. Activities gradually intensified to that point that a professional, full-time legal advisor working on a portfolio of activities was posted to the Ministry by 1995. The activities included a mixture of capacity building for the Ministry, legal drafting, and training for other institutions – the latter two elements still focused substantially on economic law.

In this period Sweden also initiated fairly large-scale activities intended to "improv[e] the mechanisms for law-making and legal training; introduc[e] new and supposedly better structures for economic dispute resolution and bankruptcy ... enhanc[e] the institutional capacity of the Ministry of Justice [and] ... assist in the drafting of specific pieces of legislation or to facilitate a swift integration of Vietnam into regional and international bodies" (Umea Project in Brief 2000).

At the same time a fairly modest series of activities intended to strengthen the two core law faculties in Hanoi and the then two core law faculties in Ho Chi Minh City were initiated by several bilateral donors as well, particularly France, Sweden, and Japan. Sweden's expanding program focused on assisting teaching and research at several law faculties (Umea Project in Brief 2000; UNDP Matrix 2000); the French government supported the establishment of the Maison du Droit at the Hanoi Law College and its training programs in Vietnam and in France, as well as provision of French law materials and other activities (UNDP Matrix 2000); Japan and the Asia Foundation separately supported conferences with and research by the Institute of State and Law in the then National Center for the Social Sciences and Humanities (now VASS).

Thus the first six to seven years of donor legal assistance to Vietnam focused first on specific elements of the economic law agenda, and then gradually expanding to capacity building within the Ministry of Justice and beyond as an institutional development strategy for which both donors and the government could readily agree, as well as some initial efforts to help build capacity for law teaching and legal research.

THE BROADENING CIRCLE: INSTITUTIONAL SUPPORT FOR LEGISLATIVE, JUDICIAL AND PROSECUTORIAL CAPACITY BUILDING

A third stage of donor support for legal reform in Vietnam emerged in 1996 and 1997, when UNDP, Denmark and other donors began substantial capacity building efforts in three legal institutions that had long been largely closed to all but the most formal discussions with westerners. These were the Office of the National Assembly, the Supreme People's Court, and the Supreme People's Procuracy. The donors' (particularly UNDP's) capacity building and institutional strengthening efforts within the Ministry of Justice had proven both successful and were not perceived as particularly dangerous within the Communist Party. With that experience in mind the Party agreed to add those three other institutions – legislature, court, and procuracy – to the mix for donor-supported institutional strengthening, at a time when the enhancement of legislative, judicial and prosecutorial expertise was on the Vietnamese political agenda.

Thus by the mid 1990s, the widening array of donor activity in legal reform encompassed: continuing work on elements of the economic law agenda with dozens of state institutions, largely at the central level; continued capacity building efforts for the Ministry of Justice as the government's focal point for legislative development and legal reform; and new activities intended to build capacity in three other key institutions – the National Assembly, the judiciary, and the powerful state prosecutor's office.

In this third stage of building broader institutional capacity UNDP was a key conceptual and operational actor. Several bilateral donors provided support for UNDP projects with the Ministry of Justice, National Assembly, Supreme Court and Supreme Procuracy, while others began to work on their own in legal reform. But the UNDP work with the Ministry of Justice, National Assembly, Supreme Court and Procuracy were arguably the most significant activities in donor legal assistance during this period. These projects conducted a myriad of activities: training and other capacity building, both within Vietnam and abroad; provision of equipment; advice in legal drafting and comparative legislative perspectives; linking Vietnamese institutions to their counterparts around Southeast Asia, East Asia and beyond; and a range of other work. They also sought, with mixed success, to link these central institutions more effectively to their provincial and local branches, and more effectively to each other.

Other bilateral donors supported institutional strengthening on their own as well – Australia, Canada, Denmark and Sweden with the National Assembly; Denmark, Japan and France on training with the Supreme People's Court; Japan with the Supreme People's Procuracy; and a wide range of donors, including Germany, Japan, Sweden, UNDP and others with the key legal institution still most widely available for work with the foreign donor community – the Ministry of Justice (UNDP Matrix 2000). Some work on institutional capacity building also moved down to local levels in the late 1990s: Norway and other donors supported the training of judges in Ho Chi Minh City and Hanoi, for example, and other donors worked in other provinces. Left largely out of this picture was a key institution that began, in the mid to late 1990s, to play a growing role in the formulation of legal policy – the Internal Affairs Commission of the Vietnamese Communist Party (*Ban Noi chinh*). Not until 2002 and 2003 would foreign donors begin working in earnest with the Internal Affairs Commission, well after when that should have been occurring.

Though UNDP and the work with the Ministry, National Assembly, Supreme Court and Procuracy dominated donor legal assistance efforts in the mid and late 1990s, a plethora of other, sometimes smaller activities developed as well. The Swedish projects remained at a fairly large scale, gradually expanding in scope toward institutional strengthening and moving away from work on particular pieces of economic legislation. And cooperation in law drafting remained an important part of this agenda. France, Japan, and UNDP worked on the Civil Code; each also worked on the Civil Procedure Code and the Criminal Procedure Code, along with Denmark. A host of donors worked with Vietnamese partners on the Enterprise Law and its implementing documents. The list of donor engagement with law drafting and redrafting is a long list, generally involving work with one of the central legal institutions or a particular ministry tasked to draft a specific law, and this work constitutes an important but often under-recognized component of the donor legal assistance agenda in the mid- and late 1990s (UNDP Matrix 2000).

Other bilateral activities at this stage were usually of a relatively small scale and carefully maintained at an institutional level, where they could be controlled and monitored effectively. Thus Australia supported work by the Centre for Asian and Pacific Law at the University of Sydney with the Ho Chi Minh National Political Academy (Party School) on international law and human rights issues; the Netherlands supported retraining of faculty at Can Tho University that included some law teachers; the Ford Foundation supported training in international law at the Foreign Ministry's Institute for International Relations and some initial activities on human rights research and translation in the Ministry and the Party School; Canada supported comparative law work at the Ministry of Justice's Legal Research Institute; France expanded its training activities to include a three year graduate program for Hanoi Law University staff; JICA supported government lawyer retraining as well; and Sweden supported an expanded program of human rights training and study visits through the Ho Chi Minh National Political Academy (UNDP Matrix 2000).

In summary, the initial forms of donor assistance to Vietnam focused on economic law, and on institution building of legislative, judicial, procuratorial and legal training institutions, largely at the central level. Standard forms of donor legal assistance generally support the types of law and state that the receiving state and the donors desire to establish. In Vietnam, the receiving state and Party, and the donors, sought market-based structural improvements to Party-dominated institutions without, at least at the early stages, substantially improving the capacity of those institutions to exercise independent authority or to respond to claims of rights from below. But perhaps more provocatively, in Vietnam the receiving Party and state and, arguably, donors, funded economic law improvements that helped to reduce poverty while also substantially benefiting the new holders of capital and their state patrons and clients.

THE COMPLEX ROAD TO LEGAL "IMPLEMENTATION" AND "ENFORCEMENT"

By the mid 1990s it was already clear to many donors that Vietnam's busy activity and significant progress in drafting legislation and regulations was unmatched by implementation and enforcement of law at each jurisdictional level. A key issue for donors became how to access and work on that important arena of "implementation" and "enforcement." Some crucial enforcement and implementation institutions were largely off limits, including the then Ministry of Interior and other police and security forces, although a few organizations, the Ford Foundation among them, were able to do some training and familiarization work with the Ministry in the mid-1990s. Several governments also worked with the Ministry of Interior (later the Ministry of Public Security) on drug control and other criminal law matters, and eventually human trafficking issues.

Donor strategies for working on "implementation" and "enforcement" took several forms: Some of the significant focus on institution building and capacity development in the Ministry of Justice, National Assembly, judiciary and procuracy began to shift toward the implementation and enforcement of law by those institutions, including execution of judgments. Other line agencies were brought into the picture. A new focus on legal information systems emerged, an area important both to implementation and enforcement and to access to justice.

Thus several donors began work on training and drafting for civil judgment enforcement with the Ministry of Justice and other agencies; Denmark began a pilot project on customs and tax collection with the customs and tax authorities; and Germany began assisting implementation and enforcement of enterprise, cooperative, investment, budget, audit and banking law with the relevant government agencies. It was in this stage that donors first turned their programmatic attention to corruption in a significant way, including Swedish studies and other activities with the Ministry of Justice and the State Inspectorate, and Switzerland with the State Inspectorate as well (UNDP Matrix 2000).

Other implementation and enforcement programs were developed as well. The Asian Development Bank, whose legal staff had long promoted the importance of secured transactions, began work with the Ministry of Justice on a securitization register. Canada, Japan, Sweden and UNDP began extensive programs of work on the registration of land and housing and the implementation of land legislation. UNDP worked on streamlining implementation of company legislation (UNDP Matrix 2000). In the relatively clear political economy of donor legal assistance to Vietnam, donors were encouraged to work on legal implementation and enforcement because those were now priorities for Vietnam's legal institutions as well – but the donors worked on those issues with and through Vietnam's central legal institutions, whose interests in focusing on important national needs and on attracting important donor funds merged effectively in the work on "implementation" and "enforcement."

An exceptionally busy agenda of work on legal information systems emerged as well, involving multiple, sometimes overlapping efforts by UNDP and the Asian Development Bank and the bilateral aid agencies representing Denmark, Japan, Sweden and other major donors. These efforts involved: provision of computers and other equipment to the Ministry of Justice and other central legal institutions; linking central and provincial legal agencies; gathering legal documents and expanding access to them through CD-Roms and databases.

"ACCESS TO JUSTICE": THE FIRST GATEWAY TO RIGHTS

By the late 1990s fissures were developing in the donor consensus on legal assistance to Vietnam. Donors had spent much of a decade working first on economic law and then on institutional strengthening, with a sometimes frustrating foray into implementation and enforcement, amidst a widening and worrying sense that inequality was rising in Vietnam and that poor peasants, urban dwellers, and domestic and overseas laborers could not access justice and assert rights. In the late 1990s the NGO and donor community in Vietnam began thinking more explicitly about rights and social justice in their work. Rights issues began to arise with more frequency at annual donor meetings and more frequent NGO gatherings in Hanoi. The World Bank's focus under James Wolfensohn on reducing poverty and consulting with domestic and international NGOs brought rights issues more to the fore in its discussions on Vietnam projects, influencing the Asian Development Bank and others. Foreign NGOs began working more directly with laborers and the poor in Ho Chi Minh City and elsewhere around the country. On behalf of a range of foreign NGOs, Oxfam commissioned a planning paper in 1999 on how a rights-based legal perspective could be brought into NGO activities in Vietnam (Sidel 1999). And, perhaps most visibly, the Vietnamese government under-took the establishment of a legal aid system to provide legal counsel to citizens who could not afford lawyers, a major development discussed in Chapter 7, and rapidly gained support from a wide array of bilateral and nongovernmental donors.

It is not surprising that legal aid led the way toward a new focus on "access to justice." The Vietnamese Party and government could come to terms with foreign donors on the problem of "access to justice" far more easily than focusing directly on rights; Vietnam itself recognized, to its credit, that in a rapidly marketizing society in which the role of law was expanding, citizens needed legal expertise and that millions of Vietnamese could not afford legal assistance. Legal aid also involved providing access to law and legal remedies rather than a more challeng-ing focus on asserting rights, and it had a natural political base in a key legal institution already fully authorized to receive and coordinate donor legal assistance – the Ministry of Justice. For its part the Ministry was eager to support access to justice, not only as a normative matter but also to continue accessing donor support, and to maintain a leading position among jockeying institutions. All of that coalesced into a concern for "access to justice," a concern that manifested itself in the late 1990s most immediately in the establishment of legal aid as a governmental activity within and coordinated by the Ministry of Justice and local justice bureaus (UNDP 2004). For bilateral donors and NGOs, legal aid was also a natural entry point into access to justice and rights issues in a highly controlled donor environment. For bilateral donors and NGOs, legal aid gave them work on access to justice while recognizing that that was as far as the Party and government were willing to go at that stage. Denmark, Norway, Sweden, UNDP, the Asia Foundation and others rapidly became significant supporters of the initial legal aid programs developed by the Ministry of Justice through its National Legal Aid Agency (UNDP Matrix 2000).

A second important area within the broad arena of "access to justice" – also acceptable to the government and largely implemented through central legal institutions – was work on disseminating legal information and legal literacy. The Asian Development Bank, Canada, Denmark, Sweden and other donors were all involved in studies, pilot projects, publications and other activities intended to bring law to the people, though it remains unclear how much success those projects actually have had (UNDP Matrix 2000).

STRENGTHENING THE ROLE OF LAWYERS

The feeble Vietnamese Lawyers Association (VLA) and the complex, divided and weak Vietnamese bar had been unable to attract much donor interest through most of the early and mid-1990s. Nor had the key central legal institutions, including the Ministry of Justice, particularly encouraged donors to consider lawyers a priority field of donor activity. But in the mid- and late 1990s the increasing concern for implementation and enforcement, and for access to justice, and a recognition that the role of lawyers would need to grow in Vietnamese society led several donors to increase their work on capacity building for and linkage with the Vietnamese bar. The Asian Development Bank included the bar in its retraining programs; Canada supported training and workshop linkages between the Canadian Bar Association and the VLA; Denmark began a small program with the VLA; Japan included bar lawyers in its training programs and helped with revising the Law on Lawyers, among others (UNDP Matrix 2000). Yet there remained a strong sense in both Vietnamese lawyer and donor communities of a mismatch between the skills donors and their foreign partners could provide and the capacities needed in Vietnam. And some of the most important work in strengthening the role of lawyers – enabling lawyers to work directly on issues of rights, and as aggressive advocates in litigation – remained too sensitive for donor engagement.

RETHINKING AND EXPANDING THE STRATEGY FOR LEGAL DEVELOPMENT HARMONIZATION

Another, again expanded fourth phase of donor legal assistance began in about 2000–2001, when the Vietnamese government invited UNDP and other donors to provide assistance to the first major legal sector planning and strategy development effort in the *doi moi* era. Law and legal institutions had grown quickly since the late 1980s; constitutional revision was on the Vietnamese agenda; and there was a strong sense that strategic planning by the Party, state and legal institutions would be needed to support the strengthening of legal institutions in the short and medium term (through 2010 or 2020). If donor legal assistance activities in the first stage can be characterized as economic law-focused and quite specific to particular ministries and agencies; and in the second and third stages broadening to an institutional and implementation focus, then in the next stage the Vietnamese government acquiesced in the continuation of all those valuable activities and added yet another circle or layer to the expanding menu of donor legal assistance – support for legal system strategy development and for legal harmonization with the globalized legal system.

What resulted was a sizable project to support the Comprehensive Needs Assessment for the Development of Vietnam's Legal System to the Year 2010, coordinated by the Ministry of Justice and supported by a number of bilateral donors, including UNDP, the World Bank, Asian Development Bank, Japan, Denmark, Sweden, and France. Studies and conferences were undertaken beginning in March 2001 and a Comprehensive Legal Needs Analysis emerged in 2002 and 2003 that provided a blueprint for Vietnam's strengthening of law and legal institutions at least through 2010 (Legal System Needs Assessment 2002).

The advantage of this process is that it brought donors directly into the development of strategy for the legal system. The disadvantage was that the process seemed to avoid a number of important and controversial debates that were beginning to flow around the Party, legal institutions, intellectuals and activists: how should the Constitution be amended? Should there be a Constitutional Court or some other way to assert constitutional violations and vindicate constitutional rights? How autonomous and assertive should Vietnamese courts and lawyers be allowed to become? What, finally, should be done about the powerful procuracy, at one time the most powerful legal institution after the police but the subject of constant debate over its role and structure since at least the early 1990s? These larger questions seemed to go largely undiscussed in the drafting of the Comprehensive Legal Needs Assessment. That is not surprising – in most cases these issues have not been thought of as being the appropriate province of foreign donors, and they were being debated at a higher level than the Ministry of Justice (though interlocutors in those debates included senior MOJ officials).

After the Comprehensive Legal Needs Assessment was completed, the Ministry of Justice moved into drafting a Legal System Development Strategy for approval by the Party and government and implementation by the Ministry and a wide array of other agencies. UNDP, Sweden, Denmark, the World Bank and ADB provided assistance to the drafting and implementation of the Legal System Development Strategy. At the same time, however, Party officials began drafting their own version of a judicial reform strategy, one that came to stress court reforms but implicated issues beyond the judiciary as well. Swedish International Development Cooperation Agency – aggressive and innovative among the legal reform donors in seeking out work with the Party and its Internal Affairs Commission when others inexplicably and mistakenly held back – emerged as the key donor supporting the Party's judicial reform strategy development efforts. The result, in June 2005, was adoption of separate, parallel legal reform strategies. One was the Legal System Development Strategy drafted largely by the Ministry of Justice and other state agencies and focusing on legislative and institutional development; the other was the Judicial Reform Strategy, drafted largely by a judicial reform steering committee led and staffed primarily by Party officials and chaired by then-President Tran Duc Luong. Donors assisted with each of these, but the results were separate, and at the beginning of 2006 there were few signs that implementation of these strategies had been coordinated by the Party or government in significant ways (Legal System Development Strategy 2005; Judicial Reform Strategy 2005).

THE MAJOR NEW FOCUS ON LEGAL HARMONIZATION

The period after 2000 saw another shift in the focus of donor legal reform activity in Vietnam, as some donor funding moved toward helping Vietnam harmonize its laws and their implementation with international practice. This shift in focus resulted from Vietnam's signing of a Bilateral Trade Agreement (BTA) between Vietnam and the United States, and Vietnam's increasing efforts to gain WTO accession in the late 1990s and early years of the new decade. The US Agency for International Development (US AID) and a few other donors became deeply involved with assisting Vietnam in reforming its legal environment "in almost all key economic and commercial sectors, as well as advancing the procedures and capacity of the courts to resolve commercial, IPR and investment disputes" (UNDP Matrix 2005). This work, funded primarily by US AID with additional programs underway supported by Atlantic Philanthropies and other donors, has been undertaken in well over thirty national agencies and more than ten provincial and city governments. Activities include redrafting of a significant number of important laws and regulations, training of government officials, English translations, revision of court and other procedures, publication of judicial documents, legislative planning at the National Assembly on WTO accession, and a host of other activities (UNDP Matrix 2005).

The key actor in this new arena of legal harmonization has been the US AID-funded Support for Trade Acceleration (STAR-Vietnam) program, which is carrying out much of this work in collaboration with Vietnamese government ministries and other state organizations. That work has gone quite smoothly, fueled by the fact that much of STAR's workplan is mandated by the BTA and WTO accession, focusing attention by Vietnamese policymakers and national and local institutions in ways that have been lacking in other programs. The result has been what appears to be a highly successful program based on its own harmonization goals, though the implementation and enforcement of new legal provisions, and particularly of the transparency processes that the BTA and the WTO require, must be watched very closely in the years ahead (STAR Vietnam 2003, 2004, 2005).[3]

ASSESSING FIFTEEN YEARS OF DONOR SUPPORT FOR LEGAL REFORM IN VIETNAM

Donor concern with how law actually worked among ordinary people, institutions and enterprises gathered steam in the second decade of donor engagement with Vietnamese legal reform, reflecting donor concerns as well as a shift in attention among some institutions and policy makers in Vietnam. Donor programs continued to build capacity within central institutions such as the Ministry of Justice, National Assembly, judiciary and procuracy, but now added a range of activities intended to promote the implementation and enforcement of law and "access to justice." The shifts in one major donor legal reform project, the key activity funded by Sweden, indicated the shifts in emphasis.

In the early 1990s, Sweden's main law reform project in Vietnam had sought to "improve the mechanisms for law-making and legal training; introduce new and supposedly better structures for economic dispute resolution and bankruptcy . . . enhance the institutional capacity of the Ministry of Justice and . . . assist in the drafting of specific pieces of legislation or to facilitate a swift integration of Vietnam into regional and international bodies." Beginning in 2001 the focus was on "strengthening the capacity for law-making and law implementation . . . improving the protection of people's rights; and . . . enhanc[ing] the administrative capacity of the Ministry of Justice" (Umea Project in Brief 2000, with slight grammatical revisions). It was a changing, hybrid era for virtually all the donors, and the Swedish project description captured it well.

In one sense, Vietnam's central legal institutions supported the expansion of donor focus to implementation, enforcement and access to justice, for the Vietnamese Party and state was already anxious about farmer, labor and urban unrest, and a perception that thousands of legal documents had been promulgated but that legal enforcement was exceptionally weak. So Vietnamese and donor interests coincided. But it is important not to omit the institutional interests of Vietnam's central legal institutions and Vietnam's political realities: the price for expanding donor work on implementation, enforcement and access to justice was twofold: the donors would continue to support capacity building in the central legal institutions, and the new work on implementation, enforcement and access to justice would be carried out through the central legal institutions.

The donors were in a complicated position, particularly as fissures had begun to develop in the Party/donor legal consensus. Tens of millions of dollars had been put into the structures of economic law and the structures of judicial and legislative administration. The Party and donors may have wanted subordinate, instrumental legal structures to serve the development of markets – but there was an increasing recognition of the costs of these policies, recognized rapidly in the late 1990s by alert bilaterals and by an increasingly assertive NGO community. Economic and political gaps were continuing to grow in Vietnamese society. Early warning signs included small but highly public demonstrations by Vietnamese farmers against corruption, bureaucracy and excessive taxation in the late 1990s and the early part of the new decade. Labor unrest grew rapidly as well, across the spectrum from foreign-invested factories to state-owned enterprises to the thriving private sector to violations of labor rights among Vietnam's highly visible overseas workers. Increasingly the thousands of pages of legal documents and the thousands of legal personnel seemed irrelevant on the ground: workers and farmers went largely unprotected by the supposedly "strengthened legal system," corruption was widely perceived to be out of control, and in Saigon, a highly visible gangland leader co-opted, utilized, corrupted and commanded a healthy swath of the new cadre of trained, supposedly "professionalized" police, prosecutors, legal officials and others to serve his private purposes rather than serving the authority of law or even the authority of the Party. In short, after a decade and a half of donor-supported legal reforms, Vietnamese law looked more modern, more detailed and more user-friendly to the business community – but either ineffective or worse to ordinary citizens, with a perception that it was primarily protecting the wealthy and powerful in Vietnamese society.

For donors, there was a general sense that law was not living up to its expectations; for the Vietnamese authorities, this was a problem of "implementation" and "participation" and perhaps even "access." It is a complicated period, for this emerging sense among donors coincided with and was strongly affected by other developments in the donor community. One such factor was the emphasis on poverty reduction and the discourse of democratic governance that has emerged from the World Bank and the NGO community. Even this notion that implementation, participation, access and poverty reduction might be moved toward the center of law and development efforts provoked institutional resistance, not only in certain countries but also in other multilateral institutions. When permeated through a Vietnamese, donor and legal lens, what emerged in Vietnam was a new focus on "implementation" and "participation" and, to some degree, perhaps less in Vietnam than in some other countries, directly linking law and poverty reduction.

There have been some successes in this new donor programming, particularly in smaller, bilateral programs that have sought to serve and build capacity in areas of law and gender, legal aid, corruption, rural economic issues, democratization, and the strengthening of a voluntary sector. At the same time, particularly in the mainstream of donor legal support in Vietnam that now includes elements of "implementation" and "participation," there are strong and disturbing parallels with the early stage of legal development to serve a market economy. This new mainstream donor approach to legal reform may well be failing to prevent the exploitation and cooptation of donor-supported legal structures from being used for exploitation by powerful actors who overwhelm the little legitimacy and authority that law currently has.

First, despite recent attention to implementation, participation and legal literacy, the donor emphasis continues to focus on creation, strengthening and support of a legal elite rather than on developing programs that serve the exercise of law by those most negatively affected by it in Vietnamese society. At the urging of Vietnamese government agencies, donors continue to emphasize traditional capacity building programs, such as training legislative and government officials, providing computers and other materials to ministries and parliamentarians and prosecutors and police – though now with an additional emphasis on implementation and broader elite participation. Despite some concern in the donor community, both among NGOs and bilateral and multilateral aid agencies, rights and justice and the exercise of rights by affected groups continue to remain the largely unmentioned and unaddressed elements of donor support.

Second, legal reform donors have not yet effectively targeted those left behind in Vietnam's rush to the market in major programs. Some may argue that donor support for legal aid programs, a new development since the late 1990s that reflects the new emphasis on implementation, participation and access, conflicts with this conclusion. It does not. Legal aid in Vietnam serves admirably to ameliorate legal problems in some individual cases without challenging structures of power that have emerged, and donor support for it is a patchwork that has not yet begun to address the issues of inequity and legitimacy that truly envelop the Vietnamese legal system.

Nor do the new donor programs that seek to broaden participation in the drafting of legislation and legal instruments effectively assist those left behind or exploited in the nexus between market and law in Vietnam. Those projects to increase participation are aimed primarily at elite legislators and at other officials, seeking to replace narrow Party fiat with a somewhat broader consensus-building cadre – but usually not including ordinary citizens who may be disadvantaged or even oppressed by the cooptation of the legal system created since the late 1980s, despite some admirable efforts to establish computer-based and other mechanisms to seek citizen input on draft legislation.

Thus we have come to a state in which donor legal support has played a major role in creating structures of law and legal institutions that existed largely as shells as recently as the early 1990s. That is a major accomplishment. Yet at the same time we are witnessing, in the cases I have mentioned and in others, failures in that project, and significant issues in the more recent project of supplementing legal construction with legal implementation, participation, and access to justice. These are the intertwined problems of legal authority and legitimacy, the failure of law to address the rapidly growing problem of social equity, and a failure of the strengthening of groups and citizens that are able to criticize, analyze and produce policy alternatives and to struggle for the authority and legitimacy of law.

THE ROAD AHEAD FOR DONOR LEGAL SUPPORT IN VIETNAM

The fundamental problems of Vietnamese law today, some twenty years after legal reform began and fifteen years after donors entered the picture are particularly intractable: law's failure to serve social justice and social equity, and the remaining weaknesses in the authority and legitimacy of law and the legal system. The reshaped focus of the major donors on legal harmonization and legal implementation shows little signs of significant capacity to affect these intertwined problems of social justice and law's authority and legitimacy. Too often the work of the major donors produces an ability to draft legislation that is used to harm the victims of Vietnam's marketization process (such as export or domestic workers) or that strengthens structures that remain highly susceptible to official and unofficial cooptation (as evidenced by Nam Cam's takeover of legal and judicial structures of Ho Chi Minh City). The broadening of donor legal support from the creation of legal structures for a market to include work on implementation, participation and access has occurred in China and other countries as well as in Vietnam. But at least in Vietnam – and probably elsewhere as well – there is a clear need for a new paradigm in donor legal support in Vietnam that clearly addresses law and authority, law and social justice, and law and the creation of critical, analytical groups with the capacity to initiate dialogues and further reforms.

This is not to say that all donor efforts are unduly tainted by these problems. For example, the United Kingdom, Australia, Sweden, Canada and other donors continue to support domestic NGOs that are seeking to use law on behalf of victimized groups, be they women or poor farmers or other sectors (UNDP Matrix 2005). This focus, exemplary but too rare, on the victims of marketization and bureaucratic corruption and on their legal capacity and strategies, should certainly be continued. And even major donor support for increasing implementation, participation and elite access in the central structures of law – the Supreme Court and higher local courts, the national prosecutors' office and the chain of public prosecutors down to the provincial and local levels, the National Assembly – while too limited, has its utility in seeking modest reforms in a system riven by internal contradictions. But the major donors should seek to do considerably more.

What might a new paradigm in law and development donor support for Vietnam look like, in a system in which the Party has imposed key limits on the scope of law's authority and legitimacy, and in which weak law serves the bureaucratic and financial interests of state officials and the holders of economic power alike? Bearing in mind the very real limitations imposed by Vietnamese policymakers, a system in which the Party continues to dominate law and in which weak law is used for bureaucratic and personal gain by state officials and the holders of capital to oppress others, there are two key directions for donor legal support that might yield some positive influence:

The first is explicitly working to build long-term capacity, including the capacity for new and broader thinking, among newer and broadened generations of legal intellectuals. This is an ironic return to traditional donor programming that has been sharply neglected since the Chinese experience of the 1980s. The donors have failed to do this in Vietnam. It is true that donors have worked with the law colleges on economic legislation; have sent law teachers and court officials and ministry cadres abroad to study foreign investment law and banking law and taxation. But donors have never done in Vietnam what was executed successfully in China in the 1980s and 1990s: intentionally seeking to build a new corps of legal scholars and teachers whose vision for the possibility of law, for the application of law, for the authority of law is wider than Party-dominated law and wider than the technical aspects of economic law, wider than the next draft of a foreign investment law, wider than "legal harmonization," wider than donors' vision for law.

In China those younger and mid-level legal scholars trained in England and America returned home with a broadened vision for the aspirations of law and its authority. They have worked in numerous fields – economic and civil law, criminal law, jurisprudence and many others. But they have set a new tone for the role of law in China, pushing the boundaries of debate at key moments (such as in 1989) while staffing and rising to leadership in the key intellectual centers of Chinese law (Sidel 1995b, 1999; McClymont and Golub 2000). Donors have failed to do this in Vietnam. It is indeed possible that most multilateral and bilateral donors even prefer, like their Vietnamese Party and state counterparts, to work with relatively narrowly focused and relatively compliant economic law officials. Many donors prefer those who draft and implement to those who challenge. And Vietnam itself may be uncomfortable with the idea of a much more independent group of public legal intellectuals who seek to vindicate rights, link to the problems of the poor and disadvantaged, and effect major reforms in the legal system.

Second, the donor community must seek to expand work with those most directly and negatively affected by the expansion of the market economy in Vietnam and the interests of officials and criminals in that market system. There are many such affected groups: peasants over-taxed and over-regulated by cadres; industrial, manufacturing and service workers in a variety of workplaces; women workers in many industries; export workers exploited by loan sharks, local police, local officials and labor export companies; and many others disadvantaged under a new system of market regulation that may have provided more law but arguably, for significant numbers of people, less rights.

The donor community, particularly smaller NGOs and some bilaterals, already work relatively directly and at the grassroots with a variety of these affected groups. To the degree possible, such work should now include legal protection and legal advocacy that is as autonomous as possible, a difficult task but one well worth undertaking. There are a number of possible ways to do this: seeking to help establish semi-autonomous or even relatively autonomous legal support centers that can help in the assertion of rights; seeking to strengthen and, just as important, help make more autonomous the legal aid centers now in formation; assisting law schools in establishing legal clinics for the assertion of rights, not merely the drafting of laws, which can have the added benefits of contributing to the formation of an innovative, challenging group of legal intellectuals and might allow law colleges and departments to play a role in protecting clinics that assert rights; directly supporting the development of newer and broadened generations of critical legal intellectuals; significantly strengthening the role and capacity of the media in exposing abuses of legal rights and demanding both redress and structural change, and other methods as well.

There are those in the Vietnamese Party, government and in the donor community who do believe that the second phase of law and development activities in Vietnam, marked by an added emphasis on legal harmonization and legal implementation, may well signify the limits of what can and should be accomplished in a socialist transitional state like Vietnam. Those efforts may be applauded, but they are certainly not sufficient, and donors continuing to pour millions of dollars into Vietnam's legal reform efforts will need to reassess their goals and activities in the years ahead in an effort to serve those who are disadvantaged in the midst of the wave of legal reform that Vietnam has promoted and institutionalized since the *doi moi* era began.

NOTES

1. The author served as litigative consultant to the US Department of Justice in the prosecution of the major case of labor slavery of Vietnamese workers that is discussed in this chapter and Chapter 5, as well as consultant to a number of the donors supporting legal reform activities in Vietnam discussed here, including the United Nations Development Programme, the World Bank, Asian Development Bank, the Vietnamese Ministry of Justice, Oxfam and the Ford Foundation. The views expressed here are the author's alone and not those of any organizations, many of which might not agree with the conclusions discussed here.
2. I have never entirely understood how "law and development" could crumble so quickly under the onslaught of a few intellectual critics based in London, Madison and elsewhere. It was only when I began working in the donor world on legal reform activities, as I have with the Ford Foundation as a program staff member in Beijing, Hanoi, Bangkok and New Delhi, and as a consultant with a number of other organizations, that I began to understand how truly skittish the donors can be, and how quick to retreat from controversial and criticized programs, especially when those criticisms are raised by local elites or noted academics.
3. One result of particular interest has been the release of the first two volumes of case documents by the Supreme People's Court, a significant event for judges, lawyers and students of Vietnamese law in Vietnam and no less a major event for scholars and students of Vietnamese law abroad (Supreme People's Court 2005).

BIBLIOGRAPHY

ABC Radio 2004. 'Vietnamese woman detained for trafficking women to China', 15 January 2004 (http://abc.net.au/asiapacific)

Agence France Presse 1994a. 'Police clash with crowd outside Hanoi trial', 14 December 1994

1994b. 'Incidents lors du procès en appel d'un policier condamné pour meurtre', 14 December 1994

1994c. 'Court upholds death penalty on Hanoi policeman', 15 December 1994

1995. 'Hanoi traffic policeman executed after controversial case', 6 March 1995

2002. 'Official sentenced to death in Vietnam for fraud', 26 November 2002

Ainsworth, Janet 1992. 'Interpreting sacred texts: Preliminary reflections on constitutional discourse in China', 43 *Hastings Law Journal* 273–300

Alford, William P. 2000. 'Exporting the 'pursuit of happiness'", 113 *Harvard Law Review* 1677–1715

Amnesty International 1996. *Socialist Republic of Vietnam: The death penalty.* London: Amnesty International

Amnesty International USA 1990. *Vietnam: Renovation (doi moi), the law and human rights in the 1980s.* New York: Amnesty International USA

An, Nguyen Van 2001. 'Doan ket chung quanh Dang ta, tiep tuc dua dat nuoc vung buoc di len', *Tap chi Cong san (Communist Review)*, July 2001 (http://tapchicongsan.org.vn)

Asia Watch and Committee to Protect Journalists 1987. *Still confined: Journalists in 're-education' camps and prisons in Vietnam.* New York: Asia Watch

Asia Watch 1993. *The case of Doan Viet Hoat and Freedom Forum: Detention for dissent in Vietnam.* New York: Asia Watch

Asian Labour News 2003. 'Vietnam: Taiwan bans 43 labour agencies', 22 November 2003 (http://www.asianlabour.org)

Bach, Pham Van and Hoe, Vu Dinh 1984. 'The three successive Constitutions of Vietnam', 1 *International Review of Contemporary Law* 105–118

Balme, Stéphanie and Sidel, Mark 2007. *Vietnam's new order: International perspectives on the state and reform in Vietnam.* New York, Palgrave Macmillan

Bao Lao Dong 2001a. 'Can tang cuong so luong dai bieu Quoc hoi chuyen trach', 26 June 2001 (http://www.laodong.com.vn)

2001b. 'Quoc hoi thao luan sua doi, bo sung Hien phap nam 1992 Can tang cuong so luong dai bieu Quoc hoi chuyen trach', 26 June 2001 (http://www.laodong.com.vn)

2001c. 'Quoc hoi tiep tuc thao luan ve noi dung sua doi, bo sung Hien phap nam 1992', 27 June 2001 (http://www.laodong.com.vn)

2001d. 'Can bo cong doan chu chot gop y du thao sua doi, bo sung hien phap', 21 September 2001 (http://www.laodong.com.vn)

2001e. 'Can co hinh thuc bo phieu bat tin nhiem', 1 December 2001 (http://www.laodong.com.vn)

2001f. 'Quoc hoi thao luan va thong qua viec sua doi, bo sung mot so dieu cua Hien phap nam 1992 Phat trien giao duc, khoa hoc – cong nghe la quoc sach hang dau', 12 December 2001 (http://www.laodong.com.vn)

2001g. 'Quoc hoi thong qua toan van du thao Luat To chuc Quoc hoi (sua doi)', 19 December 2001 (http://www.laodong.com.vn)

2004. 'Lap toa an hien phap, mo che dinh thua phat lai', 20 October 2004, (http://www.laodong.com.vn)

Bao Phap Luat 2001. 'Tra loi cau hoi vi sao lai chi sua do, bo sung dieu cua Hien phap 1992' (Interview with Nguyen Van An), 19 September 2001

2004. 'De dan can la co' (We must provide what the people need), 22 October 2004 (reprinted at http://www.cpv.org.vn)

Barrett, Jill 1983.'What's new in China's new Constitution?', 9 *Review of Socialist Law* 305–345

BBC 2003. 'US factory boss guilty of 'slavery'", 22 February 2003 (http://news.bbc.co.uk)

2005a. 'Nang vi tri luat su trong xa hoi VN' (Raising the status of lawyers in Vietnamese society), BBC Vietnamese Service, 20 September 2005 (http://news.bbc.co.uk/vietnamese)

2005b. 'Bi gat do lien quan hoat dong "Vi cong ly"?' (Rejected because of the activities of 'For Justice'?), BBC Vietnamese Service, 20 September 2005 (http://news.bbc.co.uk/vietnamese)

Beaulieu, Carole 1994. *Is it an NGO? Is it civil society? Is it pluralism wriggling along?* Hanover: Institute of Current World Affairs

Bergling, Per 1997. 'Theory and reality in legal co-operation – The case of Vietnam,' in Sevastik 1997, pp. 64–66

1999. *Legal reform and private enterprise: The Vietnamese experience.* Umea: Umea University

Bergling, Per, Häggqvist, Erik, et al. 1996. *The Vietnamese legal system.* Hanoi: Ministry of Justice

Binh Dinh Legal Aid Centre 2003. *Handbook on legal aid (So tay vu viec Tro giup Phap ly).* Ninh Thuan: Binh Dinh Thuan Legal Aid Center

Bon Nhan Van. *Giai pham truoc toa an du luan.* 1959. Hanoi: Truth Publishing House

Boudarel, Georges 1991. *Cent fleurs enclosés dans la nuit du Vietnam: Communisme et dissidence 1954–1956*. Paris: Jacques Bertoin

Bui Cong Ly 1995. 'Sang 5–3, tai phap truong Cau Nga, Ban an to hinh Nguyen Tung Duong da duoc thi hanh', *Ha Noi moi*, 7 March 1995

Cai, Dingjian 1995. 'Constitutional supervision and interpretation in the People's Republic of China', 9 *Journal of Chinese Law* 219–245

Cam, Le 2003. 'Cai cach Tu phap o Viet Nam trong giai doan xay dung Nha nuoc phap quyen: Mot so van de chung' (Judicial reform in Vietnam during the era of building a state ruled by law: Some general issues). 2003 *Vietnam National University Journal of Economics and Law*, n.p.

Can, Le Thac 2006. *Report to the Vietnamese Union of Scientific and Technological Associations and the United Nations Development Programme on the Law on Associations*. Hanoi: United Nations Development Programme

Cao, Lan 2001. 'Reflections on market reform in post-war, post-embargo Vietnam', 22 *Whittier Law Review* 1029–1057

Carothers, Thomas 1999. *Aiding democracy abroad: The learning curve*. Washington: Carnegie Endowment for International Peace

Chan, Anita, Kerkvliet, Benedict, and Unger, Jonathan (eds.) 1999. *Transforming Asian socialism: China and Vietnam compared*. Sydney: Allen and Unwin

Chan, Anita and Norlund, Irene 1998. 'Vietnamese and Chinese labor regimes: On the road to divergence', 40 *The China Journal* 173–197

Chi, Hoang Van 1958. *The new class in North Vietnam*. Saigon: Cong dan

Chinh, Hoang Minh 1992. 'Ve sua doi Hien phap 1992' (http://www.danchu.net)

CIEM (Central Institute of Economic Management) 1996. *Kinh nghiem cua mot so hop tac xa tieu bieu trong cac nghan kinh te (Experiences of outstanding cooperatives in different economic sectors)*. Hanoi: Central Institute of Economic Management

Circular 1 2004. Ministry of Home Affairs, Circular 01/2004/TT-BNV guiding the implementation of a number of articles of Government Decree 88/2003/ND-CP on the organization, operation and management of associations (http://www.un.org.vn/donor/civil)

Circular 2 2003. Ministry of Public Security, Circular no. 02/2003/TT-BCA(C11) providing guidance on registration and issuance of licenses for road motorized means of transport (28 January 2003) (http://www.luatvietnam.com.vn)

Circular 17 2005. Ministry of Public Security, Circular no. 17/2005/TT-BCA(C11) providing guidance on registration and issuance of licenses for road motorized means of transport (21 November 2005) (http://www.luatvietnam.com.vn; http://www.nhandan.com.vn)

Circular 22 2003. Ministry of Labor, Invalids and Social Affairs, Circular no. 22/2003/TT-BLDTBXH providing guidance on the implementation of

Decree no. 81/2003/ND-CP (July 17, 2003) of the Government on detailed provisions and guidance for the implementation of the Labor Code with respect to Vietnamese laborers overseas (http://www.dafel. gov.vn/ english/document/circular22.html)

Civicus Vietnam Study Group, Dang Ngoc Dinh, Norlund, Irene et al. (eds.) 2006. *The emerging civil society: An initial assessment of civil society in Vietnam.* Hanoi: Civicus Vietnam Study Group.

Civil Code of the Socialist Republic of Vietnam 1995. Hanoi: The Gioi Publishers

CNN 2003. 'Factory owner convicted of abuse', 22 February 2003 (http://www.cnn.com)

Cohen, Jerome 1978.'China's changing Constitution', 76 *China Quarterly* 794–841
    1990. 'China's influence on Vietnam's emerging legal environment', 17 *China Business Review* 43–45

Cohen, Jerome, Tai, Ta Van and Bich, Nguyen Ngoc 1999. *Investment law and practice in Vietnam.* Hong Kong: Longman

Communist Party 2002. Political Bureau Resolution 8 on some crucial tasks in legal work in the forthcoming period (Nghi quyet 08 cua Bo Chinh tri ve mot so nhiem vu trong tam cong tac tu phap trong thoi gian toi) (http://www.cpv.org.vn)

Communist Party 2005a. 'Viewpoints of the Party on legal aid work', 13 September 2005 (http://www.cpv.org.vn)
    2005b. 'Ban Cong tac lap phap cua Uy ban thuong vu Quoc hoi to chuc hoi thao khoa hoc ve "Co che bao hien o Viet Nam",' (The legal drafting work group of the Standing Committee of the National Assembly organizes a research meeting on 'the system of constitutional protection in Vietnam') (22 March 2005) (http://www.cpv.org.vn; http://www.nhandan.org.vn)

Constitution of the Socialist Republic of Vietnam 1992. In *The Constitutions of Vietnam, 1946–1959–1980–1992.* Hanoi: The Gioi Publishers

Criminal Code of the Socialist Republic of Vietnam 1989. In *Selection of fundamental laws and regulations of Vietnam 2003.* Hanoi: The Gioi Publishers, pp. 203–416

Daewoosa Judgment 2002, http://samoa.saigon.com/samoa/overview/index.html

Dallas Morning News 2003. 'Human trafficking victims find hope, U.S. visas', 18 April 2003

Dam, Vu Cao 2002. 'On the occasion of the tenth anniversary of the promulgation of Decree 35/HDBT by the government', trans. Nghiem Phu Ninh, adapted by Mark Sidel

Dang, Nguyen Huu 1956a. 'It is necessary to have a more regularized society', *Nhan van* no. 4 (5 November 1956)
    1956b. 'How are democratic freedoms guaranteed by the Vietnamese Constitution of 1946?', *Nhan van* no. 5 (20 November 1956).

Decision 7 1995. Decision 07/CP of the Government on detailed provisions on certain articles of the Labor Code on the sending of Vietnamese labor to work overseas on fixed terms (20 January 1995) (http://www.vietlaw.gov.vn; http://home.vnn.vn/english/legal_docs/doc00015.html)

Decision 135 2003. Decision 135/2003/ND-CP of the Government on the inspection and handling of legal documents (14 November 2003) (http:// www.na.gov.vn)

Decision 258 1957. Government Implementing Decree on associations 1957, Nghi dinh quy dinh chi tiet thi hanh Luat so 102-SL (14 June 1957)

Decision 370 1991. Decision 370-HDBT of the Council of Ministers (9 November 1991), at www.vietlaw.gov.vn

Decision 725 1999. Ministry of Labor, Invalids and Social Affairs, Decision 725/1999/QD-BLDTBXH on labor export (30 June 1999) (http:// asemconnectvietnam.gov.vn/laws)

Decision 734 1997. Ministry of Justice, Decision 734/Ttg on establishing the system of legal aid for the poor and other policy targets (6 September 1997)

Decree 27 2001. Decree 27/2001/ND-CP of the Government on travel and tourism businesses (5 June 2001)

Decree 35 1992. Ministry of Science and Technology, Decision 35-HDBT on the management of science and technology (28 January 1992); and implementing regulations to Decision 35 (Joint Circular 195-LB, 13 November 1992)

Decree 81 2003. Decree 81/2003/ND-CP of the Government on detailed provisions and guidance for the implementation of the Labor Code with respect to Vietnamese laborers overseas (http://www.dafel.gov. vn/english/document/decree81.html; http://www.dost-dongnai.gov.vn/ vbndung. asp?idd=15982)

Decree 88 2003. Decree 88/2003/ND-CP of the Government on the organ-ization, operation and management of associations (http://www.un.org. vn/donor/civil)

Decree 152 1999. Decree 152/1999/ND-CP of the Government on fixed term labor abroad by Vietnamese specialists (20 September 1999) (http:// www.dafel.gov.vn; http://asemconnectvietnam.gov.vn)

Decree 177 1999. Decree 177/1999/ND-CP promulgating the regulations on the organization and operation of social funds and charity funds (http:// www.un.org.vn/donor/civil)

Department of Justice 2003. 'Garment factory owner convicted in largest ever human trafficking case prosecuted by the Department of Justice', 21 February 2003 (http://www.usdoj.gov)

Directive 20 1995. Ministry of Labor, Invalids and Social Affairs, Directive 20/ LDTBXH-TT providing implementing regulations under the 1995 labor export regulations (3 August 1995) (http://law.vdcmedia.com)

Directive 28 1999. Directive 28/1999/TT-BLDTBXH of the Government on the implementation of Decree 152/1999/ND-CP (15 November 1999) (http://www.dafel.gov.vn)

Directive 33 2001. Ministry of Labor, Invalids and Social Affairs, Directive 33/2001/TTLT-BTC-BLDTBXH providing supplemental guidance and amending Directive 16 2000 on labor export (http://www.dafel.gov.vn; http://law.vdcmedia.com)

Directive 41 1999. Communist Party of Vietnam, Political Bureau of the Central Committee, Directive 41-CT/TW on the export of workers and specialists (22 September 1999) (http://www.dafel.gov.vn)

Directive 1366 2001. Ministry of Labor, Invalids and Social Welfare, Directive 1366/LDTBXH-QLLDNN on certain enterprises not permitted to continue sending Vietnamese workers and specialists to work abroad for fixed terms (21 May 2001) (http://vnlegal-info.net.vn/vnlegalinfo/dvsb; http://law.vdcmedia.com)

Document 3828 1999. Office of the Government, Document 3828/VPCP-VX on management of sending labor to work abroad for a fixed term (21 August 1999) (http://law.vdcmedia.com)

Dong, Pham Van 1980. 'May van de ve nha nuoc dan chu nhan dan', in Dong, Pham Van 1980. *Mot so van de ve nha nuoc (Some questions on the state)*. Hanoi: Truth Publishing House, pp. 80–83

Duiker, William J. 1992. 'The constitutional system of the Socialist Republic of Vietnam', in Beer, Lawrence (ed.) 1992. *Constitutional systems in late twentieth century Asia*. Seattle: University of Washington Press, pp. 331–362

Dung, Nguyen Dang 2001a. 'Can quan triet hon nua ky thuat lap hien', *Bao Nhan Dan*, 11 September 2001, republished on National Assembly constitutional amendment comment webpage, http://www.na.gov.vn

2001b. 'Ve viec sua doi Hien phap nam 1992 – Mot so van de co tinh nguyen tac', *Tap chi Cong san (Communist Review)*, November 2001 (http://tapchicongsan.org.vn)

Dung, Nguyen Dang and Tuan, Ngo Duc 1999. *Luat hien phap Viet Nam (Vietnamese constitutional law)*. Bien Hoa: Dong Nai General Publishing House

Econet 2003. 'Challenges ahead for labor export', 29 January 2001

The Economist 1995. 'Vietnam: Courts of public opinion', 6 January, 1995, p. 31.

Falk, Per 1997. 'Legal training: The case of Vietnam', in Sevastik 1998, pp. 106–144

Fall, Bernard 1954.'Local administration under the Viet Minh', 27 *Pacific Affairs* 50–57

1956. 'The labor movement in the Communist zone of Viet-Nam', 45 *Monthly Labor Review* 534–537

1959. 'North Viet-Nam's new draft Constitution', 32 *Pacific Affairs* 178–186

1960a. 'Constitution-writing in a Communist state: The new Constitution of North Vietnam', 6 *Howard Law Journal* 157–168

1960b. 'North Viet-Nam's Constitution and government', 33 *Pacific Affairs* 282–290

1966. *Viet-Nam witness 1953–1966*. New York: Praeger

1967. *The two Viet-Nams: A political and military analysis*. New York: Praeger

1975. *The Viet-Minh regime: Government and administration in the Democratic Republic of Viet-Nam*. Ithaca: Southeast Asia Program, Cornell University

Fforde, Adam 1986.'The unimplementability of policy and the notion of law in Vietnamese Communist thought', 1 *Southeast Asia Journal of Social Sciences* 60–70

Friedman, Lawrence M. 1969. 'Legal culture and social development', 4 *Law and Society Review* 29–44

Gainsborough, Martin 2003a.'Corruption and the politics of economic decentralisation in Vietnam', 33 *Journal of Contemporary Asia* 69–84

2003b. *Changing political environment of Vietnam: The case of Ho Chi Minh City*. London: Routledge Curzon

Gardner, James 1980. *Legal imperialism: American lawyers and foreign aid in Latin America*. Madison: University of Wisconsin Press

Giao, Nguyen Ngoc 1994. 'The media and the emergence of a 'Civil Society'", Paper delivered to the 1994 Vietnam Update Conference, Australian National University, Canberra, 1994

Gillespie, John 1995. 'The role of the bureaucracy in managing urban land in Vietnam', 5 *Pacific Rim Law and Policy Journal* 59–124

1998. 'Land law subsystems? Urban Vietnam as a case study', 7 *Pacific Rim Law and Policy Journal* 555–610

1999a. 'Law and development in 'the market place': An East Asian perspective', in Jayasuriya, Kanishka (ed.) 1999. *Law, capitalism and power in Asia: The rule of law and legal institutions*. London: Routledge, pp. 118–150

1999b. 'Vietnam: The emergence of a law-based state', in Tay, Alice (ed.) 1999. *East Asia: Human rights, nation-building, trade*. Baden-Baden: Nomos Verlagsgesellschaft, pp. 333–371

2001a. 'Globalisation and legal transplantation: Lessons from the past', 6 *Deakin Law Review* 286–311

2001b. 'Self-interest and ideology: Bureaucratic corruption in Vietnam', 3 *Australian Journal of Asian Law* 1–36

2002a. 'Transplanted company law: An ideological and cultural analysis of market entry in Vietnam', 51 *International and Comparative Law Quarterly* 641–672

2002b. 'The political-legal culture of anti-corruption reforms in Vietnam', in Lindsey, Timothy and Dick, Howard (eds.) 2002. *Corruption in Asia: Rethinking the governance paradigm*. Sydney: The Federation Press, pp. 167–200

2004. 'Concepts of law in Viet Nam: Transforming statist socialism', in Peerenboom, Randall (ed.) 2004. *Asian discourses of rule of law*. London: Routledge Curzon, pp. 146–182

2006. *Transplanting commercial law reform: Developing a 'rule of law' in Vietnam*. Aldershot: Ashgate

229

Gillespie, John (ed.) 1987. *Commercial legal developments in Vietnam: Vietnamese and foreign commentaries.* Singapore: Butterworths

Gillespie, John and Nicholson, Penelope 2005. *Asian socialism and legal change: The dynamics of Vietnamese and Chinese reform.* Canberra: Asia Pacific Press

Ginsburg, Tom 2003. *Judicial review in new democracies: Constitutional courts in Asian cases.* Cambridge: Cambridge University Press.

Ginsburgs, George 1962a. 'Local government and administration in North Vietnam, 1945–54', 10 *China Quarterly* 174–204

    1962b. 'Local government and administration in the Democratic Republic of Vietnam since 1954 (Part 1)', 12 *China Quarterly* 211–230

    1963. 'Local government and administration in the Democratic Republic of Vietnam since 1954 (Part 2)', 14 *China Quarterly* 195–211

    1979. 'The genesis of the Peoples' Procuracy in the Democratic Republic of Vietnam', (1979) 5 *Review of Socialist Law* 187–198

Global Standards 2003. 'Vietnam Update', 12 February 2003 (http://www.global-standards.com.)

Gray, Michael 1999. 'Creating civil society? The emergence of NGOs in Vietnam', 30 *Development and Change* 693–713

Greenfield, Gerard 1994. 'The development of capitalism in Vietnam', in Miliband, Ralph and Panitch, Leo (eds.) 1994. *Socialist register 1994: Between globalism and nationalism.* London: Zed, pp. 203–234

Guardian 2002. 'Involuntary servitude case opens', 24 October 2002 (http://www.guardian.co.uk)

    2003. 'Misery of rag-trade slaves in America's Pacific outpost', 1 March 2003 (http://guardian.co.uk)

Hannah, Joseph 2007. 'Local nongovernmental organizations in Vietnam: Development, civil society and state–society relations'. Ph.D. dissertation, University of Washington.

Hanoi Bar Association 2004. *Twenty years of construction and development.* Hanoi: Hanoi Bar Association (http://www.luatsuhanoi.org.vn/tinhoat-dong/)

Ha Noi Moi 1994. Report on trial of Nguyen Tung Duong, 22 October 1994

Heng, Russell H.K. 1992. 'The 1992 revised Constitution of Vietnam: Background and scope for change', 14 *Contemporary Southeast Asia* 221–230

Hiebert, Murray 1992. 'New directions – Press takes bolder stand on corruption', *Far Eastern Economic Review*, 20 February 1992, 21–22

Hien, Nguyen Ngoc 2001. 'Cai cach hanh chinh theo tinh than Du thao sua doi Hien phap 1992', *Tap chi Cong san (Communist Review)*, November 2001 (http://tapchicongsan.org.vn)

Hoe, Vu Dinh 1995. *Hoi ky Vu Dinh Hoe (Memoirs of Vu Dinh Hoe).* Hanoi: Culture and Information Publishing House

Honolulu Star-Bulletin 2001a. 'Feds uncover American Samoa sweatshop', 24 March 2001 (http://starbulletin.com)

2001b. 'Worker says she was threatened', 28 March 2001 (http://starbulletin.com)

2001c. 'Samoa sweatshop slapped with federal fines', 26 May 2001(http://starbulletin.com)

2001d. 'Factory owner ruled flight risk', 28 July 2001 (http://starbulletin.com)

2001e. 'Feds urge sweatshop trial stay in isles', 24 August 2001 (http://starbulletin.com)

2001f. 'Rights in question in sweatshop trial', 30 August 2001 (http://starbulletin.com)

2001g. '2 sweatshop accomplices admit guilt; woman pleads not guilty', 1 September 2001 (http://starbulletin.com)

2001h. 'American Samoa to seek legal stature', 4 September 2001 (http://starbulletin.com)

2002a. 'Lurid 'slavery' trial gets under way', 24 October 2002 (http://starbulletin.com)

2002b. 'Factory worker details alleged oppression by boss in Samoa', 25 October 2002 (http://starbulletin.com)

2003. 'Man found guilty of running sweatshop', 22 February 2003 (http://starbulletin.com)

Hooker, M. B. 1978. *A concise legal history of South East Asia.* Oxford: Clarendon Press

Human Rights Watch 2003. *World Report 2003: Vietnam.* (http://www.hrw.org/wr2k3/asia9.html)

Human Rights Watch/Asia 1995. *Vietnam: Human rights in a season of transition; law and dissent in the Socialist Republic of Vietnam.* New York: Human Rights Watch/Asia

Huu, To 1958. *Qua cuoc dau tranh chong nhom pha hoai 'Nhan van Giai pham' tren Mat tran Van nghe.* Hanoi: Culture Publishing House

Huy, Nguyen Ngoc and Tai, Ta Van 1987. *The Le Code: Law in traditional Vietnam.* Miami: Ohio University Press

Institute of Law 1977. *Hien phap xa hoi chu nghia: Mot so van de ly luan co ban (Socialist Constitutions: Some fundamental theoretical issues).* Hanoi: Social Sciences Publishing House

Instructions 1 1989. Council of Ministers, Instructions 01-CT on the management of organization and activities of mass organizations (5 January 1989)

Instructions 202 1990. Council of Ministers, Instructions 202-CT on implementation of state regulations on the formation of associations (5 June 1990)

Inter Press 2003. 'Vietnam's overseas workers get raw deal', Asia Times/Inter Press Service, 2 July 2003 (http://www.ipsnews.net/migration/stories/exports.html)

Irish, Leon E., Jin Dongsheng, and Simon, Karla W. 1994. *China's tax rules for not-for-profit organizations.* Beijing: World Bank

James, Barbara 1992. 'Vietnamese law in English: A selected annotated bibliography', 84 *Law Library Journal* 461–498

Jamieson, Neil 1992. *Understanding Vietnam*. Berkeley: University of California Press

Joint Circular 55 1992. Ministry of Finance and Ministry of Science, Technology and Environment, Joint Circular 55/TLLB (providing guidlines on taxation with respect to science and technology activities) (12 October 1992)

Joint Directive 16 2000. Ministry of Finance and Ministry of Science, Technology and Environment, Joint Directive 16/2000/TTLT-BTC-BLDTBXH implementing guidance on the financial system for Vietnamese workers and specialists going abroad to work for a fixed term in accordance with Decree 152/1999/ND-CP (http://www.dafel.gov.vn)

Judicial Reform Strategy 2005. Chien luoc Cai cach Tu phap den nam 2020 (Resolution 49 on Judicial Reform Strategy to the Year 2020) (adopted by the Political Bureau of the Communist Party of Vietnam, June 2005)

Kerkvliet, Benedict 1999. 'Dialogical law making and implementation in Vietnam', in Tay, Alice (ed.) 1999. *East Asia: Human rights, nation building, trade*. Baden-Baden: Nomos Verlagsgesellschaft, pp. 372–400

2001. 'An approach for analysing state-society relations in Vietnam', 16 *Sojourn* 238–278

2005. *The power of everyday politics: How Vietnamese peasants transformed national policy*. Ithaca: Cornell University Press

Kerkvliet, Benedict, Heng, Russell H. K., and Koh, David W. H. (eds.) 2005. *Getting organized in Vietnam: Moving in and around the socialist state*. Singapore: Institute of Southeast Asian Studies

Kerkvliet, Benedict and Marr, David (eds.) 1994. *Beyond Hanoi: Local government in Vietnam*. Singapore: Institute of Southeast Asian Studies

Kyodo News Service 1994. 'Vietnam policeman sentenced to death for murder', Kyodo News Service/Japan Economic Newswire (Hanoi), 15 December 1994

Labor Code 1994. *Labor Code of the Socialist Republic of Vietnam* (23 June 1994) (http://asemconnectvietnam.gov.vn/laws)

Lam, Tran Dinh Thanh 2001. 'Social costs of labor exports start to emerge', Inter Press Service, 14 June 2001 (http://www.oneworld.org/ips2/june01/15_23_046.html)

Law on Associations 1957. *Luat quy dinh quyen lap hoi* (Luat so 102-SL/L.004 ngay 20-5-1957) (20 May 1957)

Law on Cooperatives 1996. *Luat hop tac xa (Law on Cooperatives)*, National Politics Publishing House, Hanoi, 1996

Legal Documents on Legal Aid 2003. *Cac van ban phap luat ve luat su va tro giup phap ly cho nguoi ngheo doi tuong chinh sach (Legal documents on lawyers and legal aid for the poor and policy targets).* Hanoi: National Politics Publishing House

Legal System Development Strategy 2005. *Chien luoc xay dung va hoan thien he thong phap luat Viet Nam den nam 2010, dinh huong den nam 2020 (Resolution 48 on strategy for development and improvement of Vietnam's legal system to the year 2010, and directions to the year 2020).* Hanoi: Political Bureau of the Communist Party of Vietnam

Legal System Needs Assessment 2002. *Report on comprehensive needs assessment for the development of Vietnam's legal system to the year 2010* (http:// www.jus.umu.se/Vietnam/pdf/LNA_FINAL.pdf; http://www.vnforum. org/docs/gov/law/en/Exsum_5_8_English.doc)

Lenduong.net 2004. 'Quyen va loi thu chinh dang trong hien phap nhan ban', 5 February 2004 (http://www.lenduong.net)

Luong, Hy Van 1993. *Revolution in the village: Tradition and transformation in North Vietnam, 1925–1988.* Honolulu: University of Hawaii Press

Luong, Tran Duc 2005. Tiep tuc day manh nghien cuu ly luan, tong ket thuc tien, nham lam sang to hon nhan thuc ve chu nghia xa hoi va con duong di len chu nghia xa hoi o nuoc ta (Continue strengthening theoretical research, summarize experience, aim at creating stronger consciousness of socialism and the road toward socialism in Vietnam), 75 *Tap chi Cong san (Communist Review)* (http://tapchicongsan. org.vn)

Hoa Mai (ed.) 1958. *The Nhan Van affair.* Saigon: n.p.

Manh, Ngo Duc 2005. 'Legislative activities of the National Assembly for a socialist law-ruled state of Vietnam', unpublished paper

Marr, David 1971. *Vietnamese anticolonialism 1885–1925.* Berkeley: University of California Press

  1994. 'The Vietnam Communist Party and civil society', Paper presented at the 1994 Vietnam Update conference, Australian National University, Canberra

  1995a. *Vietnam 1945.* Berkeley: University of California Press

  1995b. *Vietnam strives to catch up.* New York: Asia Society

  1996. *Vietnamese youth in the 1990s.* Sydney: Macquarie University

McClymont, Mary and Golub, Stephen (eds.) 2000. *Many roads to justice: The law-related work of Ford Foundation grantees around the world.* New York: The Ford Foundation

McMillan, John and Woodruff, Christopher 1999. 'Dispute prevention without courts in Vietnam', 15(3) *Journal of Law and Economic Organizations* 637–658

Merryman, John H. 1977. 'Comparative law and social change: On the origins, style, decline and revival of the law and development movement', 25 *American Journal of Comparative Law* 457–483

Ministry of Justice 1995. *So chuyen de ve Bo luat Dan su cua nuoc Cong hoa Xa hoi chu nghia Viet Nam (Democracy and law: Special issue on the Civil Code of the Socialist Republic of Vietnam)*. Hanoi: Ministry of Justice

Ministry of Science and Technology 1993. *Cac van ban phap luat ve khoa hoc cong nghe (Legal documents on science and technology)*. Hanoi: National Politics Publishing House

Mulla, Zarina and Boothroyd, Peter 1993. *Development-oriented NGOs of Vietnam*. Vancouver: University of British Columbia

Muoi, Do 1992. *Sua doi Hien phap, xay dung nha nuoc phap quyen Viet Nam, day manh su nghiep doi moi (Revising the Constitution, Building a law-governed state in Vietnam, stepping up the cause of renovation)*. Hanoi: Truth Publishing House

My, Nguyen Ngoc 2001. 'Viet kieu mong co dai dien trong Quoc hoi', *Bao Nhan Dan*, 30 September 2001

Nang, Nguyen Hong 1994. *Manufacturing civil society from outside: Donor intervention and aid – The case of Vietnam*. Amsterdam: Institute of Social Studies

Nathan, Andrew 1997. *China's transition*. New York: Columbia University Press

New York Times 2002. 'Apparel maker in Samoa is told to pay workers $3.5 million', 20 April 2002

Nga, Pham Hong 1995. 'Women's magazines break new ground in Vietnam', Agence France Press (Hanoi), 23 April 1995

Nghia, Pham Duy 2004. 'Mot phuong cach giam sat day to nhan dan' (A supervisory mechanism for the servants of the people), *Tuoi Tre*, 5 April 2004 (http://www.tuoitre.com.vn)

Nguoi Dai bieu Nhan dan [People's Deputies] 2001. 'Pho Chu tich Quoc hoi Nguyen Van Yeu tra loi phong van: Sua doi, bo sung mot so dieu cua Hien phap nam 1992 phai tren co so quan triet cac quan diem, tu tuong chi dao ve tiep tuc doi moi bo may nha nuoc, tiep tuc xay dung va hoan thien nha nuoc CHXHCN Viet Nam', 1 August 2001

Nguoi Lao dong 2006. De nghi UBND TPHCM huy bo 8 van ban trai luat (Proposing that the People's Committee of Ho Chi Minh City annul eight documents that violate the law), 12 January 2006 (http://www.nld.com.vn)

Nguyen, Phuong-Khanh 1977. *Vietnamese legal materials 1954–1975: A selected annotated bibliography*. Washington: Library of Congress
　　1981. 'Introduction to the 1980 Constitution of the Socialist Republic of Vietnam', 7 *Review of Socialist Law* 347–351

Nhan Dan [The People (Party newspaper)] 2001a. Khang dinh tu tuong dai doan ket toan dan (Reaffirm the ideology of great solidarity among the entire people), 10 September 2001 (http://www.nhandan.org.vn)
　　2001b. 'Chu tich Quoc hoi Nguyen Van An chu tri Hoi nghi gop y du thao sua doi, bo sung mot so dieu cua Hien phap nam 1992' (Chairman of the

National Assembly Nguyen Van An chairs a meeting to contribute opinions to the drafter of the amendments and supplements to the 1992 Vietnamese Constitution), 12 September 2001 (http://www.nhandan. org.vn; http://www.na.gov.vn)

2001c. 'Uy ban Mat tran To quoc tinh Ninh binh to chuc hoi nghi gop y kien vao Du thao sua doi, bo sung Hien phap nam 1992', 13 September 2001 (http://www.nhandan.org.vn)

2001d. Tran Van Tho, 'Kinh te nha nuoc chi nen phat trien trong mot so linh vuc then chot'; Ngo Thi Doc Lap, 'Cau chu trong Hien phap can ngan gon, de hieu – Khong thay thanh phan thuong nhan trong khoi dai doan ket?'; Nguyen Hoai Bac, 'Can coi trong hon nua tang lop doanh nhan'; Nguyen Ngoc My, 'Viet kieu mong co dai dien Quoc hoi'; Chau Van Chi, 'De nghi sua mot so cau trong cac Dieu 15, 36, 37, 59 va 84'; 'Mot so Viet kieu o Phap, Coi trong tinh hieu qua cua viec dua luat phap vao thuc tien cuoc song', 30 September 2001 (http://www.nhandan. org.vn)

2001e. 'Thong bao Hoi nghi lan thu tu Ban Chap hanh Trung uong Dang khoa IX', 13 November 2001 (http://www.nhandan.org.vn)

2001f. 'Quoc hoi nghe to trinh ve viec sua doi, bo sung mot so dieu cua Hien phap nam 1992 va mot so thuyet trinh, bao cao', 21 November 2001 (http://www.nhandan.org.vn)

2001g. 'Thao luan o Hoi trong ve Du thao sua doi, bo sung mot so dieu cua Hien phap nam 1992', 6 December 2001 (http://www.nhandan.org.vn)

2001h. 'Thong qua tung dieu Du thao Nghi quyet sua doi, bo sung mot so dieu cua Hien phap nam 1992', 11 December 2001 (http://www. nhandan.org.vn)

2002a. 'Chu tich Quoc hoi Nguyen Van An tham va lam viec voi Vien Kiem sat Nhan dan toi cao', 16 January 2002 (http://www.nhandan. org.vn)

2002b. 'Bo Chinh tri ra Nghi quyet ve mot so nghiep vu trong tam cong tac tu phap trong thoi gian toi', 7 January 2002

2002c. 'Thong qua tung phan du an Luat To chuc Vien Kiem sat nhan dan (sua doi)', 26 Mar 2002; 'Quoc hoi thong qua toan van du an Luat to chuc Vien Kiem sat nhan dan (sua doi)', 27 March 2002 (http://www. nhandan.org.vn)

2006. '33 tinh, thanh pho ra van ban xu phat trai luat' (22 provinces and municipalities issue punishment documents that violate the law), 13 January 2006 (http://www.nhandan.org.vn)

Nicholson, Pip 1999. 'Vietnamese institutions in comparative perspective: Constitutions and courts considered', in Jayasuriya, Kanishka (ed.) 1999. *Law, capitalism and power in Asia: The role of law and legal institutions.* London: Routledge, pp. 300–329

2001. 'Judicial independence and the rule of law: The Vietnam court experience', 3 *Australian Journal of Asian Law* 37–58

2002a. 'The Vietnamese courts and corruption' in Lindsey, Timothy and Dick, Howard (eds.) 2002. *Corruption in Asia: Rethinking the governance paradigm*. Sydney: Federation Press, pp. 201–218

2002b. 'Vietnam's labour market: Transition and the role of law', in Cooney, Sean et al. (eds.) 2002. *Law and labour market regulation in East Asia*. London: Routledge, pp. 122–156

2003. 'Vietnamese law: A bibliography', 22 *Legal Reference Services Quarterly* 139–200

2007. *Borrowing court systems: The experience of socialist Vietnam*. Leiden: Martinus Nijhoff.

Nicholson, Pip and Quang, Nguyen Hung 2005. 'The Vietnamese judiciary: The politics of appointment and promotion', 15 *Pacific Rim Law and Policy Journal* 1–34

Ninh, Kim 2002. *A world transformed: The politics of culture in revolutionary Vietnam, 1945–1965*. Ann Arbor: University of Michigan Press

Notice 147 2001. Office of the Government, Notice 147/TB-VPCP providing guidance opinions of Deputy Prime Minister Pham Gia Khiem on strengthening the export of workers and specialists (29 October 2001) (http://law.vdcmedia.com)

NOVIB 2004. *NOVIB regional program Southeast Asia*. Oslo: NOVIB.

Oanh, Nguyen Thi 1998. 'Cac hoat dong xa hoi va cong tac xa hoi chuyen nghiep', in Huong, Doan Thanh (ed.) 1998. *Sai Gon – Thanh Pho Ho Chi Minh: 300 Nam hinh thanh va phat trien 1698–1998 (Saigon – Ho Chi Minh City: 300 years of formation and development)*. Ho Chi Minh City: Bureau of Culture and Information, pp. 180–190

2002. 'Historical development and characteristics of social work in today's Vietnam', 11 *International Journal of Social Welfare* 84–90

Organization Law 2002. Law on the Organization of the National Assembly (http://www.nhandan.org.vn/vietnamese/phapluat/393.html)

Palmos, Frank 1995. *The Vietnam press: The unrealized ambition*. Perth: Edith Cowan University

Pedersen, Katrine 2001. *Civil society in the context of development aid: The case of Vietnam*. Copenhagen: Copenhagen Business School

2002. *The art of manoeuvring in changing rules of traffic: A study of emerging Vietnamese NGOs in the context of doi moi and international development co-operation*. Copenhagen: Copenhagen Business School

Petition to the National Assembly 1997 (http://www.vietforum.org/ Vietforum_VN/Documents/Bao_Cu_HSP_HMQ_ThuguiCSVN.htm)

2002 (http://www.ykien.net/vd20cutri.html)

Phap luat Viet Nam 2005. 'Co che bao hien o Viet Nam: Co thanh lap toa an hien phap?' (Mechanisms for constitutional protection in Vietnam: Should a constitutional court be established?), reprinted 27 April 2005, www.vnlawfind.com.vn

Phuc, Thang Van, Hai, Nguyen Xuan, et al. (eds.) 2002. *Vai tro cua cac hoi trong doi moi va phat trien dat nuoc (The role of associations in renovation and the development of the country).* Hanoi: National Politics Publishing House

Quang, Le Chi 1992. 'Gop y sua doi hien phap 1992' (http://www.shcd.de)

Quang, Nguyen Hung 2007. 'Lawyers and prosecutors under legal reform in Vietnam: The problem of equality', in Balme and Sidel 2007, pp. 162–177

Quang, Nguyen Hung and Steiner, Kirsten 2005. 'Ideology and professionalism: The resurgence of the Vietnamese bar', in Gillespie and Nicholson 2005, pp. 191–211

Quang, Pham Le 2001. 'Hien phap phai tao khung kho phap ly moi choc he do kinh te', *Bao thoi bao kinh te*, 17 September 2001

Quigley, John 1988. 'Vietnam at the legal crossroads adopts a penal code', 36 *American Journal of Comparative Law* 351–357

Quinn, Brian 2002. 'Legal reform and its context in Vietnam', 15 *Columbia Journal of Asian Law* 219–281

  2003. 'Vietnam's continuing legal reform: Gaining control over the courts', 4 *Asian-Pacific Law and Policy Journal* 431–468

Radio Free Asia 2005a. 'Radio Free Asia Vietnamese Service report on 'For Justice'', 15 September 2005 (http://www.rfa.org/vietnamese)

  2005b. 'Radio Free Asia Vietnamese Service report on 'For Justice'', 18 September 2005 (http://www.rfa.org/vietnamese)

  2005c. 'Radio Free Asia Vietnamese Service report on 'For Justice'', 22 September 2005 (http://www.rfa.org/vietnamese)

Regulations on Democracy in Communes 1998 and 2003. Decree 29/1998/ND-CP (Regulations on the exercise of democracy in communes); Decree 79/2003/ND-CP promulgating the Regulations on the exercise of democracy in communes; Circular 12/2004/TT-BNV guiding the implementation of Decree 79/2003/ND-CP. (http://www.un.org.vn/donor/civil)

Rose, Carol 1998. 'The "new" law and development movement in the post-Cold War era: A Vietnam case study', 32 *Law and Society Review* 93–136

Saich, Tony 1983. 'The fourth Constitution of the People's Republic of China', 9 *Review of Socialist Law* 113–124

Saigon Times Daily 2002a. 'Suleco to recruit for jobs in Malaysia', 31 January 2002

  2002b. 'Labor export robust', 1 March 2002

  2002c. 'First firms licensed to send workers to Malaysia', 19 March 2002

  2002d. 'Labor exporters short of recruits', 8 May 2002

  2003. 'Vietnam to cut labor exporter numbers', 16 May 2003

Salemink, Oscar 2003. 'Disjunctive developments: The politics of good governance and civil society in Vietnam', paper presented at SOAS/EIDOS conference on 'Order and Disjuncture: The Organisation of Aid and Development' (http://www.soas.ac.uk/eidosfiles/conferencepapers/salemink.pdf)

Sang, Do Xuan 1974. 'The Constitution,' in *An outline of institutions of the Democratic Republic of Viet Nam*. Hanoi: Foreign Languages Publishing House, pp. 9–21

Seattle Post-Intelligencer 2003. Brad Wong, 'Made in misery: How 12 women escaped sweatshop slavery', *Seattle Post-Intelligencer*, 17–21 November 2003 (http://seattlepi.nwsource.com/specials/madeinmisery)

Seidman, Robert 1978. *The state, law and development*. London: Croom Helm

Sevastik, Per (ed.) 1997. *Legal assistance to developing countries: Swedish perspectives on rule of law*. The Hague: Kluwer Law International

Sidel, Mark 1992. *Law reform and legal education and research in the Socialist Republic of Vietnam*. New York: Ford Foundation

  1993. 'Law reform in Vietnam: The complex transition from socialism and Soviet models in legal scholarship and training', 11 *UCLA Pacific Basin Law Journal* 221–259

  1994. 'The re-emergence of legal discourse in Vietnam', 43 *International and Comparative Law Quarterly* 163–173

  1995a. 'The emergence of a nonprofit sector and philanthropy in the Socialist Republic of Vietnam', in Yamamoto, Tadashi (ed.) 1995. *Emerging civil society in the Asia Pacific community*. Singapore: Institute of Southeast Asian Studies and Japan Center for International Exchange, pp. 293–304

  1995b. 'Dissident legal scholars in China's cities, their organizations, and the Chinese state in the 1980s', in Davis, Deborah et al. (eds.) 1995. *Urban spaces in contemporary China: The potential for autonomy and community in post-Mao China* New York: Cambridge University Press, pp. 326–346

  1996. 'New directions in the study of Vietnamese law', 17 *Michigan Journal of International Law* 705–719

  1997a. 'The emergence of a voluntary sector and philanthropy in Vietnam: Functions, legal regulation and prospects for the future', 8 *Voluntas* 283–302

  1997b. 'Vietnam: The ambiguities of state-directed legal reform', in Tan, Poh-Ling (ed.) 1997. *Asian legal systems: Law, society and pluralism in East Asia*. Singapore: Butterworths, pp. 356–389

  1997c. 'Conflicting approaches to law in Vietnam, 1954–1995', paper presented at the Association for Asian Studies

  1998. 'Law, the press, and police murder in Vietnam: Media and the trial of Nguyen Tung Duong,' in Marr, David (ed.) 1998. *The mass media in Vietnam*. Canberra: Australian National University, pp. 97–119

  1999. *Social justice and poverty programming in Vietnam*. Hanoi: Oxfam Hong Kong

2002. 'Understanding Constitutional amendation in socialist transitional societies: The case of Vietnam', 6 *Singapore Journal of International and Comparative Law* 42–89

2003. 'Legal reform in whose interests? Text, implementation and reality in Vietnamese law: Illuminations from Vietnamese labor export and its regulation'. Paper delivered at the International Conference on the State of the Law and Rule of Law in post-Doi Moi Vietnam, Paris (Sciences Po), October 2003

2004. *The legal regulation of export labor and the revision and implementation of the Labor Code in the Socialist Republic of Vietnam: Report to the State Department.* Iowa City: University of Iowa

2007. *Vietnamese-American diaspora philanthropy for Vietnam.* Boston: The Philanthropic Initiative (www.tpi.org)

Sidel, Mark and Vasavakul, Thaveeporn 2006. *Report to the Vietnam Union of Scientific and Technological Associations (VUSTA) and the United Nations Development Programme (Viet Nam) on the Law on Associations.* Hanoi: UNDP

Sin, Bach Tan 2002. 'Civil society and NGOs in Vietnam: Some initial thoughts on development and obstacles', paper presented at meeting with Swedish Parliamentary Commission on Swedish Policy for Global Development to Vietnam

Son, Bui Ngoc 2003. 'Hoc thuyet phan chia quyen luc: Mot cach tu duy ve quyen luc nha nuoc' (The theory of the separation of powers), 3 *Vietnam National University Journal of Economics and Law*, n.p.

2004. 'Co so cua che do bao hien' (The foundations of a system of constitutional protection), *Nghien cuu Lap phap*, n.p. (http://www.nclp. org.vn)

Son, Diep Van 2001. 'Sua doi Hien phap tao dieu kien cai cach he thong tu phap', VnExpress, 5 September 2001 (http://vnexpress.net)

Son, Le Hong 2001. 'Sua doi, bo sung Hien phap nam 1992 voi van de xay dung nha nuoc phap quyen Viet Nam', *Tap chi Cong san (Communist Review)*, December 2001 (http://www.tapchicongsan.org.vn)

STAR Vietnam 2003. *Workplan for 2003 and report on project activities completed in 2002.* Hanoi: STAR

2004. *Workplan for 2004 and report on project activities completed in 2003.* Hanoi: STAR

2005. *Workplan for 2005 and report on project activities completed in 2004.* Hanoi: STAR

Stromseth, Jonathan 2001. 'Business associations and policy-making in Vietnam', in Kerkvliet, Heng and Koh 2005, pp. 62–109

Supreme People's Court 2005. *Review judgments of the Judicial Council of the Supreme People's Court, 2003–2004, Volumes I and II [Quyet dinh Giam doc tham cua Hoi dong Tham phan Toa an Nhan dan Toi cao, Nam 2003–2004, Quyen I, II].* Hanoi: People's Court Journal.

Tai, Ta Van 1989. *The Vietnamese tradition of human rights*. Berkeley: University of California, Institute of Southeast Asian Studies

Tai, Hue-Tam Ho 1996. *Radicalism and the origins of the Vietnamese revolution*. Cambridge: Harvard University Press

Tai, Hue-Tam Ho (ed.) 2001. *The country of memory: Remaking the past in late socialist Vietnam*. Berkeley: University of California

Taiwan Migrants Forum 2003. 'Taiwan: Land of dreams and tears', 13 November 2003 (http://www.twblog/migrants)

Teitel, Ruti 1997. 'Transitional jurisprudence: The role of law in political transformation', 106 *Yale Law Journal* 2009–2079

Templer, Robert 1999. *Shadows and wind: A view of modern Vietnam*. New York: Penguin.

Thai, Ho Anh 1996. 'What's *doi moi* done for literature and the press', *Viet Nam News*, 8 December 1996

Thanh, Ngo Ba 1993. 'The 1992 Constitution and the rule of law', in Thayer and Marr 1993, pp. 121–134

Thanh, Nguyen Chi 1977. 'Tiep tuc ren luyen lap truong tu tuong vo san trong quan doi (Bai noi chuyen o Hoc vien Chinh tri (May 1963))', in Nguyen Chi Thanh 1997, *Nhung bai chon loc ve quan su*. Hanoi: People's Army Publishing House, pp. 379–380

Thanh, Nguyen Van and Hoa, Dinh Duy 1999. 'Viet Nam', in Silk, Thomas (ed.) 1999. *Philanthropy and law in Asia: A comparative study of the nonprofit legal systems in ten Asia Pacific societies*. San Francisco: Jossey-Bass, pp. 355–371

Thanh Nien 2004. 'Cuc Kiem tra van ban quy pham phap luat – Bo Tu phap cam on Bao Thanh Nien', 18 March 2004 (http://wwww.thanhnien. com.vn)

Thao, Nguyen Van 2001a. 'Soan thao, sua doi hien phap va thuc hien bao ve Hien phap' (Revising and amending the Constitution and mechanisms for Constitutional protection), *Tap chi Cong san (Communist Review)*, October 2001 (http://www.tapchicongsan.org.vn)

2001b. 'Soan thao, sua doi hien phap va thuc hien bao ve Hien phap' (Editing and revising the Constitutition and undertaking constitutional protection), *Tap chi Cong san (Communist Review)*, October 2001 (http://www.tapchicongsan.org.vn)

2001c. 'Ve kiem tra tinh hop hien, hop phap cua van ban phap luat va cac co quan tu phap' (On the inspection of the constitutionality and legality of legal documents and judicial agencies), *Bao Khoa hoc va Phat trien*, 3 October 2001 (http://www.na.gov.vn)

Thayer, Carl 1992. 'Political reform in Vietnam: *Doi Moi* and the emergence of civil society', in Miller, R. F. (ed.) 1992. *The development of civil society in Communist systems*. Sydney: Allen and Unwin, pp. 110–129

1993. 'Recent political developments: Constitutional change and the 1992 elections', in Thayer and Marr, pp. 50–80

Thayer, Carl and Marr, David (eds.) 1993. *Vietnam and the rule of law.* Canberra: Australian National University

Thinh, Pham 1995. 'Vietnamese media find a new role', *IPI Report*, July/August 1995, pp. 37–38

Tho, Nguyen Xuan 1992. *Presse und Medien in Vietnam.* Köln: Berichte des Bundesinstituts für ostwissenschaftliche and internationale Studien

Tin, Bui 1995. *Following Ho Chi Minh: Memoirs of a North Vietnamese colonel.* Honolulu: University of Hawaii Press

Truong, N. N. 1994. 'Grassroots organizations in rural and urban Vietnam during market reform: An overview of their emergence and relationship to the state', paper delivered to the 1994 Vietnam Update Conference, Australian National University, Canberra

Tri, Do Van 2001. 'Hien phap phai mang tinh khoa hoc, khai quat, van phong chuan xac,' *Bao Van Hoa*, 29 September 2001 (http://www.na.gov.vn)

Trubek, David and Galanter, Marc 1974. 'Scholars in self-estrangement: Some reflections on the crisis in law and development,' 1974 *Wisconsin Law Review* 1062–1101

TTVNOnline 2004. 'Thanh lap Toa an Hien phap Viet Nam?' (Establish a Vietnamese constitutional court?). http://www.ttvnonline.net.khpl/435379.ttvn

Tuan, Dao The 1995. *Khao sat cac hinh thuc to chuc hop tac cua nong dan nuoc ta hien nay (An investigation into the forms of cooperative organization among the Vietnamese peasantry today).* Hanoi: National Politics Publishing House

Tuoi Tre 2004. 'Chu tich Tran Duc Luong: Cai cach tu phap de chu dong hoi nhap' (President Tran Duc Luong: Legal reform to advance integration), 20 October 2004 (http://tuoitre.com.vn)

Tuong, Nguyen Manh 1958. 'Concerning mistakes committed in land reform', in Chi 1958, pp. 61–80

1992. *Un excommunie: Hanoi, 1954–1991: Procès d'un intellectuel.* Paris: Que Me

Turley, William and Selden, Mark (eds.) 1992. *Reinventing Vietnamese socialism: Doi moi in comparative perspective.* Boulder: Westview Press.

Tuyet, Tran Thi 1994. 'Tac dong cua chien tranh den viec hinh thanh y thuc va loi song theo phap luat', in Institute of State and Law (ed.) 1994. *Xa hoi va phap luat (Society and law).* Hanoi: National Politics Publishing House, pp. 101–121

Uc, Dao Tri 2001. 'Ve nhu cau, muc do sua doi Hien phap nam 1992 va quan diem xay dung nha nuoc phap quyen', *Tap chi Cong san (Communist Review)* October 2001 (http://www.tapchicongsan.org.vn)

Uc, Dao Tri, and Tuyet, Tran Thi (eds.) 1995. *Binh luan khoa hoc Hien phap nuoc Cong hoa Xa hoi Chu nghia Viet Nam nam 1992 (Scientific commentary on the 1992 Constitution of the Socialist Republic of Vietnam).* Hanoi: Social Sciences Publishing House

Umea Project in Brief 2000. (http://www.jus.umu.se/Vietnam/frame.htm)

United Nations Development Programme (UNDP) 2000. *Matrix of legal assistance activities 2000*. Hanoi: UNDP (http://www.undp.org.vn)

2004. *Access to justice in Viet Nam: Survey from the people's perspective*. Hanoi: UNDP (http://www.undp.org.vn/undp/ docs/2004/a2j/a2je.pdf)

2005. *Matrix of legal assistance activities 2005*. Hanoi: UNDP (http://www.undp.org.vn)

Vasavakul, Thaveeporn 1995. 'Vietnam: Changing models of legitimation', in Alagappa, Muttiah (ed.) 1995. *Political legitimacy in Southeast Asia: The quest for moral authority*. Stanford: Stanford University Press, pp. 257–271

Vasiljev, Ivo 1973. 'Democratic Republic of Viet-Nam', in Knapp, Viktor (ed.) 1973. *International encyclopedia of comparative law: National reports*. New York: Oceana, pp. D7–13

Vietnam Investment Review 1994. 'Unable to make the big leap, cooperatives face extinction', 26 December 1994

1999. 'Officials seeking to export more workers', Vietnam Investment Review, 27 December 1999

2002a. 'Labor exporters offer escape from rural poverty trap', 18 February 2002

2002b. 'Officials temper labor offer', 25 March 2002

2002c. 'More licenses granted for Malaysia-bound labor, 14 October 2002

2003a. 'Escaping the clutches of the poverty trap', 3 March 2003

2003b. 'Labour exports continue to rise despite war fears', 10 March 2003

2003c. 'State further tackles poverty and joblessness', 24 March 2003

2003d. 'More businesses to be allowed to export labour to Malaysia', 24 March 2003

2003e. 'Labor export boom – Vietnam's foreign cash cow', 22 December 2003

2004a. 'Compensation or cop-out?', 26 April 2004

2004b. 'Job drop blamed on Malaysia', 23 August 2004

2004c. 'Migrant training plan to lift job hopes', 27 September 2004

Vietnam Labor Watch, 2001. *Report on the working conditions of Vietnamese workers in American Samoa*, 6 February 2001 (http://samoa.saigon.com)

Vietnamnet 2001. 'Ha Noi lai phat hien mot cong ty lua dao lao dong di Han Quoc', 10 December 2001 (http://www.vnn.vn/vascorient/xahoi)

2003a. 'Khoi to, bat 4 doi tuong lua dao xuat khau lao dong sang Malaysia', 19 May 2003 (http://www.vnn.vn/xahoi)

2003b. 'Phat hien mot vu xuat khau lao dong bat hop phap', 12 June 2003 (http://www.vnn.vn/xahoi)

2003c. 'Bat khan cap 2 doi tuong lua dao xuat khau lao dong sang Han Quoc', 6 August 2003 (http://www.vnn.vn/xahoi)

2003d. 'Ket an ke danh dap lao dong Viet Nam tai dao Samoa', 25 February 2003 (http://www.vnn.vn/xahoi)

2004a. 'Report on "For Justice"', 13 May 2004 (http://www.vnn.vn/xahoi)

2004b. 'Luat su Pham Hong Hai bao chua cho ong Mai Van Dau' (Lawyer Pham Hong Hai defends Mr. Mai Van Dau), Vietnamnet, 9 December 2004 (http://www.vnn.vn/xahoi)

2004c. 'Nam 2005 phan dau xuat khau 70.000 lao dong', 1 July 2004 (http://www.vnn.vn/xahoi)

2005a. '42 tinh, thanh pho ban hanh van ban "xe rao"' (42 provinces and municipalities promulgate 'fence breaking' documents), 28 August 2005 (http://www.vnn.vn/xahoi)

2005b. 'Report on the motorbike debate in Hanoi', 6 December 2005 (http://www.vnn.vn)

2005c. 'Report on the motorbike debate in Hanoi', 7 December 2005 (http://www.vnn.vn)

2005d. 'Report on the motorbike debate in Hanoi', 13 December 2005 (http://www.vnn.vn)

Vietnam News 2001. 'Law makers give imprimatur to constitutional amendments', 14 December 2001

2005. 'Lawyer accused of extortion', 18 June 2005

Vietnam News Agency 2004a. 'Labour exports to Taiwan suspended for high rate of breaking contracts', 27 August 2004

2004b. 'Illegal labour exporter sentenced to eight years imprisonment', 27 April 2004

Vietnam News Briefs 2005. 'Lawyer arrested for blackmailing nearly $200,000', 17 June 2005

Vietnam News Service 2001a. 'Gov[ernmen]t vows to press on with administrative reform', 28 February 2001 (http://vietnamnews.vnagency.com.vn)

2001b. 'Administrative reform is tied to economic renovation: PM Khai', 4 June 2001 (http://vietnamnews.vnagency.com.vn)

2001c. 'NA mulls constitutional changes', 28 June 2001 (http://vietnamnews.vnagency.com.vn)

2001d. 'Party leader tells fourth plenum to set nation on path to success', 7 November 2001 (http://vietnamnews.vnagency.com.vn)

Voice of Vietnam 2001. 'Resolution on constitution amendment published', 15 January 2002, reprinted in BBC Worldwide Monitoring (Asia Pacific), 16 January 2002

VUSTA 2006. Law on Associations (Vietnamese Union of Scientific and Technological Associations, Draft 5, January 2006). Hanoi: VUSTA.

Waldron, Arthur 1995. 'China's coming constitutional challenges', 39 Orbis 19–35

Washington Post 2003. 'Va. aid group helps victims of human trade', 6 March 2003

Wischerman, Joerg 2001. 'The relationship between "civic organizations" and "governmental organizations"', 2001 Vietnam's Socio-Economic Development, pp. 19–34

2002. 'Vietnam in the era of Doi Moi: issue-oriented organisations and their relationship with the government', 43 *Asian Survey* 867–89

Wischerman, Joerg, and Vinh, Nguyen Quang 2005. 'The relationship between civic and governmental organizations in Vietnam: Selected findings', in Kerkvliet, Heng and Koh 2005, pp. 185–233

Xin, Chunying 2003. 'What kind of judicial power does China need?' 1 *International Journal of Constitutional Law* 58–78

Yeu, Nguyen Van 2005. 'Xay dung Nha nuoc phap quyen XHCN Viet Nam cua nhan dan, do nhan dan va vi nhan dan (Constructing a state ruled by socialist law in Vietnam of the people, for the people, and by the people)', *Bao Nhan Dan*, 9 November 2005, published in *Tap chi Cong san (Communist Review)*, October 2005 (http://www.tapchicongsan.org.vn)

Young, Stephen B. 1979. 'The legality of Vietnamese re-education camps', 20 *Harvard International Law Journal* 519–538

Yu, In-son 1990. *Law and society in seventeenth and eighteenth century Vietnam.* Seoul: Asiatic Research Center, Korea University

Zinoman, Peter 2002. *The colonial Bastille: A history of imprisonment in Vietnam, 1862–1940.* Berkeley: University of California Press

VIETNAMESE NEWSPAPER AND WIRE SERVICE REPORTS

An ninh Thu do [Capital Security] 1994a. 23 October 1994
   1994b. 24 October 1994
   1994c. 30 October 1994
   1994d. 4 November 1994

Dai Doan ket [Great Unity] 1993a. 11 June 1993
   1993b. 25 June 1993
   1993c. 13 August 1993
   1993d. 20 August 1993
   1993e. 20 September 1993
   1993f. 24 September 1993
   1994a. 21 January 1994
   1994b. 4 March 1994
   1994c. 25 March 1994
   1994d. 20 May 1994
   1994e. 27 May 1994
   1994f. 3 June 1994
   1994g. 7 October 1994
   1994h. 21 October 1994
   1994i. 4 November 1994

1994j. 6 November 1994
1994k. 9 November 1994
1994l. 23 December 1994
1994m. 30 December 1994
1995a. 3 March 1995
1995b. 17 March 1995
Ha Noi Moi [New Hanoi] 2005a. 16 November 2005
2005b. 22 November 2005
2005c. 24 November 2005
2005d. 25 November 2005
2005e. 26 November 2005
2005f. 27 November 2005
2005g. 3 December 2005
2005h. 5 December 2005
2005i. 6 December 2005
2005j. 8 December 2005
2005k. 9 December 2005
2005l. 13 December 2005
2005m. 14 December 2005
2005n. 22 December 2005
2005o. 26 December 2005
2006a. 3 January 2006
2006b. 25 January 2006
Phu nu Thu do [Women of the Capital] 1993a. 5 May 1993
1993b. 20 July 1993
1993c. 23 July 1993
1993d. 30 July 1993
1993e. 20 September 1993
1994a. 20 April 1994
1994b. 18 May 1994
1994c. 25 May 1994
1994d. 1 June 1994
1994e. 7 June 1994
1994f. 15 June 1994
1994g. 29 June 1994
1994h. 17 August 1994
1994i. 7 September 1994
1994j. 26 October 1994
1994k. 2 November 1994
1994l. 9 November 1994
1994m. 16 November 1994
1994n. 21 December 1994
1995a. 7 March 1995

Tien Phong [Vanguard] 2005. 12 December 2005
Tuoi Tre [Youth] 2005. 8 December 2005
VnExpress 2001a. 22 November 2001 (http://vnexpress.net)
  2001b. 25 November 2001 (http://vnexpress.net)
  2001c. 30 November 2001 (http://vnexpress.net)
  2001d. 1 December 2001 (http://vnexpress.net)
  2001e. 5 December 2001 (http://vnexpress.net)
  2001f. 12 December 2001 (http://vnexpress.net)
  2001g. 28 March 2001 (http://vnexpress.net)
  2001h. 31 January 2001 (http://vnexpress.net)
  2002a. 18 March 2002 (http://vnexpress.net)
  2002b. 19 November 2002 (http://vnexpress.net)
  2002c. 29 November 2002 (http://vnexpress.net)
  2003a. 9 January 2003 (http://vnexpress.net)
  2003b. 7 February 2003 (http://vnexpress.net)
  2003c. 11 February 2003 (http://vnexpress.net)
  2003d. 14 February 2003 (http://vnexpress.net)
  2003e. 1 March 2003 (http://vnexpress.net)
  2003f. 8 August 2003 (http://vnexpress.net)
  2003g. 14 August 2003 (http://vnexpress.net)
  2003h. 23 September 2003 (http://vnexpress.net)
  2004a. 12 March 2004 (http://vnexpress.net)
  2004b. 17 March 2004 (http://vnexpress.net)
  2004c. 17 April 2004 (http://vnexpress.net)
  2004d. 5 May 2004 (http://vnexpress.net)
  2004e. 5 July 2004 (http://vnexpress.net)
  2004f. 10 May 2004 (http://vnexpress.net)
  2004g. 11 May 2004 (http://vnexpress.net)
  2004h. 12 May 2004 (http://vnexpress.net)
  2005a. 6 July 2005 (http://vnexpress.net)
  2005b. 27 August 2005 (http://vnexpress.net)
  2005c. 28 August 2005 (http://vnexpress.net)
  2005d. 22 November 2005 (http://vnexpress.net)
  2005e. 24 November 2005 (http://vnexpress.net)
  2005f. 25 November 2005 (http://vnexpress.net)
  2005g. 26 November 2005 (http://vnexpress.net)
  2005h. 27 November 2005 (http://vnexpress.net)
  2005i. 29 November 2005 (http://vnexpress.net)
  2005j. 30 November 2005 (http://vnexpress.net)
  2005k. 5 December 2005 (http://vnexpress.net)
  2005l. 7 December 2005 (http://vnexpress.net)
  2005m. 8 December 2005 (http://vnexpress.net)
  2005n. 9 December 2005 (http://vnexpress.net)

2005o. 10 December 2005 (http://vnexpress.net)
2005p. 12 December 2005 (http://vnexpress.net)
2005q. 13 December 2005 (http://vnexpress.net)
2005r. 14 December 2005 (http://vnexpress.net)
2005s. 15 December 2005 (http://vnexpress.net)
2005t. 19 December 2005 (http://vnexpress.net)
2005u. 21 December 2005 (http://vnexpress.net)
2006. 24 January 2006 (http://vnexpress.net)

INDEX

"For Justice" group of public interest lawyers, 183–188
Ford Foundation, 203, 208, 209
foreign aid donors, 195–222
    access to justice, 189–191, 210–212
    beginnings of aid to Vietnam, 204
    economic law, overemphasis on Daewoosa case and, 195–197
    initial aid to Vietnam, 204–205
    public interest law, consequences for, 169
    future directions for, 216, 219–222
    historical development of legal aid from, 200–204
    implementation and enforcement, 209–210
    initial lack of aid to Vietnam, 202
    institutional capacity-building, 205–209
    lawyers, retraining and strengthening role of, 204–205, 212
    legal reform and strengthening, unintended consequences of, 197–200
    legal system strategy development and harmonization, 213–215
    Nam Cam case lessons learned from, 197–199
    National Assembly, 206–209
    Procuracy, 206–209
    public interest law and (See under public interest law)
    review and enforcement of constitution, influence on, 56
    social justice issues, interest in, 215–219
    to transitional socialist countries, 195, 202–204
foundations and funds, social and charitable, 150–152
France
    Constitutional Court of, 56, 58
    foreign aid from, 206, 207, 208, 213
funds and foundations, social and charitable, 150–152

Galanter, Marc, 201
garment industry and export labor. See Daewoosa export labor case
General Department for Inspection of Legal Documents, 59–60, 77, 91
Germany
    Constitutional Court of, 57
    export labor to East Germany, 99
    foreign aid from, 207, 210
Gillespie, John, 1, 2, 13, 205
Ginsburg, Tom, 69, 70–72
global economy
    legal system strategy development and harmonization, foreign aid for, 213–215
    Vietnamese labor in (See export labor law)

governance requirements, nonprofit and voluntary sector, 161
Gulf region, export labor to, 99, 100

Hai, Pham Hong, 177, 180–181, 182, 188
Hai, Tran Vu, 180–181, 183, 185, 186, 188
Hanh, Tran Mai, 177, 178
Hanoi, motorbike restrictions in. See motorbike constitutionalism
harmonization and strategy development for legal system, foreign aid for, 213–215
Hien, Nguyen Van, 177
Ho Chi Minh, 4, 9, 10, 11, 142
Hoang, Tran Huu, 112
Hoe, Vu Dinh, 9–12
Hong Kong, export labor to, 194
Hundred Flowers Movement
    in China, 4, 14, 142
    in Vietnam, 142
Hung, Cao Van, 181, 182
Huy, Bui Quoc, 177, 178
Huy, Nguyen Ngoc, 1

implementation and enforcement
    amendment of constitution, 42–44
    constitutional (See review and enforcement of constitution)
    of export labor law (See under export labor and export labor law)
    foreign aid for purposes of, 209–210
India, foreign aid donors in, 200
Indonesia
    Constitutional Court of, 58
    foreign aid donors in, 201
Institute of State and Law group, academic approach to legal thought of, 3, 8–13
institutional capacity-building, foreign aid for, 205–209
instrumentalist approach
    to constitutional issues, 18–22, 44–48
    to law in Vietnam, 141

Jamieson, Neil, 2
Japan
    Confucian ideology, effects of, 57
    Constitutional Court of, 58
    export labor to, 100
    foreign aid from, 201, 206, 207, 208, 210, 213
judicial system. See also prosecutors
    activist lawyers (See under public interest law)
    foreign aid for, 206–209
    retraining and strengthening role of lawyers, 204–205, 212

Kerkvliet, Ben, 2
Kim Ninh, 2